Branding

a

Main

"Whether you're dying to launch your own company, or are more of a reluctant entrepreneur, you face the imperative to build your brand. Catherine Kaputa has made this challenge her personal and professional study, and in this book she shares secrets worth many times the cost of admission. Now go forth and brand!"

—Daniel H. Pink, Author, *DRIVE and A WHOLE NEW MIND*

"*Breakthrough Branding* is engaging, vital and packed with branding power. With examples from around the world, it's a must read for entrepreneurs and intrapreneurs who have a business ide but need the tools to grow it into a big brand."

—William H. Roedy, Former Chairman & Chief Executive of MTV Networks International, and Author, *What Makes Business Rock*

"If you aim to be an entrepreneur and already have a big idea, but you never studied marketing and branding, this book will give you a running start. Catherine is a superb coach and her book delivers a wonderful collection of marketing steps and real world entrepreneur success stories."

—Philip Kotler, Marketing Professor, Kellogg School of Business, Northwestern University

"Anything that Catherine writes is worth reading. She was one of my best students on the subject of 'Positioning' and building brands. She won't steer you wrong."

—Jack Trout, World Famous Marketing Strategist

"If there's one thing you've just got to know about—but is tough to learn about—it's branding. Catherina Kaputa tells you what you must know in this valuable book. Read it before your competitors do."

—Jay Conrad Levinson Author, Million-Selling *Guerrilla Marketing Series*

"If brand building were courting and marrying, Kaputa's strategies would be the best dating advice around! She shows you how to romance the marketplace with your package, your name, and your image without sacrificing the heart of your brand."

—Dr. Wendy Walsh, America's Relationship Expert, Co-Host, *THE DOCTORS* and CNN's *Human Behavior Expert*

BREAKTHROUGH BRANDING

How SMART ENTREPRENEURS and INTRAPRENEURS Transform a SMALL IDEA into a BIG BRAND

CATHERINE KAPUTA

NICHOLAS BREALEY
PUBLISHING

BOSTON • LONDON

This edition first published by Nicholas Brealey Publishing, in 2012.

20 Park Plaza, Suite 610   Spafield Street, Clerkenwell
Boston, MA 02116 USA   London, EC1R4QB, UK
Tel: + 617-523-3801   Tel: +44-(0)-207-239-0360
Fax: + 617-523-3708   Fax: +44-(0)-207-239-0370
www.nicholasbrealey.com

Printed in the United States of America
15   14   3   4   5

ISBN: 978-1-85788-581-1

Library of Congress Cataloging-in-Publication Data
Kaputa, Catherine,
   Breakthrough branding: how smart entrepreneurs and intrapreneurs transform a small idea into a big brand / Catherine Kaputa.
      p. cm.
   Includes bibliographical references and index.
   ISBN 978-1-85788-581-1 (pbk.)
   1.   Branding (Marketing) 2.   Success in business.   I. Title.
   HF5415.1255.K37 2012
   658.8'27--dc23
      2011044338

To my heroes:
All the entrepreneurs and intrapreneurs
growing businesses around the world

Contents

Never in history has there been so many opportunities for entrepreneurs to become wealthy beyond their wildest dreams.

Mark Zuckerberg, a college dropout, is twenty-six years old and is worth $13.5 billion.

Dustin Moskovitz, a former roommate of Zuckerberg's, is eight days younger than Mark and is worth $2.7 billion. The third employee of Facebook, Dustin left early to start a software company.

Over in Japan, another entrepreneur, Yoshikazu Tanaka, is thirty-four years old and is worth $2.2 billion.

All over the world, the stories are the same. If you want to become really wealthy, forget the traditional path of getting an entry-level job at General Motors, General Electric, or General Dynamics and working your way up from the bottom.

The way to become really wealthy is to start at the top and not at the bottom. Be an entrepreneur and not an employee.

That's the good news. The bad news is that more than 90 percent of entrepreneurs never become truly successful. They struggle for years and never seem to break out of the pack.

Why is this so?

Perhaps it's because entrepreneurs are different. There's an old saying: You can always tell an entrepreneur, but you can't tell them much. To be an entrepreneur and start a company, you need a thick skin. You need to be able to shrug off advice like, You're going to start a WHAT?

Years ago, I worked with an entrepreneur with zero experience in publishing who started a publishing company. Yet in the five or six consulting assignments I conducted with this company, the entrepreneur took none of my advice.

I learned from this experience. You don't tell an entrepreneur, you sell an entrepreneur. You have to explain the marketing principles behind the advice, with a heavy emphasis on case histories and analogies.

Which is exactly what Catherine Kaputa has done with her book. She has isolated the principles most relevant to entrepreneurs and then presented them in an organized way with a liberal use of relevant case histories.

But that's not the most important aspect of her book. The most important aspect is that these principles are difficult to learn and difficult to put into practice because they are counterintuitive. That's why they are so helpful.

Everything about marketing is illogical, including Catherine Kaputa's shocking first principle of entrepreneurship: "Forget the big idea, go for a small idea."

Imagine that. Small is better than big. When Mark Zuckerberg started Facebook, he didn't try to sign everybody up. He tried to sign up only students at Harvard, one of the smaller colleges in the country. His success at Harvard was the solid foundation for what later became the world's largest social media site.

I have known Catherine Kaputa for three decades. As a matter of fact, we worked together when I ran an advertising agency in New York City. A successful entrepreneur herself, Catherine has assembled an awesome array of principles that are bound to be of enormous help to anyone who has the inner fire to become an entrepreneur.

That may be you.

My Story

I'd like to tell you that I became an entrepreneur as a result of a lot of careful planning and a blinding flash of insight—a big idea that I knew couldn't fail. But...it didn't happen that way. The truth is, I was forced into entrepreneurship when I lost my high-powered corporate branding job right after 9/11.

Saying goodbye to a Wall Street job—the security, the prestige, the good paycheck—was scary but exciting at the same time. (Never mind that it felt like my *only* realistic option.) The demand for what I was doing—marketing financial services companies and products—was drying up, and that situation was unlikely to turn around anytime soon. I had periodically harbored thoughts that I'd do something entrepreneurial at some point (particularly after a bad day at the office). Now, I had to do it. I may have been a reluctant entrepreneur at first, but after the initial shock of job loss wore off, I was determined to find an idea and develop a business plan quickly. I had to start selling something soon if I was going to survive.

The Circuitous Path to Entrepreneurship

I knew that, as an entrepreneur, I would have to learn to rely on myself and my own resources. I would have to make things happen, be independent—be a leader. I would have to attract clients and make money on my own. When I looked at the situation honestly, I had to admit that for many years I had been a follower—and that had started long before I entered the business world.

As a child, I had been an obedient schoolgirl, laboring to live up to the exacting standards of the nuns at St. James Catholic School in Miami, Florida. I remember learning how to write each letter neatly and perfectly, following the rules of the Palmer Method of Penmanship. I was a quick study and it was so satisfying—I had found the way to succeed! Follow directions. Abide by the rules. Don't deviate from the pattern. Don't get noticed. Above all, don't be creative! Those rules applied equally well to my studies in other areas too, and my world felt orderly—black and white with no nuances of gray.

Following the rules served me well throughout grade school, high school, and even at university. Then I entered the real world, and guess what? Those old rules still worked like a charm—until I was put in charge of leading a department and later became an entrepreneur. In those positions, you have to be willing to stand up and stand out. You have to come up with new ideas and solutions, and that means breaking from tradition.

I majored in journalism at Northwestern University and thought I was off and running, until I experienced what I now call my first personal branding crisis. It was the kind of identity crisis quite common at the time, and I abruptly switched gears in my junior year to major in art history. For the next eight years, Japanese art was my brand, and I was in deep: I spent four years as a curatorial assistant at the Seattle Art Museum, coauthored two books on Asian art, spent a summer as a Smithsonian fellow, and got a two-year grant from the Japanese Ministry of Education to study at Tokyo University. I entered the Ph.D. program at Harvard because I thought Harvard was right for my brand (though I wouldn't have thought about it in those terms at the time). As I started to write my dissertation, I had my second personal branding crisis and decided that Dr. Kaputa, Japanese art historian, was not who I was after all. It wasn't my brand. (And I hoped these personal branding crises weren't becoming a habit.)

Next stop, New York City. After my experiences in the Asian art world, I had an intuitive sense that my original passions in college—journalism and advertising—were my deepest ones and should dictate my future. Perhaps partly because I had a personal connection there, I couldn't resist the lure of New York. My heart and head were both telling me to go. I wasn't quite sure what I would end up doing, but I knew I would find it in the capital of the world.

Through networking, I got my start as a junior copywriter at Trout & Ries Advertising, a small agency that was known for strategy and position-ing. Four years later, I landed at Wells Rich Greene, supervising the "I Love

New York" campaign. The account was high profile, and the television commercials we made won many awards. Part of my job was to enlist celebrities and the casts of Broadway shows to be in the commercials.

Celebrities are experts at personal branding, but their carefully constructed public brands—who we think they are—are not always real. I could tell lots of indiscreet stories about backstage tantrums and the need for pampering, but...let's just say that it was an interesting gig. One of the highlights was shooting Ol' Blue Eyes himself, Frank Sinatra, and I quickly realized that Sinatra was a brand apart. He paid his own way, gave an unforgettable performance, and seemed to leave magic dust in his wake.

My next career move was the big one: I landed a job as a corporate ad director on Wall Street. It wasn't easy to get. Networking my way through six degrees of separation, I finally landed an interview at Shearson Lehman Brothers (then part of American Express), got the job, and ended up staying more than ten years—through four mergers, two spin-offs, and more restructurings than I care to recall.

As a branding and advertising executive, all of those changes kept me busy. Each merger meant a name change, and with each spin-off and restructuring came a pressing need to manage and adapt the brand. By the time I left in 2001, the firm was known as Citi Smith Barney, and it was still a highly prestigious and trusted brand, thanks in part to the way we managed all of those changes. Which brings me back to the beginning of my story: starting my new life as an entrepreneur.

What's the Big Idea?

Whether you're an entrepreneur working independently or an intrapreneur, a corporate entrepreneur working inside a company, you're in the business of taking an idea and growing it into a successful product or service—one that offers something new or works better than what's out there. Every business begins with an idea, and perfecting that idea is your first and most important task. It has to incorporate your strengths, be the right thing at the right time, and carry with it a certain kind of excitement that makes it memorable and marketable. In the branding business, when looking at a new enterprise, we always ask, "What's the big idea?"—meaning what's its *unique selling proposition* (USP), its new and competitive angle. This book will show you how to find your own individual brand idea.

All of this wisdom was running through my mind as I contemplated launching my own business brand. Given my background, it seemed logical that I would start a marketing consultancy business, but I knew that would put me in direct competition with a lot of established businesses—and in a very tough economy. Could I figure out a way to rise above the competition? I wasn't sure. At the same time, I had started coaching other downsized refugees of 9/11, some of whom were looking for corporate jobs while others planned to start businesses. I had an epiphany. There was more to branding than promoting big brands. Why not focus on what's been overlooked?

Personal branding was a new idea in the marketplace at that time, so there weren't many competitors out there. I knew there was a need for it because I was helping to fill that need with my coaching. Looking back at my own experience, I realized that building a durable and fulfilling career takes careful, calculated branding efforts at every turn. It's true that few personal branding transformations are as dramatic as mine was when I moved from Japanese art historian to advertising executive; but to some degree, I had to rebrand myself for every move I made (even within the same industry), and so does everyone else. My own business idea was clear: combining my personal experience and my professional expertise, I would focus on neglected areas of branding—employees and executives at companies, and entrepreneurs and their businesses.

I named my company SelfBrand and set about targeting executives, professionals, and fellow entrepreneurs—people who were smart and good at what they did but needed help with branding themselves and their businesses in order to rise to another level. Unlike other executive and business coaches, I became a brand strategist. My approach was to apply the principles and strategies from the commercial world of brands to another, equally important product: you.

The Entrepreneur Era

It's the age of the entrepreneur. Many people who had dreamed of opening a business are doing it. For some, it's the desire for independence from corporate politics (or, as in my case, the need for reinvention after downsizing).

For others, it's a vision of riches. For many, it's all about doing something they love.

In today's challenging market, many people of all ages are facing an uncertain future and embracing entrepreneurship as a way to take control, make money, and create a job for themselves and hopefully many others. New college graduates who find limited opportunities at corporations are starting businesses.

Many baby boomers are not retiring to a life of leisure and golf. Instead, they are starting businesses around a hobby or passion. They may be reluctant entrepreneurs but they are starting businesses in record numbers, too. There are also social entrepreneurs who want to change the world for the better.

These days, you don't need bricks and mortar to run a business, either. The digital world has made it easier to hang out a shingle than ever before. All you need is a website. And many of the fastest-growing businesses are based entirely on digital technology.

As for the corporate entrepreneur, within today's larger, flatter corporations, there are more opportunities to be an *intrapreneur* or, to use today's trendier name, a *corporate entrepreneur*, within a large company. To think and act like an entrepreneur while working for others means thinking like an owner with a stake in growing the business. It can power your corporate career in a new way. Rather than thinking like an employee or even a manager, you'll be working for yourself and for the good of the enterprise. The rewards are bound to follow. And that will repay you in results and recognition.

Brand Your Business! Brand You!

Building a business is a very personal and a very human activity. Every business is built by someone like you or me, an ordinary person trying to do something extraordinary.

To build a successful business, you have to be willing to leverage every asset and pursue every opportunity—whether your dream is to create a large-scale enterprise or a successful solo venture. That's why it's important to think brand and build a personal brand—Brand You—in tandem with your business brand. There is no doubt that this will increase your impact and, ultimately, your success.

Your business is an important asset. Branding can help you maximize that asset by identifying a clear *promise* to consumers—something that your business does in its own unique way.

 Brand:

> A PRODUCT: something that is interchangeable with other similar items.

> A BRAND: a special promise of value that is admired and recognized.

Likewise, you are an important asset, and personal branding can help you maximize the value of Brand You in terms of achieving success as represented by money, fame, or whatever is important to you. But personal branding is also about self-actualization and becoming who you were meant to be.

 Brand You:

> A PERSON: an individual with a skill set that is interchangeable with those of other people.

> BRAND YOU: a personal brand, a special promise of value that sets you apart.

There are many legendary entrepreneurs who took the Brand Your Business/Brand You route. Think Richard Branson at Virgin, Steve Jobs at Apple, Martha Stewart at Martha Stewart Living Omnimedia (MSLO), and John Mackey at Whole Foods. More recently, entrepreneurs like Tony Hsieh of Zappos and Reed Hastings of Netflix have taken the same double-barreled approach. They are all big names today, but they started out small and built strong businesses in part by simultaneously managing their personal and business brands. They are what I call *brand entrepreneurs*, leaders who weave their personalities, leadership styles, and values tightly into their business brands. And what a difference that can make.

It's hard to talk about personal branding without evoking the T word. Donald Trump is perhaps the poster child for building a personal brand in tandem with a business brand. (And there are many lessons to learn from him.) There's no doubt that Trump's success in personal branding contributed to his business success. And he's still building his personal brand today, long after he needs to, via television shows, books, products—even a foray into presidential politics! Branding can be subtle or grating, up-to-date or outdated, classy or over-the-top, but one thing is clear: if you don't participate, you will be left behind.

As an entrepreneur, you have to compete every day. Why not leverage all of your assets in the effort, including your personality, your leadership philosophy, your worldview, and your visibility? Why not tie together your personal and business brands? Especially in today's digital world, people want to know who you are. They want to see if the Wizard of Oz is a charlatan or the real deal. They want to know your story. This book will show you how to develop it and get it out there.

Like It or Not, Your Brand Is Out There

In this digital world, people don't have to know you personally to love you. Or research you. Or post something about you. Or unfriend you.

Privacy and anonymity are things of the past. Social media such as Facebook and Twitter, along with the massive proliferation of blogs and consumer sites, connect your customers to one another—and to *you*—twenty-four hours a day, seven days a week. Consumers want to find you and learn your story. Finding your business story (the one you want to put out there or a very different one that has been created by others outside your control) is just a Bing or a Google away.

Can there be any doubt, then, that branding is something you must take seriously? If you don't take charge of your brand, someone else will. If you leave things to chance, you risk ceding control to others. Because if you don't brand yourself, other people will—and they are not likely to brand you in the way you want to be branded. If you don't actively work at branding yourself and your business, you will be left unable to compete with those entrepreneurs who do.

 If you don't brand your business and yourself, other people will.

The first thing today's consumers do when they need a product or service is check the Internet. A nonexistent or poorly executed web presence can brand you as weak or a B player. Bad reviews on online forums might define you as second rate or worse. With all of the choices out there, consumers are looking for a way to narrow their options. Why should they take a chance on you when they can select a business with "A+" reviews?

This has always been true but has never been more relevant: your brand isn't what you say it is, it's what other people say about it. Branding is all about perception, and the perceptions of others, the comments they make, and the value they assign to your business are key factors in today's marketplace.

A Weak Digital Footprint Is Like a Weak Reputation

Your brand—your image and reputation—is valuable. That's why you need to take charge of building and nurturing it.

In the digital world we live in today, people will search for information about you and your business on the Internet, whether you are trying to create the next billion-dollar technology start-up or open a local retail store. People will check you out on the Internet and they'll find *you*, whether you work for a company or are looking for a job, whether you're blogging about your hobbies or just want a date. They're going to do it whether you want them to or not. Checking out people, products, and companies on the Internet is how we operate today.

Entrepreneurs have always had to strive for maximum impact at minimum cost when it came to marketing and compete every day to succeed. Now the competition—and the marketing possibilities—has grown to encompass the much larger digital playing field. Without breakthrough branding, you won't be able to compete as well as other people—your competitors—who use this resource (as well as other media) to create a strong brand impression. You won't be making the most of your two most important assets: your business and yourself.

Today, it's not just business owners who have to think brand. We're all entrepreneurs now. Employees at a company have to think like entrepreneurs—corporate entrepreneurs. You have to rely on yourself, be innovative to stay at the front of the curve, and demonstrate your value every day to succeed. No one can rely on long-term employment or a pension. Chances are, given the ebb and flow of traditional jobs and up-and-down economies, you'll be an actual entrepreneur at some point, not just a corporate entrepreneur.

This is the way it is now.

The Brand Entrepreneur in the Digital Age

This fast-paced new media world has completely changed the way people relate to brands, companies, media, and each other. Marketing is no longer a one-way, top-down, manufacturer-to-consumer selling effort; rather, it is a two-way, bottom-up, consumer-to-manufacturer buying culture.

Consumers may want to buy, but they are skeptical and selective—they feel empowered as never before. The digital era has armed consumers with information and choice. People feel that they know their brands and they want to be involved in analyzing them. They want to connect with brands and with each other in the buying process. And the Internet makes it easy for them to do this.

Digiworld has made branding more important and more accessible than ever for business owners. Branding is turning into a process of image-making that touches the emotions and presells a product or service in an intensely personal way. There is no doubt that you'll have a harder time overcoming objections and making a sale if your business is not branded well. And the marketing job of getting more customers won't be so easy, either.

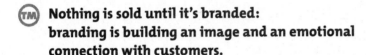 **Nothing is sold until it's branded: branding is building an image and an emotional connection with customers.**

In the digiworld, there are so many more media channels and opportunities to build visibility and engage consumers.

Visibility creates a brand. If something is visible—all over the Internet, the top television shows, on billboards, wherever—consumers tend to think it must be better than a competitive product that lacks visibility. I call this the *visibility premium*. And the digiworld gives you low-cost, high-impact avenues to build visibility for your business brand and for yourself, so you can take advantage of this visibility premium.

Today, there are no hard-and-fast rules. Yes, there are timeless branding principles, as well as new branding principles brought about by the digital age. But what worked last year may not work now. Then again, it may, so it is important to stay plugged in and current.

As an entrepreneur, you need to monitor and reevaluate. You need to improvise and have the pluck to make up rules as you go. Your competitors are moving faster too, so you must constantly rethink your product, your company culture, and the ways in which you connect with your customers. You'll need the confidence to develop your own product and branding ideas, your own ways of engaging your customers, and your own company culture. This book will provide you with the tools to do all of these things.

Power to the People

Today, companies aren't the only ones who control brand messages. On the web, consumers have a lot of clout and their opinions are powerful. They aren't afraid to say what they think, either, and they can be downright negative and trash your brand. What's more, because of the instantaneous nature of the Internet, it can all happen quickly. The brand you've taken months or years to build can be compromised in a matter of days, hours, or even minutes.

For example, no less a brand than the mighty Proctor & Gamble had to scramble to put out Internet fireworks over the safety of its Pampers Dry Max diapers, when some moms started believing that the diapers caused rashes and even chemical burns on their babies. It started when one particularly vociferous mom started a Facebook page with the headline "P&G, Bring Back the Old Cruisers/Swaddlers" and posted descriptions of her baby's rashes, presumably a result of using the new diapers from the company.[1]

Word spread fast. Soon, other moms signed on to the Facebook page and posted similar complaints about rashes with the new P&G diapers. As many fervently expressed in the posts, mothers know best! The demand that "P&G must recall the diapers!" gained traction.

Before long, the Facebook page had over 11,000 "friends" who had similar complaints or supported the efforts of this large band of mothers to get P&G to recall the diapers.

It may not surprise you that the accusation had little credibility. P&G had ample research to prove that the rashes were not due to the new diapers. Many babies get rashes no matter what kind of diapers they use. But considerable damage was done to the brand.

Initially, P&G tried to defend itself in the media, and the sides became polarized as more reporters and producers picked up on the story. Then P&G invited a group of moms, including some who were involved in the Facebook page, to a personal meeting and shared the company's research findings and listened to the moms' complaints. Sometimes the personal touch—even in a digital age—is what it takes. The story started to lose its traction.

The digital age has launched a faster-paced, customer-centric brand world, for sure. You need to be a branding-oriented entrepreneur to deal with it. This book will show you how to manage your business brand and your customers in the digital age.

Branding Cornucopia

Today's democratization of media is something every entrepreneur must embrace. In the digital world, you have more access and control. There are so many options and you don't have to appeal to gatekeepers, as you do with traditional media (though you should consider leveraging those avenues, too).

With the Internet at your disposal, you have a huge megaphone you can use to fan the flames of your brand, reach customers, and build your brand reputation—all for a relatively small investment. Of course, your competitors can holler their messages with digital tools and have these same advantages too, so it behooves you to learn how to use them better than anyone. Anybody can be a fan or critic on Yelp or other online forum. In this book, you'll learn tactics for managing your business brand and your personal brand effectively on the Internet.

It's important not to become intimidated by the digital onslaught. How do you deal with digital technology and run the business, too? How do you use social media to raise your profile, disseminate your message, and make money? Within these pages, you'll learn a lot about the traditional principles of branding—most of which still apply to every business owner—as well as the new principles that have emerged to help you reap the advantages of the digital age. Digital media gives you a way to be close to your customers and understand what they want and then give it to them.

Who Is This Book For?

Breakthrough Branding is for anyone building any kind of business anywhere:

- ► Entrepreneurs with a dream and a purpose
- ► Reluctant entrepreneurs who can't find a "real" job

- ▶ Corporate entrepreneurs running a business area inside a company
- ▶ Anyone aspiring to run or build a small business
- ▶ Solo practitioners of a trade or profession
- ▶ Aspiring social or nonprofit entrepreneurs who want to make a difference in the world

When it comes to the basics, these various entrepreneurs are more alike than different. What drives the best entrepreneurs and leaders is a quest to make a difference, to achieve success or riches—maybe even to change the world. Entrepreneurs are leaders on a mission to make their mark. They, I believe, are the lucky ones who get to make the most of their gifts and apply them to an enterprise that fills a need while making them successful on whatever terms matter to them.

You've Got to Brand

My goal in writing this book is to provide a comprehensive branding guide for entrepreneurs and intrapreneurs—a how-to and how-to-think book for entrepreneurs who want to launch a small business and grow it to a big brand. The only way to do that is through breakthrough branding. The book will show you how to go from business idea to positioning your business successfully, from establishing a verbal identity and a visual identity to packaging the brand with a distinctive look and feel, from marketing the brand to scaling it into a bigger business.

The book is full of stories—inspirational, practical, and real—of entrepreneurs and intrapreneurs and their businesses, their problems, and how they solved them to build a business that could grow into a big brand. Each chapter has "brainstormer" exercises so that you can apply the ideas to your own business as well as Brand You. At the beginning of each chapter is a quote from legendary "Mad Man" Bill Bernbach, the cofounder of Doyle Dane Bernbach, who ignited the creative revolution of the 1960s and '70s and lauched many breakthrough branding campaigns that changed the world of communication and business forever. For me and for many others, Bill Bernbach is the branding writer who continues to offer inspiration for anyone involved in breakthrough branding.

In short, you will learn how to think B.R.A.N.D.:

Brand idea: The best brands are built around what I call a "small idea"—an idea that's simple and focused and different—an idea that you could write on the back of a business card. This is your *brand promise* to your customers.

Represent the brand: "Package" your business brand and Brand You so that you have a strong visual and verbal identity and personality that conveys your brand idea. *This is your brand DNA.*

Analyze your customers: No brand is for everyone or solves every problem. Define your "typical" customer as if you were casting a person in a movie, so that the brand and branding resonate with their specific needs and desires. *This is your brand persona.*

eNgage your customers: In the digital world, customers want to be involved with your brand. They want information. They want to interact and participate. *This is your brand experience.*

Digital touchpoints: Take advantage of the digital world to expand your *brand DNA* exponentially and connect with your audience. Everything should be consistent and resonate with your *Brand Idea. These are brand touchpoints.*

Looking for True Grit

Over my years of working with entrepreneurs and budding leaders, I have come to realize that I can't always coach someone into being a successful entrepreneur. I can't provide the grit, enthusiasm, and courage you'll need as an entrepreneur. It's risky taking the entrepreneur's journey. You have to rely on yourself. You have to come to terms with standing up and standing out as a leader. You can never, ever give up.

You have to be willing to say yes to all the challenges you'll face as an entrepreneur or corporate entrepreneur. You have to be willing to fail. You have to keep doing it, adapting, and trying until you come up with a win.

And if you say yes to the challenges—and you're open to learning how the principles of breakthrough branding can help you build your business brand and your personal brand in today's digital world—then you have a much stronger chance of success. This book is dedicated to you in that endeavor.

A Final Word

Some things never change.

Your personal brand and your business brand have to come from what's true and what's best about you: your talents, values, and ideas.

Nothing will replace authenticity.

Nothing will replace *entrepreneuring*, creating more value through innovating new products and services, whether you own a company or work in one.

 ENTREPRENEURING: Thinking creatively and strategically about how to innovate, improve and market your products and services so they are more valuable to your customers.

Nothing will replace a unique insight into a consumer's need or a new solution to a problem. The solution can become a brand, and the brand can meet that need.

Nothing will replace a strong bond with your customers. That bond will lead them to spread the word, to tell their friends about you and your company. Word of mouth is a huge asset in the digital world. It has always been and remains an entrepreneur's strongest card.

Nothing will replace a company culture that people are banging at the doors to be a part of.

But if you have "true grit," if you are determined to succeed despite all the pitfalls and warnings, this book is for you. You'll feel the joy shared by entrepreneurs of all kinds: those who are following their hearts and minds, doing what's important to them, and making their own decisions despite the risks and naysayers.

The tools of breakthrough branding are for all those who say yes to being an entrepreneur.

Chapter 1

What's the Brand Idea?

*Find the simple story in the product and present it in an articulate,
intelligent, and persuasive way.*

—Bill Bernbach, Legendary "Mad Man"

Destiny is a dramatic word—but really, the first step in starting a new venture is identifying your business destiny, determining what specific business you—and only you—were born to create. The best idea for you will involve the perfect convergence of your skills, talents, and passions with the needs of the marketplace.

The hardest part of launching a business is beginning. You need to find the brand idea that's right for you. Yet, it's the most important step. Finding your business idea is like examining your DNA. It's finding what's different, relevant, and special about you so that you can share it with others. It's discovering where you belong in the world so you can embark on the journey that will take you there.

The Valley of Death

Entrepreneurs brand the time between coming up with a business idea and having a successful start-up as "The Valley of Death." As the name implies, the beginning period is no picnic. It's a tough time to get through intact. You don't have enough financing. You don't have all the skills and resources you need. You can die in the valley if you don't get enough customers and money to cover cash flow.

Yet, in so many ways, this starting period is the most valuable time you will ever have as an entrepreneur. It's the time when you can create tremendous value out of nothing. You're creating a new product or service where there was none before. You're positioning the brand so it can stand out in the marketplace. You're creating *intellectual property* with a brand name and with your brand's look and feel. You're starting to build a reputation for the new brand and for Brand You. You're developing tangible assets such as your product, equipment, and even real estate.

As a bootstrapping entrepreneur, you're creating many valuable brand assets during the beginning phase that will set the course for brand success or failure. The beginning period, this Valley of Death, may be your riskiest time, but it is also your most valuable time creatively and strategically.

Yet, many entrepreneurs rush to market, shortchanging the formulation phase. They want to have a business, yet they don't have a fully formed and viable idea. Or they have a copycat idea. Or a gargantuan, overly complicated idea. Or an idea that tries to appeal to everyone and therefore is destined for failure. When you try to appeal to everyone, you appeal to no one. If you don't use this beginning phase to build a solid foundation of brand assets, you will likely not survive the Valley of Death.

The Paradox: Small Ideas Are Big

It all begins with an idea. In the branding business, people talk a lot about the "big idea."

But I say, "Forget the big idea, go for a *small idea*."

There's a fundamental paradox of business ideas: the bigger the idea, the simpler and more focused it will be. Big ideas are small—simple, focused, and specific—so that they can occupy a unique niche and dominate their category. The best business and product ideas come from drilling down and being very targeted and specific. Drill down until you come up with a way that your brand can be superlative.

That way, you're building a business on something that's small enough to own and create a brand identity around and that will get you big results. You and your business will stand for something, rather than being a mashup of who knows what.

All good branding involves sacrifice—you must sacrifice the things that don't belong to the core business idea. Too many entrepreneurs stumble over this simple reality. When expressing their business idea, they ramble on and on for fifteen minutes, leaving their listeners (investors, potential clients, potential employees) scratching their heads. Either they haven't zeroed in on what they want to accomplish or they haven't figured out how to express it simply. Whatever the case—they are not yet ready for business.

So get a clearly focused business idea. You don't want to be an apple and orange business. You want a clear-cut business that you can define easily and effortlessly. Your simple sentence that defines your business will serve you well when pitching your idea to investors, attracting talent, talking to the press, and, most especially, connecting with your customers.

(TM) **"SMALL" IDEA: a simple, focused brand promise that defines what's special about your brand.**

Your brand idea is your tagline or mantra for your business that expresses the core concept. It's the promise of what your brand will offer customers that others don't. For example, FedEx's brand promise is its advertising tagline: "Your package will get there overnight. Guaranteed." The Japanese retailer Uniqlo's tagline is "Made for All," reflecting its mission of creating stylishly simple casual clothes for all to wear. For its fruit smoothies, the U.K. company Innocent uses the tagline, "The fruit, the whole fruit, and nothing but the fruit."

In breakthrough branding, you'll find that you always convey the most when you say the least. So make it simple. You must figure out a way to articulate clearly, for yourself and others, what the business is, who it's for, why it's needed, and why it will be a success.

Your business idea should be short enough to write on the back of a business card. You want a phrase or sentence, not an elaborate paragraph. Another way of looking at it is, if you can't explain your business idea successfully to a ten-year-old, you don't have a clear-cut idea for your business. You need to be able to sum up what your business is and why it matters. As Einstein said, "Everything must be as simple as possible, but not simpler."

Your sentence should contain a keyword or phrase that you want everyone to associate with your brand. Think of the way big brands try to own a word or phrase, like Google owns "search," Volvo owns "safety," and FedEx owns "overnight." So when people think of your brand, they think of "X." Or when they think of "X," they think of your brand.

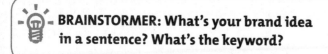

BRAINSTORMER: What's your brand idea in a sentence? What's the keyword?

When Your Heart Talks, Pay Attention

To be a successful entrepreneur, your goal has to be more than just making money. Entrepreneurship and finding your business idea are about finding your purpose. Your goal must be tied to your deeper story, your sense of destiny for yourself and your business. It must feel authentic and right for you. It's discovering your personal vision that reveals your essence, your passion, and your values. That vision comes from your heart, not your head.

Great brands are always built on *authenticity*, on who you are and what your business can be, not what you want it to be. For a decade in the 1990s, Las Vegas marketed itself as a family vacation destination. Think about it, positioning Vegas as a *family* destination. Nobody goes to Vegas for family stuff, well, almost nobody. Vegas is about drinking and gambling like crazy and doing things you want to keep under wraps afterward. Its nickname is "Sin City," after all. In 2003, when Vegas adopted authentic positioning, the city came up with its famous slogan, "What happens in Vegas, stays in Vegas." And the branding was a smash success. Now, here was a positioning line that came from Vegas's DNA. It was a brand promise that people could believe in.

⒯ Branding has to come from who you are and what your business can be, not from what you want it to be.

Great brands didn't get that way by failing to deliver on an authentic brand promise. When customers and prospects believe what you say, you get a *trust premium* over competitors. Procter & Gamble found that its businesses that were growing faster than average, including Pampers, Tide, Downy, and Crest, had a trust advantage that gave these brands a market share advantage. A global study conducted by the former chief marketing officer of P&G found that the quality of a company's external and internal communications around a shared customer ideal led to business success and the ability to grow.[1]

When we believe something is honest and comes from its true nature, what psychologists call *essentialism*, that even gives us pleasure.[2] And that pleasure is lost when we find out something is "fake" or not what we thought it was. The pleasure of a good wine is influenced by whether we think it's expensive or cheap. Just as we enjoy a painting that we trust is authentic, and don't enjoy it when we are told it is a reproduction or a fake.

You need to build a business based on authenticity, based on what the business is and can be, and who you are and can be. More than working for others, entrepreneurship offers you the opportunity to be who you were meant to be, to succeed on your own terms. You don't have to do it the company way anymore—you can and must do it your way. That's the good news *and* the bad news, of course, because you won't have the company to lean on or to blame when things go wrong. You can't be fired or even reprimanded—but you can lose everything.

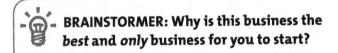

> BRAINSTORMER: Why is this business the *best* and *only* business for you to start?

The Mouse That Roared

Small, "high-concept" ideas are different. They're not copycat ideas but try to break new ground. They provide a fresh benefit, appeal to a hungry target audience, have a new process—a different something. Even though you're a small business now, having an important difference will give you a loud voice in the marketplace.

Being different is a cardinal rule of branding. You don't have to have a big idea, but you do have to have an idea that is different from your competitors' ideas. Having a different idea for your business is powerful. Just being different from everything else in your category in some way is immensely helpful for your brand because you can position your business and products as unique, occupying their own niche.

You can't own what someone else owns, so don't even try. Once you've claimed your position in the market, no one can easily move in on your spot, either.

There are a lot of ways to be different. The ultimate way is to create a whole new product category and, in the process, to create a consumer need that no one has previously exploited—possibly even a need that consumers didn't know they had. Apple has been wildly successful at this. But while not all of us are brilliant (or capitalized) enough to create a whole new product platform, we can make changes in the existing ones and be successful.

You could utilize a new technology that gives your product a competitive edge, as the various smartphone makers do every year, in an attempt to outmaneuver their competitors. Or your product might be made out of ingredients or by a process that's different.

The television cook and author Sandra Lee created a new cooking concept she called Semi-Homemade. She came up with the name while walking down the aisle in a grocery store one day and seeing bags of semisweet chocolate for cooking. That's sort of what I'm doing, she thought, because her dishes are made up of about 70 percent packaged ingredients and 30 percent fresh foods. While Lee's concept is more than semi-controversial with many cooks, she has a thriving business with adoring fans who love her easy-to-prepare recipes and her appealing personal brand. Sandra Lee's tagline for her cooking concept is "Keep It Simple, Keep It Smart, Keep It Sweet, Keep It Semi-Homemade."[3]

Each target market has its preferences and hot points, and your product could tap into the mindset of a specific group or generation. Axe positions its grooming products for teenage boys and young men and what's on their minds. Its "Axe effect" marketing is compelling for this target, namely, smell good with Axe and get the girl.

Price is a differentiator. Most cultures revere innovators, but cheapeners are critical, too. If you come up with a new manufacturing technique or a supply chain process that saves money, you can pass that on to your customers and beat the competition handily, as Wal-Mart has shown.

Customer service could be your differentiator if you develop specific service advantages that competitors don't offer. For example, Amazon took an early and decisive lead in online retailing based in part on the user-friendliness of its interface and in part on its competitive discounting structure and low shipping costs. Amazon started as the "world's largest *bookstore*" but parlayed its early success in a narrow retail category into vastly expanded offerings, including music, housewares, drugstore items, clothes, you name it. Amazon's small idea wasn't books, after all, it was online retail sales. A slew of useful business books have been written about Amazon and other retailers (online ones, such as Zappos, as well as brick-and-mortar businesses such as Nordstrom's and Starbucks) who quickly turned "small ideas" into big profits.

Even something as simple as a new and exciting design can be the differentiator. In the era of iPad, design matters.

Bottom line: you need a different mental angle for your brand, one that shows how your brand is different or superlative. And you need to express that in every communication about your business. You must always be ready to answer the question, "What do you have to offer that's different from what's already out there?"

In short, you will never be a breakthrough branding star unless you aim for that small, unique, clearly focused idea—an idea that's crisp and offers something different. Reaching for something focused and unique pays off. You may not end up on the *Inc.* list of America's Fastest-Growing Companies, but you won't end up with a handful of dirt, either.

> **BRAINSTORMER: My brand is the only**
> _____ **that** _____.

Let Your Mind Dream

During the period when you are looking for and refining your business idea, let your mind wander. Dream. Free associate. What calls out to you, even though you're not sure why? What do your find yourself drawn to? When you're walking around, what attracts your attention? When you're on the Internet, what do you find intriguing? Why? What is it telling you?

If you could do anything you wanted, what would it be? What other businesses and entrepreneurs do you admire? Why is that?

What do you find easy to do or easy to learn? What feels good? What gives you satisfaction?

Whether or not you want to start a business in an industry that you have already worked in (and that is something you should certainly consider), it makes sense to examine business areas that you are familiar with. Look at what you know well. What rules have never been questioned in your industry or area of expertise? What would happen if they were? What are the problems that everyone complains about? How could they be solved? Could this lead to an opportunity for you? When you start paying attention, you'll find lots of areas ripe for exploration.

As we all know, successful entrepreneurs look at the same things that everyone else looks at and see something different. They see opportunities. Then we all look at what they've created and say, "Why didn't I think of that? It's so obvious." And the entrepreneur thinks, "I didn't really do it. I just saw something."

Set the Stage for Ideas

While you can't make a business idea come to you on a schedule, there is much you can do to impel the creative process and open your mind to insight.

Think about your business idea then leave the subject behind and do something different. Forget about the question at hand for a while and let your mind wander. Sleep on it. (My most fruitful time for breakthroughs is early in the morning, when I'm half asleep.) Take a walk. Soak in the tub.

Scientists believe that big breakthroughs often seem to come out of nowhere, when we're doing something else. The unconscious mind takes over and makes connections, helping us solve problems we haven't been able to crack consciously—maybe because we were *trying* too hard. This is "peripheral thinking," because it is analogous to peripheral vision. (You've probably noticed that something glimpsed out of the corner of your eye can make a clearer impression than something you are staring directly at.)

Try it and see if a lightbulb goes off. Maybe you think that lightbulb line is a cliché. But you know what? It kind of *is* like that—a "lightbulb" does go off in your mind when you come up with a new idea. Studies have shown that when you have a new idea, there is a burst of brain activity that looks like a light show on brain scans.

This phenomenon is actually gamma waves emanating from the brain's right hemisphere. That's the area of the brain involved in handling associations and assembling elements of a problem. The only difference between you and me and all of those serial entrepreneurs who come up with business ideas right and left is that they have the courage to act upon their own bursts of insight.

 BRAINSTORMER: What business ideas come to you when you let your mind wander?

Hypothetically Speaking

Brainstorming can be easier with the help of a group. Try putting together a small, diverse "focus group" to help you explore your ideas. (Of course, you'll have to invite them over for dinner first.)

Don't ask the group to prepare by reading or studying something in advance. Make your initial meeting a session of "freestyle brainstorming" to come up with your initial hypothesis. The initial hypothesis is a technique that many management consultants use successfully. It's based on the concept that the best ideas often come through on-the-spot brainstorming and by developing an initial hypothesis without the benefit of any research. As we discussed earlier, many ideas come from the unconscious mind—and that is true in group brainstorming sessions as well.

Spontaneous brainstorming involves free thinking without the limitations of conventional thinking or what the experts or skeptics say. Deep down, we already all have a lot of smart ideas and know the answers. The trick is letting them out!

The reason the initial hypothesis can be insightful is simple: it may seem counterintuitive, but conventional wisdom often steers us in the wrong direction. The answer to a question like "What's the best business for me to start?" is often right in front of your nose. Look first for the obvious solution—or what your intuition tells you. Your hunch is often as accurate or better than the answer derived through careful study.

In your brainstorming and informal focus groups, pay special attention to two things:

Big picture: What are the recurring themes that keep coming up?
Nitty-gritty: What words, phrases, or nuggets of insight could be useful in developing your business idea and its branding?

So, when tackling something as important as your business idea, don't begin by doing a lot of research. You can do that later. Begin by tapping into your gut and the free associations of your brainstorming pals.

When you are in the business idea–generation phase, remember that censoring is taboo. What appear to be dumb ideas often turn out to be good ideas, or they serve as catalysts to better ideas. One thing I observed while working in ad agencies was that the top creative people generated tons of ideas. They didn't self-censor like the rest of us. Nine out of ten ideas were bad, but there was the one gem. So make it your goal to come up with lots of ideas, crazy as well as logical. You can put your ideas on index cards, and if you have dozens, you can lay them out on the floor and gradually remove the weak ones from the group until you have your gem of an idea.

 BRAINSTORMER: What would be the dream business for you based on your unique talents, interests, and abilities?

Find the White Space

You know you have a viable business idea when you find the "white space," which is really just a need in the marketplace that no one is filling or that no one can satisfy in quite the way you will. Look for a powerful emotional need, a big want that people have.

In 1980, Fred Carl Jr., a fourth-generation builder, was designing a kitchen for a new house that he and his wife, Margaret, were building. Margaret wanted a heavy-duty gas range like the one her mother cooked with—a 1947 Chambers range. It turned out that Chambers ranges weren't made anymore, so Carl looked into commercial ranges used by restaurants. But he was told that those weren't really suitable for homes.[4]

Not one to give up when challenged, Carl decided to work nights and weekends to design and make a professional-quality range for his own home use. He did research whenever he went out to dinner with his wife, often embarrassing her by going back into the kitchen to check the ranges and ask about how they performed. Carl found out what it was about commercial ranges that made them unworkable for homes—for one thing, they gave off as much heat as your average furnace.

Carl called all the major manufacturers of ranges in the United States and told them about his idea: a commercial-style range for the home. Everyone thought he was crazy. No one would want a range like that in his home, manufacturers told him.

That's when Carl realized that he had a business idea. It was a small idea: simple, focused, and different. He knew there was a need. His wife wanted one, and no one was making them so it stood to reason that other home cooks would love to have a heavy-duty, commercial-style range as well.

Carl pitched a group of range manufacturers to make about a dozen of the residential commercial ranges he had designed. He'd pay for them, of course, with an added bonus of purchasing more if sales took off. The manufacturers were skeptical, but he finally persuaded one appliance manufacturer to produce his ovens on a limited basis.

Perhaps you've guessed this by now: Carl called his oven "Viking." He chose the name because he thought of Vikings as tough, substantial, and enduring. He started out using his own money and credit cards but soon brought in a small group of investors from his hometown in Mississippi. His first shipment went out in 1987, and the Viking stove was an immediate success.

Fred Carl Jr. had a winning business idea, but that was just the beginning. Very quickly, he had to learn about manufacturing, marketing, and signing up a dealer network. After he got the range launched, naturally his wife wanted all of the appliances in her kitchen to match. Soon, Carl was developing accessories and companion products such as ventilation hoods, built-in ovens, and refrigerators. What had started out as a personal renovation project turned into the hugely successful Viking appliance business.

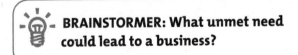

BRAINSTORMER: What unmet need could lead to a business?

What's Your Passion?

What do you love to do? What are your hobbies? What do other people compliment you about? Is there a business there? Is it a brick-and-mortar business or an online business? How can you make money?

It's powerful to create your business idea out of something that you love to do, because it means that you'll be building your business right smack in the center of your personal sweet spot, and running it may not even seem like work.

The Gilt Groupe was launched in 2007 by two young, fashionable women, Alexis Maybank and Alexandra Wilkis Wilson, who had met at Harvard Business School. Both were working in New York City, and at lunchtime, when they had the chance, they would often steal out of the office and go to designer sample sales, hunting for discounts on clothes and accessories. But they couldn't always spare the time, and they didn't always hear about sales in their neighborhood.[5]

That gave them an idea. What if they brought the sample sale concept online? It was a small, different idea. It was simple and focused. It was different—no one was doing it. They knew there was a need because they had often witnessed the excitement of sample sales firsthand, as had many of their friends.

The duo thought a lot about the sample sale experience (it's a kind of contact sport for New York City women!) and realized that to succeed, they had to replicate some of the frenzy that characterizes an actual New York City sample sale—right down to the tug-of-war matches between fashionably dressed women. How could they create that urgency and competition online, they wondered, along with the sense of exclusivity that comes with being on the mailing lists for the sales? The answer they came up with involved online membership, along with the "flash sale" concept used by online retailers to push limited-time-only sales on the Internet.

In order to participate, shoppers must become Gilt Groupe members—usually by invitation from other members. Every day, just before noon, Gilt Groupe sends out e-mails to its membership about that day's designer fashions on sale. There is a sense of excitement and surprise engendered by the e-mails that is integral to the brand concept. Its status as a member-only site gives it an air of exclusivity. There's also the sense of scarcity. Each item is on sale for that day only—and only while supplies last. This creates an online frenzy that replicates what happens at "live" sample sales in stores.

The two partners chose the name because they felt that the word *Gilt* (meaning covered in gold leaf) sounded timeless and beautiful, like the items they'd offer for sale on the web. They also liked the little bit of wordplay with the word *guilt*. And finally, the two words created a nice alliteration that would make the name easy to remember. The French spelling of *Groupe* connoted fashion and a certain sense of *je ne sais quoi*. Clearly, they gave the idea and the name a lot of careful thought—and the result has been a stellar success.

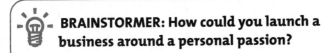

> **BRAINSTORMER: How could you launch a business around a personal passion?**

Ask Why? What If? How About?

What attracts your attention? What's in the news? What business ideas look intriguing? What's working in one area but might also work in another area with a little tweaking? What are the hurdles? How can they be eliminated?

In 1999, when he was approached with the idea of an online shoe business, Tony Hsieh was uncertain whether people would buy shoes online without being able to try them on. A comfortable fit is crucial and can be tricky.[6] Would women, the real shoe fanatics, really buy shoes through the Internet?

But Hsieh did some research and was impressed with the sheer scale of the shoe market. Catalog shoe sales already made up 5 percent of the market. Hmm, thought Hsieh—why not online sales, then, where we can offer a truly vast selection? Hsieh realized this could be an interesting business. It was a small, different idea: an online shoe store offering the largest variety of styles imaginable.

Hsieh's partner suggested calling the company *Zapatos*, after the Spanish word for shoes, but Hsieh thought that might be hard to pronounce, spell, and remember, and he shortened it to Zappos.

Realizing that the biggest hurdle for customers would be their reluctance to pay shipping fees when returning merchandise that didn't fit or suit them, Zappos offered free shipping both ways on all shoe orders, no questions asked.

Knowing that customer service is key, even in an online business, they emphasized their toll-free help number (unlike many companies, who hide it in the fine print on their websites). This emphasis on service became their mantra, and Zappos made it big. Zappos realized that customer service wasn't a cost but a powerful part of the company's branding. It was a small idea: simple, focused, and different, and Zappos executed it brilliantly.

 BRAINSTORMER: Is there something from the brick-and-mortar arena that you could launch on the Internet?

A Marriage Made in Heaven

Some breakout ideas come from connecting with the right partner—someone with complementary strengths.

In 1997, Seth Goldman was looking for a refreshing drink after a run with a friend, but all the choices were too sweet. Figuring that there was a need in the market for healthier, less-sweet drinks, Goldman e-mailed Barry Nalebuff, one of his professors at Yale Business School. Nalebuff had just returned from India, where he had been writing a case study about tea.[7]

Tea is one of the world's cheapest luxuries, Nalebuff told him, yet all of the bottled teas in the United States were made from the poorest quality tea. Goldman and Nalebuff decided to launch a business together based on a perceived gap in the market and an idea for a healthy drink. Now, they had their product to fill it. They'd hit upon a small, different business idea.

The two began brewing tea in Goldman's kitchen, experimenting with different ingredients and recipes. In 1998, they brought thermoses of their best concoctions to Whole Foods, including a sample bottle—an empty Snapple bottle with a pasted-on label—and after one taste, the buyer ordered 15,000 bottles. Over the next two months, the partners had to raise money, manufacture the tea, design the branding and packaging, and bottle the tea.

They discovered that using less sweetener saved them enough money to afford natural sugar. That meant they could advertise their product as "organic"—and get in on the burgeoning trend toward healthy drinks. Their timing was perfect, as the trend toward healthy drinks contributed to their success.

The team called its product Honest Tea (sounds like *Honesty*!), and the initial product line included bottled teas, tea bags, and bulk tea.

In the early years, Goldman focused on building distribution.[8] The beverage industry can be fickle. If you're not on the shelves and restocked, you're out of business. He and his team went to a lot of trade shows and spent nights in cheap hotels, sometimes doubling up in the same room to save money as they marketed the company's drinks and lined up distributors.

After about five years, the partners realized that the standout aspect of their real business idea was in the "Honest" part, so they enlarged their brand footprint to include Honest Kids and Honest Ade. (They own the rights to Honest Food, as well.)

After ten years in business, Goldman and Nalebuff sold 40 percent of the company to Coca-Cola. Of course, that partnership has had some growing pains. Not long after the deal, the two companies had a dustup over the label on Honest Tea products that promised, "No high-fructose corn syrup," which some at Coke saw as a rebuke of their products.

In 2011, Coca-Cola bought all of the company under an agreement that leaves Goldman and his management team in place in "recognition that, especially with early-stage brands, the entrepreneurs continue to be relevant and important," said Goldman.[9]

Chalk up this success story to one thirsty guy who found the right partners.

 BRAINSTORMER: Is there someone you could partner with who complements your strengths?

You Should Open a Store!

Branding is a competition. It's a competition over product ideas, and it's a competition over customers. Nowhere is this competition more cutthroat than in the fashion and retailing businesses.

Korean immigrants to the United States Do Won and Jin Sook Chang came to Los Angeles in 1981, a time when Korean immigrants were starting to work their way into the garment industry there. While performing menial jobs, they saved enough to open a 900-square-foot retail store in a gritty area of the city in 1984. They initially called the store Fashion 21, a rather generic moniker, but refined it to Forever 21, a name with a concept and a cheeky edge.[10]

The Changs were targeting teenage girls, but they understood that fashion is aspirational and that teens would love the idea of looking and feeling "21." And, let's face it, there are plenty of older women who shop there who want to feel twenty-one, too!

Their small idea was fast fashion—cutting edge today but inexpensive enough to replace tomorrow. They were all about cheap chic, turnover, and youthful energy.

From the beginning, the Forever 21 concept was built-in obsolescence. Rather than put out tons of items like other stores did, the Changs put out small groups of hot styles, positioning the newest items at the front of their stores and changing them daily. There was a treasure hunt aspect to the shopping experience. Items were priced so that customers weren't making a big investment—just buying some hot items they could wear for a while and then discard in favor of the next new thing. (Most items are priced between $5 and $40.)

Every day, trucks pulled up to the stores with new merchandise. Fashion-conscious teenagers quickly realized that if they liked something, they'd better grab it, or it wouldn't be around the next time they were in the store. A typical Forever 21 store might turn over 20 percent of its merchandise in a week, about twice as much as other retailers.

Forever 21 stores look different from any other chain. The interiors are designed to "pop," with large-scale mannequins and graphics. Some stores have an electronically revolving rack that girls can stop when they want to look at a particular piece—an idea the Changs got from the movie *Clueless*.

The Changs had a small idea, simply focused on teenage girl power and their scramble for affordable, fun fashion. It's an idea they parlayed into a business encompassing more than 350 Forever 21 stores in the United States and dozens more around the world.

 BRAINSTORMER: Could you create a retail store that targets a special niche?

Party Girl

Frustrated that she couldn't find fun, quality, and affordable party items for her three young children's parties, Carole Middleton began sourcing and creating party paraphernalia herself. It led to her small idea. Why not launch a mail-order party business for frustrated moms like herself?

Launched in 1987, Party Pieces was the United Kingdom's first mail-order party company. Initially, it was just Middleton working from the shed in her back garden. Carole developed in-house branded items such as party boxes and party food boxes. They were such a success that Party Pieces created specialty boxes and other products for every party theme. Before long, her husband left his job as a flight dispatcher to help run the business, and their three children got involved. Today, with more than thirty employees and working out of three converted barns, Party Pieces is the U.K.'s leading online and catalog party company. And they keep expanding the party line beyond children's parties to the adult party and celebration category.[11]

Of course, Party Pieces got some unexpected publicity when the Middleton's eldest daughter, Catherine, became engaged to and then married Prince William, and traffic to the website has spiked dramatically. Mindful of a conflict of interest, the royal family buys its party supplies elsewhere, but the rest of England orders through Party Pieces.

 BRAINSTORMER: Is there something missing in the market that you could supply?

The Mashup

When you're trying to come up with a new business idea, you might try putting together two related but unlike things and see what you come up with.

Jack Dorsey first came to fame—and fortune—as the creator of Twitter. The idea for that groundbreaking innovation grew out of his fascination with the way people communicated within cities, especially the "haiku" of people such as bike messengers, delivery truck drivers, firefighters, and taxi drivers who stayed in touch with one another via GPS devices, CB radios, and cell phones. He was intrigued with the code words and special language they developed to communicate with each other quickly and efficiently. The only problem, as he saw it, was that this form of communication was confined to the members of these specific groups. The rest of us were left out—there were no regular people in these networks.[12]

Breakthrough branding connects things that weren't connected before.

Like lots of people, Dorsey was using the instant messaging and texting functions on his cell phone as a way to communicate with his friends. He started thinking about how he might use these means of communication to create networks among groups of friends or colleagues—just as he'd observed within communities of taxi drivers or messengers. In essence, the small idea for Twitter was a mashup of instant messaging and texting with the networking capability of CB radio that ties a group together.

The inspiration for limiting tweets to 140 characters came from the realities of texting. Most basic phones limit messages to 160 characters before they start to split the messages into segments. So to avoid splitting messages, Dorsey decided that Twitter would take twenty characters for the user name and leave 140 for the content. And that's it. Having only a limited number of characters to communicate a thought has changed the way people frame what they have to say to one another.

Twitter fans created branded words like "tweet" for the act of producing the messages and the messages themselves. In the early days, Twitter also used the word "watch": you could "watch" or "unwatch" someone. But it soon hit upon a better word. On today's Twitter, we "follow" or "unfollow" someone, because that's a more accurate description of the process.

Launched in 2006, Twitter quickly upended the traditional way people communicate. It has become one of the web's most rapidly growing information channels. Twitter began with a simple idea—a simple way of sharing information that came about by combining two different things: texting and the networking systems of CB radios.

 BRAINSTORMER: Can you put together two different things to create a new business service?

Hip to Be Square

Having founded Twitter, Dorsey was looking for a new start-up idea in 2008. He got into a conversation with a friend who was a glassblower. His friend was exploring ways to use a smartphone to sell his artwork, because traditional credit card machines were bulky and expensive to use at outdoor art shows or other locations outside his studio.

The small idea that they hatched together was bringing a "Twitter-like simplicity to the complex world of credit card processing."[13] Named after the small, square devices you plug into your smartphone, Square makes it easy for anyone to accept credit card purchases without bulky equipment and monthly fees.

Unlike credit card companies, who charge to set up a merchant account then charge monthly fees for the service and also charge for the credit card reader (or require a long-term contract), Square simply charges vendors a fee per transaction. It's not only cheap but also simple. Square is signing up tens of thousands of new small businesses a month, including entrepreneurs with no fixed location such as flea market vendors, food trucks, and itinerant artists.

The design of the Square device is sleek and minimal and reflects Dorsey's interest in design aesthetics. He had studied botanical drawing and clothing design after all.

 BRAINSTORMER: What needs updating to be in sync with today's mobile world?

Imitation with a Twist

You don't have to come up with your small idea from scratch to be wildly successful as an entrepreneur, either. But you do have to tweak it to make it work for your country or region.

In 2009, after the Chinese government blocked Twitter for the twentieth anniversary of Tiananmen Square, Chinese entrepreneur Charles Chao saw an opportunity.[14] He realized that microblogging was a small idea that could be big in China. There was the natural conciseness of the Chinese language that made the text limitations less limiting than it is in English. In Chinese, a single character can represent an entire word or part of a word, not just an individual letter of the alphabet like in most other languages.

But Chao had to make the idea work with the restrictive government of China, where news and open communication can be a problem. He also had to make the concept right for a Chinese audience and to cut off the

Chinese microblogging sites that were starting to pop up. Chao got Beijing's approval based on his track record at keeping sensitive information off the blogs in his existing Internet company, Sina.

Chao called his company Sina Weibo (Weibo means "microblog"), and in 2011 he shortened the domain name to Weibo.com. In essence, Chao owns the domain name for the word that denotes the entire microblog category!

To make his microblog become a daily must-read for a Chinese audience and stand out from Twitter and the other Chinese Twitter clones, Chao actively sought celebrities—actors, singers, TV hosts, economists, and other VIPs—to post their news and doings on Weibo.

The celebrity connection helped Weibo take off like a rocket. Just two years after its launch, Weibo is the biggest microblog in China, with more than 140 million users and more than 60,000 celebrities. Every day, millions of Chinese log into Weibo.com to see what their favorite celebrities and friends are up to and to check who's on Weibo's Top Ten List of Celebrities, the ones with the highest number of fans that day.

Chao's small idea has been a big winner. According to iResearch, Weibo has 56.5 percent of the microblogging market based on active users and 86.6 percent based on browsing time. It is censored, but as Chao points out, it is also one of the most open online platforms in China.

 BRAINSTORMER: Is there a successful business in another part of the world that you can adapt for your market?

Up the Ladder

While working at Hotjobs.com, Marc Cenedella noticed a puzzling gap in the online search world. Jobs boards were full of possibilities great for entry- and mid-level job seekers but didn't hold much work for executives. Those job seekers looking for higher-paid jobs were frustrated, and many companies and recruiters didn't post jobs for senior candidates.

Cenedella's small idea was to create a job site focused exclusively on $100k+ jobs.[15] He launched his company, The Ladders, in 2003. To encourage as many companies as possible to post their openings on his site, the original business model offered free job posting for companies and charged a fee to job seekers who wanted access to the site.

The Ladders site quickly attracted upscale, out-of-work executives. While small and midsize companies were posting any jobs they had that paid over $100k+ on the site, large corporations weren't using it. Cenedella was puzzled until one of his sales reps brought back the answer. Corporate human resources people questioned the company's value: "How good could the site be if it's free?" Cenedella took this to heart and adjusted his business model. As soon as he started charging companies a fee, the site took off. Today, it's the number-one site in the world for filling $100k+ jobs.

 BRAINSTORMER: Is there a market segment your current employer is not serving well that you could build as a separate business?

Trend Watcher

After getting his M.B.A. from Stanford in 1954, Joe Coulombe became a researcher with a specialty in convenience stores. In 1958, he acquired his own convenience store chain, called Pronto Markets, and became more than a researcher.[16]

In the early years, Coulombe had trouble finding a winning business formula and experimented with different strategies. One day in the mid 1960s, he was intrigued with an article he was reading in *Scientific American* about baby boomers. It pointed out that a change was taking place and that, unlike their parents, the majority of baby boomers qualified to go to college were now going.

That article gave Coulombe his small idea. He speculated that those well-educated baby boomers of Depression-era parents would want a more sophisticated yet offbeat and fun food-shopping experience. His name was Joe and he decided to call his new concept grocery store Trader Joe's, launching the first store in 1967. Coulombe was targeting a specific persona, what one marketer called "a Volvo-driving professor who could be CEO of a Fortune 100 Company if he could get over his capitalist angst."[17]

Coulombe's second breakthrough came in the 1970s, again after reading an article in *Scientific American*. (That subscription certainly paid off!) This time it was about the biosphere, and Joe became what is today called "green," again years ahead of his time. Trader Joe's became a champion of organic products.

Coulombe is believed to have adopted the South Seas motif for his stores after a vacation in the Caribbean. Over the years, Trader Joe's has developed a wide range of branded products. People talk about their favorite Trader Joe's foods, and the store has made private-label goods chic. It has a small-store vibe in a big-store body, and because of its particular qualities and the way Coulombe has tapped into the zeitgeist, it has a devoted cult following.

 BRAINSTORMER: What are the new trends that might lead to a business idea?

Want to Change the World?

Some small ideas are motivated more by altruism than any profit motive. In 1989, Wendy Kopp, a senior at Princeton University, was thinking about becoming a New York City schoolteacher—but she couldn't get an entry-level teaching job because she didn't have a master's in education or a teaching certificate. Frustrated, she applied to a Wall Street investment bank and wrote her senior thesis about her idea for a teaching corps: an organization that would attract the best college graduates in all fields to teach at the lowest-performing urban and rural schools.[18]

It was a small idea. It was simple, different, and relevant: a teaching corps for the best and brightest college graduates (with or without teaching credentials) to teach for two years in the nation's worst schools.

Today, over 10 percent of college graduates apply for a two-year teaching stint via Teach for America. Unlike school systems that select teachers based on who applies, Teach for America works like a consulting firm, actively recruiting the most talented people and training them throughout their employment. Kopp may not have gotten rich from her idea, but she found her calling and created a powerful nonprofit that was named one of America's best companies to work for in 2011.

There are lots of different ways to make a difference with a nonprofit. Marjorie James was promoting diversity and inclusion in big companies in 2006 when she noticed a group no one was paying much attention to at the time: wounded soldiers and other service people returning to the United States from Iraq and Afghanistan. When she started investigating, James discovered there was a big chasm between the military and the corporate workforce. The military should be part of corporate diversity and inclusion efforts, she realized.

The more James got involved, the more passionate she became about the plight of returning military trying to get corporate jobs in a tough job market. Here were people who had sacrificed and served the country, and many were struggling to find meaningful employment.

Her daughter got engaged to a former soldier who had successfully transitioned to a career in banking, so she knew the leadership skills and other military experience were valuable in the corporate arena, but many military people had always been in the military and didn't know how to market themselves in the corporate world, whether it was for a technical job or a managerial job.

James had found her small idea and her vision for making a difference. She launched a nonprofit, Hire America's Heroes, initially in Washington state, where she has lined up corporate sponsors. She's staging corporate job fairs and training programs specifically for military veterans with the goal of eliminating the chasm between the military and corporate worlds.

 BRAINSTORMER: Is there a nonprofit or social entrepreneurship idea you could launch to make the world a better place?

However you go about looking for your idea, a breakthrough brand idea will be obvious when you find it:

It will be *small*: be simple and focused.
It will be *relevant*: solve a problem and satisfy a human need.
It will be *different*: have a different mental angle than competitors.
It will be *authentic*: play to your strengths and values.
It will *connect emotionally*: appeal to feelings not just reason.

The Alchemy of the Brand Entrepreneur

However much we would like advertising to be a science, because life would be simpler that way, the fact is that it is not. It is a subtle, ever-changing art, defying formularization, flowering on freshness and withering on imitation; what was effective one day, for that very reason, will not be effective the next, because it has lost the maximum impact of originality.

—Bill Bernbach, Legendary "Mad Man"

You've got to love the game.

Being an entrepreneur will take everything that you've got. It involves tapping into the dreamer and innovator inside you, demanding the best of yourself and others, and finding the intersection between your creativity and the marketplace.

You're in the *imagining business*. Once you've dreamed up and perfected your winning business idea, you need to know how to unlock the creativity in others, too. With your own skills and a motivated team, you can do breakthrough branding, continually imagining new possibilities and solutions as unexpected situations arise in today's dynamic business world.

You're in the *leadership business*. You are a professional inspirer who must charm, coach, and motivate the best talent in your field. A boss can make you do something, but a leader makes you want to do it. And that's a big difference. Successful entrepreneurs are terrific at expressing what they want to achieve and why and selling it. They have plans, sometimes giddy plans, for the future and are able to make others believe wholeheartedly in those plans.

Leaders *empower* their employees to do things they couldn't (or wouldn't) have done on their own, instilling in them the courage to try and the permission to fail. They never make you feel small. In fact, quite the opposite: they enlarge you and help you see the best qualities in yourself. When they believe in you, you believe in them.

You're in the *growth business*. Entrepreneurs realize that there are two main ways to fuel growth, either by increasing revenues or by cutting costs, and they aim to master both. Successful entrepreneurs are on the offensive—always—looking for new opportunities, new innovations, new communications, new customers, and new systems for growth. They are great salespeople who attract investors and customers. They are constantly on the search for new customer insights to grow the business.

You're in the *problem-solving business*. Successful entrepreneurs use every resource—intellect, friends, money—to solve a problem and launch and sustain their creation.

In fact, problems are good for you—they are opportunities. More entrepreneurs appear when there is a new problem to be solved, a new technology to be exploited, or a new need in the marketplace. These are the situations in which innovation is welcomed and motivated entrepreneurs are rewarded. Think of the way the iPhone propelled thousands of entrepreneurs to create apps for its mobile phones. And now other players and devices are jumping on the app bandwagon, creating a thriving industry.

You're in the *talent business*. Successful entrepreneurs are talent magnets, for employees and for business friends. Most people attract people who are like themselves. Successful entrepreneurs attract people who can add to their skills—people who have abilities, resources, and knowledge they lack.

Like it or not, you're in the *technology business*, even if you are launching a decidedly low-tech, high-touch business. Today, technology, business, and brand building are all intertwined, and for every business, technology and clever software are part of the solution. When you learn something about software and programming, it affects your mindset. You see that big problems are made up of smaller problems that have to be solved first. The possibilities through technology and social media are leading from a command-and-control business model to a more engaged and collaborative way of connecting with others.

Above all, if you want to be a successful entrepreneur today, you need to be in the *branding business*. Branding is not just a name or logo design or physical product. It is everything you do to communicate and market the real, tangible value that your business or product offers and build relationships with customers. In the early go-to-market stage of your business, branding and marketing is going to take up a lot of your time, particularly if you want to create a breakthrough brand that goes big. And don't just think brand in terms of customer interaction, you need to think brand in terms of the internal company culture as well, so that everything resonates inside and outside.

(TM) **Breakthrough branding is everything you do to build a brand that stands out and grabs people at every touchpoint.**

Today, it's a tremendous asset to be a great brander as an entrepreneur. Breakthrough branding—corporate identity, advertising, public relations, digital campaigns, internal communications—leads to engaged relationships externally and internally that will help you grow the business. And brand *touchpoints*, the contact points where customers come into contact with your brand, are increasing every day with the explosive growth of digital channels. That's why you've got to realize that communications and branding are integral to what you are building and watch over every aspect of it.

Business Brand + Personal Brand = Breakthrough Brand

Successful entrepreneurs understand what it takes to be in control and in demand. They built a business into a brand, and they tapped into themselves to create a unique personal brand that complements their business brand. They are what I call *brand entrepreneurs*.

BRAND ENTREPRENEUR: a business owner who thinks strategically and creatively about creating a brand—for the business and personally.

Brand entrepreneurs have good gut instincts about what people really want, even if market research tells them otherwise. For example, no research study anticipated the popularity of the Internet or social media, but some super-savvy brand entrepreneurs like Jeff Bezos of Amazon and Mark Zuckerberg of Facebook positioned themselves well ahead of the curve in these areas by envisioning what was to come.

Brand entrepreneurs have a vision, and it's more than just making money and being a CEO. They want to make a difference in some way, and they have the savvy to sell that vision. They have a knack for personal branding—or they acquire it. They learn how to harness the power of words, symbols, and story not only to build their businesses but also to position themselves as the leaders of those businesses.

As a budding entrepreneur, you need to create a unique brand that resonates with your business idea, values, and culture, and that will help drive your business success.

Taking charge of your business brand and intertwining it with your personal brand pays off. At its core, branding is about taking even something common like water or food and making it valuable and uncommon. Not so long ago, chefs were anonymous working stiffs, toiling away amidst the pots and pans in the kitchen. Nobody knew who was back there, except perhaps at a Michelin-ranked restaurant, and chefs rarely mingled with patrons.

Today, celebrity chefs are the rage—and they have a bent for branding. Wolfgang Puck was one of the first chefs to brand himself, and a legion of others followed. Emeril Lagasse, Anthony Bourdain, Tom Colicchio, Alice Waters, and Mario Batali, to name just a few, have books, TV shows, and product lines. Some of them are as recognizable as film stars and politicians. They have all become experts at using their personal brands to enhance their business brands—leveraging their distinctive personalities, cooking styles, and images to achieve success.

But brand entrepreneurship isn't just for top chefs and Michelin-ranked eating destinations. It has become a trend among smaller and more local culinary businesses as well. Chefs are the brand at many neighborhood restaurants today, and they promote their cooking credentials and specialty dishes along with such factors as location, value, and type of cuisine. Chefs greet customers personally, have web pages and a presence on social media sites, hire PR firms, and make appearances on local talk shows and at bookstores and malls. They know that raising their own profiles will help give their restaurants special cachet and make them stand out from the competition.

> **BRAINSTORMER: What specific traits make you different, even better than others?**

Hard Is Soft and Soft Is Hard

The brand entrepreneur realizes that in today's business world, branding power—what I call "soft power"—trumps hard power. It's the intangible assets that mean so much.

For your business, *hard power* consists of those quantifiable things you put on your balance sheet: the bricks and mortar, your inventory of goods, your equipment and supplies, your cash on hand, investments, and receivables. In terms of your personal brand, *hard power* consists of those quantifiable things you list in your bio or resumé, such as companies where you've worked, your job titles, years of experience, education and training credentials, awards, and the like. Hard power is important, but it's not enough to succeed in today's dynamic, competitive marketplace.

 Soft power is the brands, intellectual property, reputation, alliances, and relationships that mean so much.

For your business, *soft power* consists of the *brands* and the *intellectual property*—the brand names, inventions, patents, advertising campaigns, taglines, and ideas—your business owns. Soft power is the image and reputation of your business. It's the relationships your brand has with its people—customers, employees, vendors—who value your business and what you stand for. It's having a company or products that your core group of prospects recognize. It's having visibility in the industry, the community, and the larger world.

Soft power is what people say about you and your business on social media or at business gatherings when you're not around. Soft power comes from taking a stand for something that people recognize and value.

For your personal brand, *soft power* consists of the intellectual property people associate with you personally—the ideas, initiatives, sound bites, and phrases that are associated with you. Your personal soft power arises from your ability to speak effectively and frame your ideas so that they capture the hearts and minds of others. It's your ability to persuade and motivate others.

Soft power is your relationships with your customers, your employees, and your network of alliances. Soft power is your ability to inspire and "click" with people so that they identity with you and your business.

Soft power consists of all of the intangible assets that attract customers to your business and to you as its leader. Soft power puts creativity into the leadership equation, both in how you think about yourself as a leader and how you approach your business. Strengthening your soft power involves developing abilities to motivate others and attract customers: your image, your voice, your words, your body language, and your stage presence.

Soft power is the carrot that attracts people to your business and makes it a moneymaker. Your soft power is what's special about you and what makes you a successful leader. And you must dare to be different in order to harness it.

 BRAINSTORMER: List your hard power and soft power assets:

Hard Power Assets

FOR YOUR BUSINESS:	FOR YOU PERSONALLY:
Tangible assets you can list on your balance sheet, such as real estate, inventory, etc.	Tangible things you can list on your resumé such as education credentials, years of experience, job titles, training programs, etc.

Soft Power Assets

FOR YOUR BUSINESS: Your business idea, brands, intellectual property, customers, reputation, etc.

FOR YOU PERSONALLY: Your image, reputation, network, communication skills, alliances, speaking, visibility, intellectual property (articles), etc.

Be a "Liberal Arts M.B.A."

As an entrepreneur, you need to grow your business constantly or you won't stay in business. The best entrepreneurs, those who take a small business and grow it into a big brand, are doers and brand thinkers, not financial analysts. Because the future is impossible to predict, you need to figure out what your business is, who your customers are, and how your business is going to work.

 It used to be, the bigger your business plan, the bigger its potential. Now, it's the smaller your business plan, the bigger its potential.

Most entrepreneurs learn quickly that no business plan survives contact with the market. The future is too unpredictable. Focus on the important drivers of your business without the pie-in-the-sky forecasts. (A business plan of twenty pages or fewer is a good rule of thumb.)

Many business schools emphasize financial and analytical skills, and those are certainly important. In today's digital world, there is an increasing stream of data from the Internet and other new technology sources, and you or someone on your team needs to be good at *data mining* to make sense of all the numbers that are available. As an entrepreneur in today's marketplace, what you need is what some have called a "Liberal Arts M.B.A."[1] You need a big-picture brand and people sensibility along with financial and analytical skills.

Indeed, many top business schools are adding "soft skills" business courses to prepare students to be leaders. One study found that the skills actual business executives felt were most important—managing others and decision making—were barely covered in most business schools.[2] Only about 10 percent covered these topics in a study of more than 350 business schools. Indeed, many companies have found that people who are good in soft skills usually end up leading, no matter what their functional background is.

Adopting a mindset that is part liberal arts education, part business school means you need to look at business problems from multiple perspectives. This mindset prizes financial acumen and business analysis, yes, but also creativity and intuition. Both are essential for branding, selling, and communicating. You certainly need to understand money and how to scale an idea. And you need the ability to rally the team as well as relate one-to-one, to charm investors and give honest feedback. From a liberal arts M.B.A. perspective, you can see, as Einstein did, that "not everything that counts can be counted, and not everything that can be counted, counts."

Crossing the Divide

There's a chasm to cross when you move from the traditional business mindset to the "liberal arts" mindset of the brand entrepreneur. The chart below outlines the key shifts you must make.

Traditional Business Person	Brand Entrepreneur
Focuses on the business metrics	Focuses on metrics and building a brand
Avoids visibility	Is a visible brand ambassador
Manages the business	Innovates through change
Delegates marketing	Engaged in branding and marketing
Values winning	Values winning and making a difference

Traditional Business Person	*Brand Entrepreneur*
Manages people	Creates a culture
Is remote from staff	Engages and "clicks" with employees
Favors hierarchy and processes	Works collaboratively yet decisively
Is cautious of new media	Embraces new digital media
Stresses customer service	Stresses customer engagement
Is a factual communicator	Is a storyteller and performer
Communicates formally	Communicates in an interactive way

The Agony and the Ecstasy

Handbag designer Devi Kroell used to be branded as the "queen of exotic skins" when she had her own label and stores in posh places like New York's Madison Avenue. After a fight with her deep-pocketed investors, Kroell walked out the door. And she didn't even own the rights to her own name in business anymore.

Kroell launched her first company in a boom economy. Now she works out of her apartment, where she is designer, saleswoman, business manager, and administrative assistant.

But Kroell had something very valuable for a start-up entrepreneur, whether it's the first time or second time around. She has an extensive network of business acquaintances. And that gave her wide-ranging sources of advice and introductions. For example, initially Kroell was thinking like a corporate executive who had strong financial resources. She was talking about setting up offices and hiring people until one of her mentors told her flatly, "Forget it, you have to do it yourself."[3]

Kroell used her extensive network to do her own market research to develop the concept for her new brand of handbags and accessories. Here again, she at first resisted the advice she received to design less expensive bags for today's economy. Rather than flying to Italy for production like she did when she had wealthier backers, Kroell's advisors suggested that she find a factory in China. Unlike Italy, where manufacturers catered to her every whim, product developers in China questioned Kroell's designs and suggested ways to produce them more efficiently. Kroell had to learn fast how to design high fashion for today's buyers.

Kroell named her new brand Dax Gabler, after her grandmother, since she couldn't use her own name for the label. Rather than indulging her wild creativity and a luxury-has-no-boundaries mentality, Kroell had to learn to create things people could afford in today's marketplace. Gone are the $25,000 crocodile handbags and in are bags priced from $395 to $995. The bags aren't inexpensive, but they don't inhabit the stratosphere, either.

Marketing Your Life Story

One way to build positive perceptions about your business and Brand You is to use your life story in your marketing. U.K. entrepreneur Chris Dawson loves his image as a barrow boy made good. He openly admits that he still has trouble reading and writing, but boy, can Dawson sell.

The son of a market trader, Dawson cut his teeth in sales when he was seven years old in the jumble stall at a church sale. Later, as a teenage dropout, Dawson became an open-air market trader selling goods out of his truck. On cloudy or rainy days, he attracted customers by making his truck look warm and inviting by putting straw on the ground and setting up spotlights pointed at his truck. He always outsold the other vendors.

Dawson's ability to sell and negotiate a good deal led him to start The Range, a mid-price store for home, leisure, and garden that has now grown to forty-nine stores across the United Kingdom.[4] You can read Dawson's backstory on The Range's website under the tab, "Chris Dawson, The Boy Done Good."

It's hard to imagine a more amazing personal story than American entrepreneur Oprah Winfrey's journey. Oprah was born poor in rural Mississippi to a teenage single mom. She was originally named Orpah, after the biblical character in the Book of Ruth, but the spelling was changed to make it easier to pronounce. Winfrey was raped at age nine and pregnant at fourteen. (She lost her son in infancy.)

In her teens, Winfrey went to live with her father. At nineteen, her life changed dramatically: she landed a job coanchoring the news at a local radio station. Later, Winfrey coanchored a news show on local television. Her gift for ad-libbing as an anchor got her into daytime talk shows, where she has been the undisputed star for twenty-five years.

Winfrey runs a media empire spanning a host of media properties including her new cable network, named OWN (Oprah Winfrey Network). Its purpose is to help people find their "inner light."[5] Today Winfrey is a billionaire and one of the world's most powerful women, a position she achieved by baring her soul and urging millions to follow her credo of self-empowerment.

You: Brand Ambassador

Once you have decided to be a brand entrepreneur, you have to be willing to stand up and stand out. You have to step forward and take the initiative. You have to be a leader.

You may not think of yourself in the same category as Steve Jobs, who as head of Apple was viewed as the quintessential brand entrepreneur. Who does? But you still have a unique opportunity to personify *your* ideals and vision and become a leader to your employees and customers—to be the human embodiment of your company. To *be* a brand as well as create one.

Given the business he started, it's not surprising that John Mackey is one of the world's most influential advocates of organic food. Whole Foods was one of the first grocery chains to establish standards for humane animal treatment, and that's just one example of the ways Mackey has changed the game in the food retailing industry.

But Mackey doesn't limit his advocacy to food talk and the expected. He isn't afraid to shake up the status quo and share his opinions on his blog or in media interviews. Being candid can be refreshing, but it can also be tricky and can even get you into trouble. A libertarian and an admirer of the writer Ayn Rand, Mackey ventured into the debate on health care reform in the United States. He made public comments to the effect that Americans don't have an intrinsic right to health care, angering many of his own customers and leading to calls for a boycott of Whole Foods.[6]

(TM) **Breakthrough brands stand out as much for what they think as for what they make.**

At the same time, Mackey has endeared himself to many customers by taking a bold stand on executive overcompensation. To prove that he walks the talk, he pays himself a salary of just $1 a year. No Whole Foods employee can have a salary of more than nineteen times what the average employee makes ($16.50 in 2009). Compare that rule of thumb with the salary structure for the average CEO in an S&P 500 company, where the CEO makes 319 times what a production worker does. It's quite a difference!

With Whole Foods, Mackey has not only created a grocery chain brand that is synonymous with quality "whole" food, but he has infused the brand with his persona, ideals, and ideas. It's another way the business stands apart.

 BRAINSTORMER: How are you and your business brand intertwined in terms of messages and values?

A Rebel with a Cause

Aim to develop a distinctive voice though your blog, website, social media, articles, and other avenues. In China, countercultural rebel Han Han eclipsed a movie star to become China's most popular personal blogger.[7]

Han Han came on the cultural scene in China as a tenth-grade dropout when he wrote his first novel, *Triple Door*, the story of a bored Chinese high school student slogging through endless exam preparation classes with a Tiger mom who made him pop pills to boost his IQ. The first printing sold out in three days.

Han went on to write other novels, but his real influence is through his blog, where he's had half a billion visitors so far. Han is a person who says what everyone is thinking but is afraid to say. He blogs about China's hidden side: party corruption, censorship, and the plight of poor, young factory workers. He wrote, "Why are our politicians able to stand on the world stage, playing political chess games, honing their politics? Because of you, the low-wage worker!"[8] One of his well-known writings was, "It is better to fail the course on Thought Morals than not to have your own thoughts." (Thought Morals is a required class at Chinese colleges.) While many blogs have been shut down in China, so far Han has been adept at coming close to but not crossing the line.

Han's blogging has made him an entrepreneur who's a celebrity in China, and it has supported his passion, sports car racing (he's even won some competitions). He's the only Chinese blogger to have attracted corporate sponsorships, from Vancl, the Chinese online retailer, and Johnny Walker.

Perceptions Make the Brand Leader

When I was young and another kid called me names, I would run to my mother. She always said, "Don't pay any attention to what people say, and she'd recite that old rhyme, 'Sticks and stones may break your bones,' blah, blah, blah…"

Most of my mom's advice was great, but this particular bit of wisdom was dead wrong—at least in a business context. It doesn't matter what other people say about you? I beg to differ. Brand leaders realize that the perceptions and comments of others are immensely important to their success. The business world doesn't operate on objective reality alone; perceptions matter.

Having a great business idea and being a smart entrepreneur are important, but what really matters is which company people *think* is best, which entrepreneur they *think* is best.

 **Better entrepreneurs don't win.
Entrepreneurs who are perceived as better win.**

Your future success depends on your customers' perceptions, as well as those of prospective employees and investors. Other people decide what companies they want to do business with and what products they want to buy. Other people decide whether to fund your venture. Other people decide whether they want to work for you or for a competitor.

Successful entrepreneurs realize that branding is about leading in a way that creates positive impressions—of their brand and of themselves as leaders. You'll find that people pay more attention to what you do and the way you do it than what you say. As McDonald's was expanding in the 1950s, CEO Ray Kroc listed cleanliness as one of the burger chain's core values, along with service and quality. Employees from the early days recount how they would see Kroc pick up garbage and scrape up chewing gum with a putty knife. It left a clear message that cleanliness mattered.

When you're starting out as an entrepreneur, it's important to make tangible gestures that communicate strength and credibility for your business and yourself as you look for funding and initial customers. You need to create the perception that you are an up-and-coming entrepreneur. Make sure that you have a polished website with your client list on the site, good business cards, and other marketing or presentation materials. Having your office in a good location and meeting in upscale places also communicates credibility and success.

Above all, as a starting entrepreneur, you need to convey personal credibility with your personal story and the creation story for your business. You also gain a lot of credibility if you invested your own money in the business. It's a lot more credible to ask others to invest in your start-up if you have skin in the game.

 BRAINSTORMER: What perceptions do your customers and investors have about you and your business?

Think Outside-In

Brand entrepreneurs keep a pulse on what's happening in the industry, in their company, with their customers, and with their competitors. Brand entrepreneurs have what I call an "outside-in" orientation. They begin with the larger context—the outside—and work inward.

They don't think, "I," but "You." They think, "What needs aren't being met? What can I do to fulfill those needs?" Then, "Can this become a moneymaking business?" Thinking outside-in keeps you grounded in the marketplace.

Robin Chase and Antje Danielson, the cofounders of Zipcar, saw a gaping hole in the car rental marketplace. There was no practical way to rent a car for just a couple of hours to run an errand or get to an appointment. Rentals tended to be by the day and expensive—and were often unavailable on short notice. And, of course, car ownership is costly and wasteful if you only need to use a car occasionally. The two women came up with a small idea that became Zipcar, a car-sharing service where you pay only for the amount of car time you use, which saves you money and is easier on the environment.

Zipcar started out with a fleet of a dozen cars and a few hundred members in Cambridge, Massachusetts. Now, the company has more than 8,000 cars in the United States and the United Kingdom. Powering Zipcar is its high-tech approach. You reserve the car online, use your Zipcard to open the car door, and are billed electronically. But the brand also has a high-touch element. Every Zipcar has a name, some generated by its marketing department, some from loyal customers, some from the naming contests that Zipcar has on Facebook and other social media sites. There's the BMW called Bigfoot, a Mini Cooper called Miss Daisy, and a Honda Civic named Coach Parker after Boston University's hockey coach.[9]

Think Reaction, Then Action

Another way of thinking outside-in is to ask, "What reaction do I want from my customers?" and "What do I have to do to get that reaction?" Tony Hsieh, the founder of Zappos, wanted to get a "Wow!" from his customers, so he freed his telephone sales reps from prepared scripts and empowered them to satisfy each caller individually. Wow!

To be and to stay successful, you need to get out and sell, talk to customers and prospects, test new ideas and approaches. You can always scrap what doesn't work. Brand entrepreneurship is a journey full of unexpected developments that you can't plan for. It's not a destination you can see on the horizon and eventually attain. What fun would that be, anyway?

Thinking outside-in means not limiting yourself to your direct reports for news but rather building a rapport with a wider group. What do the employees on the front lines have to say? What problems are they encountering and how do they suggest fixing them? What are customers saying about your products and your service? What are their complaints?

In the digital age, it's easy to gather customer and prospect information. There are reams of information on the Internet or other electronic sources you can tap for trends and other information. You can do your own proprietary market research online or do a focus group with your target market. For many new businesses, the target market for their products is people like themselves, so they round up their friends for cheap market research in the start-up phase.

To get immediate feedback on customer service, you can create a pop-up response form after each online transaction—but keep it simple. You don't want to turn your customer's shopping experience into homework by making it too long, or evaluation fatigue will set in. Alternatively, you can check out the buzz about your company and its competitors by visiting online forums and consumer sites. You can even plant questions about your products yourself to get the conversation going.

Of course, you shouldn't abandon the old-fashioned way of finding out how people feel. Just ask them directly. That was the trademark behavior of former New York City mayor Ed Koch, who went around the city asking just about everybody he met, "How'm I doing?" He got answers, too, and the gambit endeared him to his constituents.

One of my clients, an entrepreneur with a small manufacturing business, set up regular office hours each week like a university professor, during which he would be in his office with an open door. Anyone who worked at the company could drop by during this time to tell him what's on their minds. His open-door policy is a big hit and says a lot about his brand of entrepreneurship.

Entrepreneurship Is about Fixing Things

Sometimes, it takes a bit of experimentation to arrive at the right execution of your business idea. Entrepreneurs tend to be good at looking at random things and putting them together differently than others.

Netflix founder Reed Hastings reportedly came up with the concept of a DVD-by-mail business after he got dinged with a $40 late fee on a videotape rental of *Apollo 13*.[10] That fine proved to be a costly one for Blockbuster. In 1997, when Hastings started thinking about the movie rental business, it was mainly focused on VHS videotapes in brick-and-mortar stores. Hastings's initial business idea was to focus on DVDs, not videotapes, and delivery through the mail, not stores.

To test the concept, Hastings went to a Tower Records, bought a couple of movie DVDs, and sent them to himself in an envelope. When they arrived a day later unscathed, he got very excited. The DVDs were small, light, and didn't need extra packaging to mail safely. Hastings created the distinctive red packaging that is one of the best, most recognizable brand packages of its time. Its special square-shaped envelope meant the DVDs went through a separate flat mail service and wouldn't get crushed at the post office.

In the early days, Hastings imitated a key aspect of the way Blockbuster and other video stores did business. You know the routine: you pay a fee for each movie you rent and if you're late returning it, you incur additional fees.

The model didn't work very well for Netflix, and sales were anemic.

So Hastings looked out a different window. He switched to a subscription model with no late fees. At the time, it was a desperate move. Hastings thought his business might go under. It was risky, too. No one had ever rented movies by subscription before.

Very quickly, Hastings realized he'd struck gold. Eighty percent of the people who signed up for the introductory free trial subscription became paying customers. After a while, his competitor, Blockbuster, filed for bankruptcy protection.

When the ability to stream movies and television to consumers' computers became practical, Netflix was nicely poised—with a large and loyal customer base—to expand into digital streaming. Now it's a new ballgame as a host of competitors like Apple, Amazon, Google, YouTube, and cable networks get into the business of streaming movies and TV programs.

Of course, no brand entrepreneur, even someone as savvy as Hastings, doesn't make mistakes, and sometimes they can be doozies. In July 2011, Hastings announced a 60 percent price increase for its combo streaming and DVD-by-mail package. Angry customers began canceling their subscriptions and the stock started to drop.

Then, things got even dicier for Netflix and its relationship with its 25 million subscribers. In a blog post on September 17, 2011, Hastings announced a breakup plan into two companies: Netflix for its online streaming business and Qwikster for its old-fashioned DVD-by-mail business. Tens of thousands of subscribers responded with a "Quitster" to that announcement by canceling Netflix and posting furious comments on its website and other forums.[11] Netflix stock dropped dramatically. In a Facebook status update three days after the announcement, Hastings wrote, "In Wyoming with 10 investors at a ranch/retreat. I think I might need a food taster. I can hardly blame them."

Three weeks later, Hastings reversed his plan and announced Netflix will keep its services together. He acknowledged in a statement that "there is a difference between moving quickly—which Netflix has done very well for years—and moving too fast, which is what we did in this case."

 BRAINSTORMER: Are there new solutions to life's irritations that could lead to a business idea?

Visionaries Look Elsewhere

It's impossible to talk about breakthrough branding without mentioning Apple and Steve Jobs. Before they came along, computers, phones, and other electronic gadgets were drab, utilitarian devices. They had their relative merits, but one company's gadgets looked much like another's. Clearly, competitors were studying one another's designs—looking out the same window—rather than seeking a distinctive view.

Except for Steve Jobs, that is. In the early days, Jobs looked to Italian car designers for ideas on the shape, finish, materials, and color for his Apple products.[12] For packaging ideas, he studied the work of Japanese and luxury goods manufacturers, adopting their attention to the quality of the paper, printing, color, and graphics and the shape and fit of each package component.

There's a Tiffanyesque "open me first" feeling about Apple product packaging. Everything looks and feels fresh, inviting, and different—and that includes the Apple store you buy it in.

As an entrepreneur, you need to be a fanatic about the user experience, too. If your desire is to be a visionary like Jobs, developing cutting-edge products, it's not helpful to go out and ask, "What do you want?" Nobody knows. You have to create desire by giving people something totally new and different from what they have previously experienced. The usual rules of product development research don't really apply. We can't all be visionaries—but we should all be open to the occasional "vision," and when it comes, we must be confident and passionate enough to follow through on it, sometimes in *spite* of what our research tells us. That's how truly innovative products are born (and great fortunes are made).

 BRAINSTORMER: Where do people look for design and operational inspiration in your industry? Where else could you look?

Brand ideas come to people who say "Why not?" rather than "No." Brand entrepreneurs are people who ask, "Why?" "What if?" "How about?" They are people who pay attention and respond. When you start paying attention, you'll find lots of areas ripe for exploration.

You'll find that the more you explore, learn new things, and challenge yourself, the more ideas will come your way. Learning new things even makes your brain cells grow, and before long, things that once were difficult aren't anymore. You'll learn that you can achieve most goals through purposeful, repeated, and focused attention and by encouraging the creativity inside yourself.

As a brand entrepreneur:

You want to be *open and receptive.*
You want to be *strategic and creative* about your brand.
You need to be *willing to take risks but not crazy risks.*
You want to *create a business that works better* than any other.
You want to *grow your small business into a big brand.*

Chapter 3

Power Positioning

"Finding out what to say is the beginning of the advertising process. How you say it makes people look and listen. And, if you're not successful at that, you've wasted all the work, intelligence, and skill that went into discovering what you should say."

—Bill Bernbach, Legendary "Mad Man"

S trategy is the brains of breakthrough branding. It's setting up the underlying code that defines your business and your brand.

While you may have your "small," relevant business idea, now you need to make sure that you strategically *position* your business. You need to find the best competitive angle so that it is clearly different from your competitors and offers a unique brand promise or benefit to your customers so that it can become a breakthrough brand.

 POSITIONING: a clear benefit or promise of worth that your product can own in the minds of prospects and that is different from that of its competitors.

Positioning your brand is like attaching an idea to your business and an idea to yourself. It's finding your *brand promise*—something that your business and you stand for that no one else owns or that no one else does in quite the way that you do.

Positioning will help you get visibility for your brand in a crowded, competitive marketplace because it forces you to think strategically—not just about your brand's strengths and weaknesses but about your competition's too. Most important, as I learned from my mentors Al Ries and Jack Trout when I worked at their ad agency, "positioning is not what you do to a product. Positioning is what you do to the mind of the prospect. That is, you position the product in the mind of the prospect."[1]

The Two Big Motivators in Branding

There are two ways to appeal to people in branding. You can appeal to *benefits and consequences*—if you use this brand, you'll have better performance; if you don't, you'll lose money, have problems, or suffer pain in some way. You choose to stay at a Hilton on your next business trip or take the kids for lunch at a McDonald's because you know exactly what you'll get no matter where you are. These companies are both leaders in their categories with clearly defined brand characteristics and benefits.

The second appeal is to *identity*—appealing to the emotions and aspirations of people. This is emotional branding, and it's very powerful because identity strategies appeal to who we are at our core (or who we'd like to be). When you buy an iPad or drive a Porsche, you're doing more than buying an electronic gadget or a car. You're signaling a certain mindset and lifestyle to others.

Let's look at some of the most popular brand positioning strategies that you might want to use for your business or product. In the "benefits and consequences" camp are strategies such as owning an attribute, being the leader, and having a special ingredient or a new process. In the "identity" camp are owning a target market, being a maverick, or having a celebrity connection. You can try each on for size to see which one might have the best potential for positioning your business in the marketplace.

When you find a breakthrough positioning strategy, it will show your brand to be:

- ▶ **Superlative:** better than your competitors in an important way
- ▶ **Different:** not a copycat of your competitors
- ▶ **Believable:** authentic and true for the brand
- ▶ **Memorable:** fresh and interesting in some way

Let's explore the most popular positioning strategies.

Positioning Strategy 1: Own an Attribute

The most common way to position your brand is to *own an attribute*. Every product or business category has specific attributes that are important to customers. If you have a financial services business, key attributes would be integrity and trust, client focus, range of products, and the quality of financial advisors. If you own a restaurant, key attributes include quality of the food, restaurant atmosphere, quality of waiters and service, location, and pricing.

Building your business brand around a desired attribute—called *attribute* or *benefit positioning*—appeals to the left side of the brain, the rational side that wants clear-cut distinctions about brand benefits and characteristics. It appeals to our desire for clear benefits and to avoid bad consequences.

Attribute positioning can give you a competitive advantage, particularly if you can align your brand around an important attribute that no one else has claimed in the category. In your marketing, you demonstrate your superiority with research or other support. Pantene reframed hair care by positioning the brand as "healthy," so healthy that your hair shines.

(TM) **ATTRIBUTE POSITIONING: the brand that is (list attribute).**

Look at mobile phone marketing. Wireless telecom companies compete for important attributes such as superior cell phone reception, better pricing, and the like. For years, Verizon Wireless positioned the brand around having a *superior cell signal* with its "Test Man" and its breakthrough "Can You Hear Me Now?" advertising campaign. Having a better cell signal was a great attribute to own because it means more reliable service. It gave Verizon a competitive attribute positioning that helped drive its mobile phone sales.

You can evolve your attribute positioning over time. When Zappos, the online shoe retailer, launched in 1999, Tony Hsieh positioned the brand as having the *largest selection* of shoes.[2] It seemed like a good attribute to own because no brick-and-mortar shoe store could compete with Zappos on largest selection. Yet, seeing Zappos's success, copycat entrepreneurs came on the scene, and these competitors could replicate the online shoe store model and its large selection.

So in 2003, Zappos moved to a new attribute positioning—*best customer service*—and adopted the tagline, "Powered by Service." The new positioning was a harder position for competitors to copy because Zappos backed up the claim with customer service innovations that few competitors were willing to match. Zappos offers free shipping both ways—a huge benefit for shoe buyers. Imagine. There is no charge to return shoes, not even a postage fee. You could order ten pairs in various sizes and colors if you wanted and send everything back—no questions asked.

Zappos breakthrough branding didn't stop there. The company freed its telephone reps from scripts. The reps' job: say and do what was needed to create a "Wow" reaction from customers who called with a complaint. Zappos also made its toll-free telephone number prominent on its website. This may seem like a small thing, but try to find the phone number on some online retailers' websites. Most online retailers want to drive all communication online because it's more cost efficient, so they hide the 800-number in small print somewhere or don't list one at all. Zappos realizes the power of the personal touch even in the online world.

In 2005, Zappos CEO Hsieh changed the brand's positioning once again to a new attribute: *special values and culture*. Hsieh felt that Zappos had a special culture that made the company a breakthrough brand profoundly different from its competitors. To support the claim to a special culture, Hsieh asked each of his employees to write a 200-word essay on the Zappos culture, and he put these together into an e-book and posted it on his website. Each essay was published verbatim, with only minor spelling and grammar corrections.

What the book portrayed was a fresh, lively culture, and it created quite a stir as thousands downloaded the book from the Zappos website. The company also began offering tours of the Zappos headquarters in Las Vegas so customers could see the zany culture in action. And that was a success, too.

In 2009, Hsieh tweaked the positioning yet again to come up with a unique attribute, *delivering happiness*. Alas, he realized that his brand promise wasn't just delivering a wide range of shoes or providing great customer service or building a special culture. He realized his brand was delivering happiness—happiness in a box to customers and happiness in a work environment to employees, a shift he chronicles in his best-selling book, *Delivering Happiness*. His latest plans are to host indie concerts and build small crash pads—with a bed and closet—that people can rent for $100 a month. Hsieh's still delivering happiness and creating a breakthrough brand.

As a brand entrepreneur, you want to stake your claim to the attribute that is best for *you* to own: true for your business, important to customers, and *available*—it is an attribute that is not owned by a competitor.

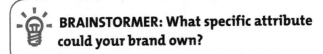

BRAINSTORMER: What specific attribute could your brand own?

Positioning Strategy 2: Target a Specific Group

Appealing to the identity of a specific target group of customers—to their quirks, preferences, and attitudes—can be a powerful positioning strategy. You connect to people emotionally at their core, with who your customers are as people. Often, marketers go after a target audience that is aspirational for many people, to attract the "in crowd" but also all of us wannabes.

Look at the old "I'm a Mac and you're a PC" campaign. Who do you identity with? The hip Mac guy or the conservative PC guy? The Mac guy appears on the right and is much younger and dressed in jeans. The PC guy wears nerdy glasses, ill-fitting khakis, and a jacket and tie. The campaign appeals to people who aspire to hipness, and it helped propel Apple's share of the computer market, attracting large numbers of former PC owners to make the switch.

TARGET AUDIENCE POSITIONING: the brand for (name target audience).

Look at the auto market. They're all cars, but they come in all different styles and prices—different strokes for different folks. While a muscle car might not get your blood pumping, you can probably imagine just the sort of young guy who owns one or aspires to. That person is very different from a Prius owner or a Mercedes owner. In fact, cars are such a great metaphor for people's identity that a popular question on product focus groups has been, "If this product were a car, what car would it be and why?"

It helps when you are creating a target audience positioning to write up a *persona*, a description of a specific person who represents the group. That way, you can easily visualize and understand what makes your target tick. You're not positioning your brand for men eighteen to twenty-four but to Jonathan, an eighteen-year-old high school senior who plays football, likes to have a fun time, and, above all, wants to feel cool and confident, particularly around girls.

When you niche your brand, don't worry that you'll lose customers who don't fit the target audience characteristics. It's counterintuitive, but niching your brand to a target group will bring in a bigger catch. You'll reach the desired demographic and people who aspire to this group. By trying to appeal to everyone, you appeal to no one. Don't forget, branding always involves sacrifice. You don't want to be everything to everybody, you want to be something specific to somebody.

Look at U.S. entrepreneur Russell Simmons. He saw a red-hot target audience that no one was going after, the urban market. He pioneered the hip-hop label Def Jam and launched the urban design phenomenon with his clothing line, Phat Farm, in 1992. His music contacts at Def Jam helped build a breakthrough brand for the clothing as he got the top hip-hop and rap artists to wear his clothes. The brand took off way beyond the urban market and now has universal appeal.

 BRAINSTORMER: Is there a specific target audience you could define your brand around?

Positioning Strategy 3: Be the First

Being the first in a category is powerful. We've all heard of the first-mover advantage. Being first accelerates breakthrough branding. After all, most of us can't remember who was second in any category. Being first gives you a breakthrough edge because people assume you must be good since you created the category.

Many firsts maintain a leadership position. Michael Dell was the first direct seller of personal computers, and Dell is still a dominant player in that business. Jeff Bezos created the first online retail book store, is still number one, and has expanded his online concept successfully beyond books.

There are two ways to be first: the hard way and the easy way. In the hard way, you create a whole new category from scratch. This is hard to do and takes a certain amount of genius, but we still continue to see new categories created, particularly in technology businesses. Mark Zuckerberg and Facebook revolutionized how people communicate and share information. So did Jack Dorsey and his partners with Twitter. Steve Jobs was a serial player with firsts in multiple categories, including music players, tablet PCs, and mobile phones.

 FIRST POSITIONING: the first brand that _____.

There is an easier way to create a first. (Creativity is required but not genius.) Find an existing product or category and carve out an extension or subset of the category that is new or "first" in some way. What you are doing is creating a new category that diverges from the main category in an important way. And, most important as a brander, you give your new category a name that your product is first in.

This type of first can be a game changer, too. On a business trip to Thailand in 1982, Austrian entrepreneur Dietrich Mateschitz discovered a local drink called Krating Daeng that miraculously cured his jet lag.[3] With his Thai partner, Mateschitz decided to introduce the drink in the West with one important modification—he added carbonation. He named the drink Red Bull, which is a close translation of its Thai name (Daeng means "red" and Krating means "water buffalo" in Thai).

Mateschitz's real branding genius was in positioning the brand. He didn't position Red Bull as refreshing or energizing (attribute positioning) or for young men (target market positioning) or as a Thai beverage (heritage positioning). Mateschitz took the "first" route. He didn't simply introduce a new beverage brand—he invented a new category he called "energy drinks."

Mateschitz hired an Austrian ad agency, which came up with fifty different designs for Red Bull before he found breakthrough branding he liked: the distinctive tall, slim, eight-ounce blue-and-silver can with the logo of two muscular bulls smashing heads in front of a yellow sun. The can is smaller than a typical soda can so people immediately got the idea that this energy drink was strong stuff!

When Mateschitz first tested the Red Bull name and the concept, people didn't like the taste, the logo, or the name. Based on the research, it didn't look like a breakthrough brand but a broken brand. But he ignored the research and went ahead with his energy drink and branding anyway, launching first in Austria and then expanding globally. Today Mateschitz has a net worth in the billions.

The interesting thing about the firsts that are subsets is that new ones are being created every day. You just have to see the need for something new in an existing category that you carve out and own as the first, like Procter & Gamble did when it introduced the Swiffer, creating the quick-surface-clean category.

Another entrepreneur who saw a fresh way of looking at a well-established category is London-based Natalie Massenet. When she approached investors, Massenet was told that women wouldn't buy high-end fashion online. Massenet proved them wrong, launching Net-a-Porter, the first ultra-high-end online fashion business, which has changed the way women shop for high fashion.

And there's Sara Blakely, who reinvented women's foundations. Her invention came about in 1998, when she chopped the feet off a pair of control-top pantyhose and created a new category of foundation garments—shapewear.

Blakely just wanted to look svelte with no telltale seams or stockings protruding from her pants legs. A part-time fax machine saleswoman and a part-time stand-up comic, Blakely called her first invention "Footless pantyhose" and launched her business, Spanx, in 2000 with $5,000 in savings. Since then she's sold more than nine million pairs and spawned the industry of bodyshaper foundations.

 BRAINSTORMER: Is there a new category you could create, where your business can be first?

Positioning Strategy 4: Be the Leader

When you have a leadership claim, you can appeal to people who want to do business with the leading player in an industry, the brand the most people are buying. You can take advantage of the *leadership premium*. Leadership, in and of itself, gives you a halo effect. As the leader in your category, people will assume that you are better than others who are the number two, three, or ten players.

You must be better, or why else are you the leader? You've got proof, too: the ubiquity of your brand in the marketplace. The visibility and sales of your brand everywhere breed further success.

There are many ways to stake a claim to leadership. You can be the biggest player in terms of locations or employees or revenues. Or you can claim to be the leader globally, nationally, regionally, or in your city. For example, you could be the leading car dealer in the country, in a specific region, or in your city. You could be the leading Brand X car dealer in your region or city. Any of these measures can give you a credible claim to leadership.

 LEADER POSITIONING: the #1 brand in _____.

Bill Gates set out to be the leader in computing with this mission: "A computer on every desk and in every home, all running Microsoft software." It was a breakthrough branding statement for computing in 1975, when few people had a computer or could see a use for one in their personal lives. The PC envisioned by Gates was cheap, utilitarian, and everywhere. And his leadership vision revolutionized the computer industry.

As a leader, you'll want to do leadership things, like speak about the industry in your blog, post white papers on your website, be visible at industry meetings, and be cited as an authority in the trade or business media. And you have a good reason to be selected to speak at the next industry conference or be quoted in the media, because you are a leader in your industry. Because you are a leader, people will pay more attention to what you have to say than they will to the also-rans. Think of the most important thing that you have to say and become known for that. Try to come up with a fresh idea or have a new twist on an old idea.

Leaders have to play a defensive role. There will always be competitors trying to topple you from your leadership perch, but it won't be easy for them to do unless you lose the edge that got you the leadership position in the first place.

 BRAINSTORMER: How can you make a credible claim to leadership for your business?

Positioning Strategy 5: Be the Maverick

As much as we love the prestige and aura of leadership, we also admire underdogs: gutsy rebels who defy convention and don't follow the establishment path.

For every Microsoft, there is an Apple—a brand that symbolizes the opposite of the dominant leader to its customers. We just looked at Bill Gates and Microsoft's leadership vision for PCs as cheap, utilitarian, and everywhere. That's very different from Steve Jobs's view of computers as expensive, exclusive, and cool looking.

Apple emphasized its maverick positioning with its "Think Different" marketing campaign. Here are the opening lines of the kickoff ad: "Here's to the crazy ones. The misfits. The rebels. The troublemakers. The round pegs in the square holes. The ones who see things differently." Of course, the maverick positioning can work so well that you overtake the leader, like Apple has done in key areas.

(TM) **MAVERICK or REVERSE POSITIONING:_____ brand is the opposite of the leader.**

The maverick position is *reverse positioning* and can be a great strategy for entrepreneurs. You build your company's brand as the antidote to the leader or large corporations by positioning the leader's strengths as weaknesses. An especially powerful tactic of the maverick positioning strategy is casting the dominant leader as the evil empire. You, in contrast, are the underdog. You stand for the good empire: fresh, honest, and full of purpose.

The maverick position is simplicity itself. Everything the leaders stand for, you are the opposite or the reverse. They are the stuffy establishment, you are a breath of fresh air. They're big and slow, you're small and fast. They are out of touch, you're cutting edge. They're bureaucratic, you're nimble and entrepreneurial. The leaders are expensive, you're good value.

Another way to look at maverick positioning is to zig when everyone else is zagging. If the leading brands are adding options, be the simple product choice without the bells and whistles. If everyone is marketing complicated pricing structures, have a simple, easy-to-understand price for your product or service.

In the 1990s, when the big airlines were offering personal service, televisions at each seat, and special perks, JetBlue came along in 2000 with maverick positioning: cheap prices, no meals, and second-tier airports. So take a step back and look at what your key competitors are doing. When you see everyone doing the same thing, ask yourself if you could diverge, do the opposite, and use that as your maverick positioning.

The maverick position is a brand strategy that offers a great PR platform, particularly if you want to play a role as the face of the brand. Think Richard Branson and Virgin. Branson has made his zany personality work for the brand. Branson may have been knighted by the Queen and be Sir Richard now, but he plays up his maverick, antiestablishment cred through his PR stunts. He's shown up in an astronaut's space suit for the launch of Virgin Galactic, dressed up as a Malay warrior for a press conference in Kuala Lumpur, and appeared as a sheik for the launch of new Virgin routes to the Middle East, to cite just a few of his PR antics.

While Branson might be a tad over the top for your style, as the maverick, you do want to have an opposite image from the leaders in your industry. If they all wear suits and ties, be a casual dresser or have more stylish attire. Being the maverick in your industry gives you a natural media pitch. When the media do stories on what's happening in an industry, they look for quotes from leaders but also from players with a radically different point of view. That's you—the maverick. So be prepared with a quotable quip.

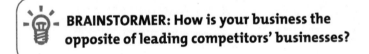

BRAINSTORMER: How is your business the opposite of leading competitors' businesses?

Positioning Strategy 6: Have a Magic Ingredient

Having a "magic ingredient" is one of the oldest positioning strategies, going back to patent medicine days in the seventeenth through nineteenth centuries. It's a great strategy to explore if you make a product where a new ingredient or a different formula can be your branding magic.

Remote parts of the world can be a great source for discovering "magic" ingredients. Intrapreneur Zanna McFerson works for agriculture giant Cargill, a dominant player in the high-fructose corn syrup market. The company had no position in the no-calorie sweetener market dominated by Sweet'N Low, Splenda, and Equal until McFerson and her team started thinking like entrepreneurs within the organization.[4]

(TM) MAGIC INGREDIENT POSITIONING: the brand with _____ special ingredient.

McFerson's magic ingredient was the stevia leaf, a natural sweetener discovered in Paraguay over one hundred years ago. She figured there was a wide-open opportunity for a natural no-calorie sweetener. Everything else on the market used chemical additives.

After all, the consumer she was targeting was someone like herself and the other members of her heavily female team at Cargill. She called her target consumer the Yoga Momma, a harried yet well-intentioned working woman who was interested in low-calorie whole food for herself and her family. As the company explains the persona of its target customer, "The Yoga Momma wears yoga pants but may never make it to class." This is a woman who has a complicated relationship with sweeteners and is a top spender on health-related supermarket items.

McFerson wanted to get the right name to reach these women and went with Truvia—it sounds like *true* plus *stevia*. And Cargill's green halo is paying off at the cash register.

Tribal regions can be a rich source for magic ingredients. Aveda has had a twenty-year partnership with the Yawanawa, an Indian tribe in western Brazil. The tribe uses a spiky fruit called urukum as a coloring agent, and it is the magic ingredient Aveda uses in its popular Uruku line of lipsticks, eye shadows, and face bronzers.[5]

Acai was unknown outside Brazil until Ryan and Jeremy Black and their friend Edmund Nichols began exporting it to the United States. Ryan Black and Nichols first tasted the fruit in December 1999 on a trip to Brazil, where they went to celebrate the millennium New Year. Served with bananas and granola at beachside acai bars, acai was a hot food in Brazil in the late 1990s, and it gave the Americans their small business idea. They would import acai to the United States.[6]

When they returned home, they discovered that acai had an unbelievably high antioxidant count. It was particularly high in anthocyanins, which can be powerful in fighting cancer, diabetes, heart disease, and aging, according to research studies. The trio called their company Sambazon, a combination of "samba" and "Amazon," and secured the exclusive rights to distribute acai from major producers in Brazil. The team had its magic ingredient. The Black brothers, with their California surfer good looks, were picture perfect brand ambassadors for acai, a "magic" ingredient that claimed to enhance youth, health, and beauty.

Like the acai team, Denis Simioni recognized a magic ingredient when it popped into his life. A relative from Central America gave Simioni a baby-food jar filled with brown goop that was good for adding shine to hair.[7]

Simioni, who was running an ad agency in Canada at the time, was intrigued and began researching and playing with the product. He traced the goop to the ojon nut from the Honduran rain forest and to local Indians called "the people of the beautiful hair," who used it for its moisturizing properties. "I didn't know how it worked at the time, but I knew it worked and it was special," Simioni says. In 2003, Simioni launched his first product, Ojon Restorative Hair Treatment, containing ojon oil, a magic ingredient that he branded as "nature's golden elixir." In 2007, Simioni sold his line of Ojon hair products to Estée Lauder, and Simioni became the face of the brand on the QVC cable shopping network.

 BRAINSTORMER: Is there a special ingredient or a new material or component that gives your brand a competitive advantage?

Positioning Strategy 7: Have a Special Process

Having a special process that you use in your business and that delivers better results can be a powerful strategy for all types of businesses, from hairstylists to chefs, from financial advisors to advertising agencies, from manufacturers to technology companies.

Your special process can be a computer code or algorithm that gives superior results that you can patent and build a business around. Look how Google came out of nowhere and blew away entrenched competitors Yahoo!, AOL, and MSN with its search technology, a special process that has kept Google at the lead in search since its beginnings. Originally, Google was a Stanford University doctorate project of Larry Page and

Sergey Brin on one of the Internet's thorniest problems: how to sort information. Their PageRank algorithm was the solution. The duo launched Google in 1998.

Around the same time that Page and Brin were developing their algorithm for search in the mid to late 1990s on the West Coast, a Chinese computer scientist was working on a similar project on the East Coast. Robin Li was also intrigued with the problem of sorting information on the Internet and developed a search process he called "linked analysis" that involved ranking the popularity of a website based on how many other sites linked to it. Li received a U.S. patent for the process in 1996.

Li was working at Dow Jones at the time, on the online edition of the paper, and then joined Infoseek to oversee search engine development. Disney moved the company into content and away from search, so Li formed his own Internet company with a colleague in 1999. They raised money in Silicon Valley and returned to China to launch Baidu, the Google of China. (Or Google is the Baidu of the United States, depending on your perspective.) Li named his company Baidu (literally, "hundreds of times"), from a famous poem from the Song dynasty about the search for the ideal.[8]

Today, Google is banned in China. Chinese have to "go over the wall" and get to Hong Kong to access Google. In exchange for letting government censors oversee its website, Baidu is allowed to operate and is the dominant player in China with some 70 percent of the search business.

(TM) SPECIAL PROCESS POSITIONING: the brand with the _____ proprietary process.

Having a special process can be a winning positioning strategy for service businesses like consultants, doctors, marketers, and the like where you can market your company's process as different and better than competitors'. Many advertising, marketing, and research agencies claim a special research process that leads to exceptional insight for their clients.

A hot area in marketing today is neuromarketing, a new area of market research that studies people's reactions to marketing stimuli by using fMRI and other technologies to study what's actually going on in the brain. As we all know, people don't always tell the whole truth in focus groups. Now, researchers can see what's going on inside the brain so they can discern your true reactions. The leading players in neuromarketing brand their own special processes and methodologies that lead to consumer insight.

 BRAINSTORMER: Is there a special process that you could brand and market for your business?

Positioning Strategy 8: Connect with a Celebrity

Brands have long recognized that a celebrity connection can power sales. It's not that people don't recognize that celebrities are generally paid for their endorsements. But people pay more attention to ads that feature celebrities and remember more of the message.

Early pioneers of this strategy were Pond's Cold Cream, which featured Queen Marie of Romania in ads in the 1920s, and Lux soap, with its famous (and unsubstantiated) claim from the 1930s that "nine out of ten stars use Lux." Through the years, hundreds of the world's most famous female celebrities have been in Lux ads: Marilyn Monroe, Sophia Loren, Brigitte Bardot, Demi Moore, Catherine Zeta-Jones, and Sarah Jessica Parker.

Many entrepreneurs in service businesses don't pay for a celebrity endorsement but leverage the fame of their celebrity clients to attract regular folks. Look at the personal training industry. Jake "Body by Jake" Steinfeld became the first celebrity trainer to build an empire from Hollywood A-list clients.[9]

Steinfeld's business started accidentally. Three decades ago, he was relaxing by the pool in his apartment complex in California when a woman asked him if he could help her get into shape for a commercial she was going to be in, but she wanted to be trained at her home. When he went to the woman's home, Francis Ford Coppola opened the door. "I didn't know who he was," Steinfeld related. "I just thought he could use a workout." Not long afterward, Steinfeld signed up Harrison Ford, Bette Midler, and Michael J. Fox. He branded himself as the "trainer to the stars," a phrase he copyrighted. He built an empire that included celebrity clients, books, and cable fitness shows all under the "Body by Jake" brand.

(TM) **CELEBRITY POSITIONING: brand _____ is used by celebrities like _____.**

Now there are dozens of fitness trainers who position their brands around celebrity connections. Tracy Anderson in New York trains Gwyneth Paltrow and Shakira and charges $900 a month at her gym plus a $1,500 initiation fee. Then there's Gunnar Peterson in Beverly Hills, whose clients include Halle Berry, Sylvester Stallone, and Kim Kardashian, as well as pro athletes. Because he has an upscale background, having attended Swiss boarding schools and hopped around in a Gulfstream jet, Peterson is unfazed by his celebrity clients, and that makes him perfect for his clientele. He bills his brand as "the celebrity trainer who does not care about celebrities."

Oprah has launched numerous brands, including Dr. Phil and Dr. Oz, who both have television shows and books, and she has supercharged the companies she features as "Oprah's favorite things" on a special yearly show. Sam Greenberg was a small purveyor of smoked turkey in East Texas when Oprah called in 2003. She wanted to give away 400 of his hickory-smoked turkeys on her show. At the time of the call, Greenberg didn't have a website and didn't accept credit cards, and the give-away show was twelve days away. Oprah mentioned his product for forty-two seconds and Greenberg sold over $1 million dollars–worth of turkeys as a result of her celebrity endorsement.

Most of us will never open a door and be greeted by a Hollywood celebrity or get a call from Oprah, but you could build your business around local "celebrities"—local politicians, civic leaders, or media personalities. The celebrity connection can be a smart positioning strategy for a wide variety of businesses such as accounting, law, coaching, medical doctors, estheticians, hair stylists, interior decorators, clothes designers, jewelry and accessory manufacturers, and the like.

A plastic surgeon won't tell you directly that he did so-and-so's face, but his front office people or other patients will spill the beans, or you can easily find out the gossip online. The media loves to report who's wearing whose clothes, shoes, and accessories, and the manufacturers love it too because it propels sales.

The celebrity connection has gotten so crazy that women's and lifestyle magazines regularly report not only who's wearing what, with detailed information on where you can get it yourself, but also what fragrance they like, what brand of sheets they sleep on, what soap they use—you name it. So getting a well-known person to wear your clothes or carry your bag or wear your jewelry—or mention that you style her hair—can add cachet to, and increase demand for, your products and services.

The celebrity connection is also a popular positioning strategy for restaurants, where your "celebrities" can be local politicians, on-air media talent, models, your chef, or anyone with a claim to fame in some way. The celebrity connection gives the media an added incentive to cover your business and can lead to photo ops or interesting stories for your blog or your tweets. Part of the success of hip frozen-yogurt company Pinkberry is the star power of devotees like fashion designer Isaac Mizrahi and rocker Bret Michaels.

One of the imperatives of the celebrity positioning is a high price. After Kim and Kourtney Kardashian stayed at the Smyth TriBeCa in New York City, the owner of another penthouse in the hotel increased its price by $195,000 and advertised, "Want to live where the Kardashians lived?" The celebrity connection can give your profit margins a boost, whether you're a lawyer, doctor, hairstylist or own real estate.

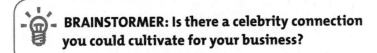

BRAINSTORMER: Is there a celebrity connection you could cultivate for your business?

Positioning Strategy 9: Be a Cheapener

We revere innovators and tend to dislike cheapeners, but both have tremendous value to the economy and to consumers. As appealing as a high price can be for profit margins or being revered as the leader can be for your sense of self-worth, brands that make things cheap deserve a lot of applause, too. When things become cheap, more people can use them, and that can have an immense impact on the world, as the cheapening of computers has shown us.[10] So the real power is not just when an idea is created but when it has entered the mainstream and many people can use it.

One of the most famous cheapeners was Sam Walton, who revolutionized discount retailing. He would travel the world to get ideas. Every time Walton heard of a new discounter, he visited it to study the concept, scribbling down ideas in his yellow legal pad. Before Walton and Wal-Mart, very few stores concentrated on buying low, selling cheap, and making their profit by selling a huge quantity.

 CHEAPENER POSITIONING: brand _____ is the best value.

Innovative technology companies can be important cheapeners. TenKsolar recently announced that it will soon be able to cut the cost of rooftop solar power in sunny locations to around eight cents a kilowatt-hour—almost the same price as current electricity rates. TenKsolar uses an idea from computer memory technology to wire up solar panels in a special pattern so that the output of each panel is not limited to the output of the lowest-performing cell. It may not seem like a big innovation, but this entrepreneurial company is playing a vital role in the cheapening of solar power so that masses of people can produce and use this low-cost form of energy.

You can explore a value positioning for your brand by developing a product that is less expensive than the big brands. The convenience store 7-Eleven has its Santiago beer to counter Mexican favorite Corona, and Wal-Mart has Equate health and beauty products, Spring Valley vitamins, and White Stag clothing. All of these value brands have names and package designs that enable them to compete with the big brands.

 BRAINSTORMER: Is there a way you can offer a stronger price/value equation than competitors?

Positioning Strategy 10: Align with a Cause

Charitable work can be a brand differentiator in a crowded product marketplace. Blending commerce with good works as a brand strategy has been around for several decades, but what's new today is tying the brand and charity so closely that you can't think of the brand without thinking of its charity work.

Look at TOMS Shoes: for every pair of its iconic cloth, rubber-soled "alpargatas" shoes sold, TOMS Shoes gives away a pair to someone who needs it.[11]

Blake Mycoskie, the thirty-something entrepreneur behind TOMS Shoes, got the idea because he was bored with his previous start-up, Drivers-Ed Direct. He Googled "polo lessons" and ended up outside Buenos Aires, where he saw wealthy city people giving their old shoes to poor village children. He found out that many kids couldn't go to school because they didn't have shoes.

"It just hit me," Mycoskie says. "Instead of a charity with handouts, why not create a company where that's the whole purpose?" The concept was, "Buy one pair of shoes today so we can give one tomorrow." That led him to the name Tomorrow Shoes. After thinking about it, he decided to shorten the name to TOMS Shoes (TOMS refers to "tomorrow" not a person's name). The brand's tagline, "One for One," communicates the brand's mission of the shoe giveaway.

CAUSE POSITIONING: brand _____ supports _____.

The company culture is a cross between "Peace Corps" and "dot-com" with plywood cubicles and large wall photos of shoe drops in Rwanda, Guatemala, Argentina, and other places around the globe. The shoes have a cult following with teens and twentysomethings.

The success of the business shows that doing good can be good for business and not just PR. The company gave away 600,000 pairs of shoes in its first four years. With each pair sold going for about $55, that adds up to $33 million in cloth shoes sales. The company was ranked in the top ten on *Fast Company* magazine's list of most innovative retailers.

Believing that business leaders should help those who lack economic stability, humanitarian aid has always been part of Guy Laliberté's business model.[12]

Laliberté started out as a fire breather and street artist, a livelihood where you pass a hat and are lucky to get enough for a bargain dinner. Yet Laliberté had a dream of creating a circus of street performers that was global in its appeal. He named his troupe of performers Cirque du Soleil, Circus of the Sun, because he loved to watch sunsets on the beach, and the sun is a symbol of youth and energy.

Supported by the Canadian government in its early years, Cirque du Soleil sold more than 10 million tickets in 2010, with an average ticket price of $75. Giving a percentage of its revenues to philanthropic efforts is integral to the brand. In 2007, Laliberté pledged $100 million personally to start the One Drop Foundation dedicated to clean water issues.

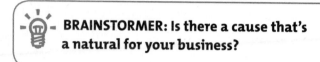

> **BRAINSTORMER: Is there a cause that's a natural for your business?**

Positioning Strategy 11: Highlight a Special Heritage

Heritage can be a strong selling point. Think Swiss watches, German engineering, Belgian chocolates, Russian vodka, Persian carpets, or French cuisine. The fact that Veuve Clicquot is from the Champagne region of France gives it authenticity from its special heritage.

Julia Child introduced French cuisine to the American public with her debut cookbook, *Mastering the Art of French Cooking*. She wrote more than twenty books and went on to star in the popular television show *The French Chef.* Child was the recognized authority on French cuisine in the United States during her lifetime.

Part of her heritage positioning was her training at Le Cordon Bleu. What's amazing and not talked about very much is that her training at Le Cordon Bleu was rather short, measured in months not years, and she didn't apprentice in a restaurant, as is typical for French chefs.[13]

**HERITAGE POSITIONING:_____ brand comes from
_____.**

But Child cowrote the first French cookbook in English for an American audience, and her television shows and string of books solidified her heritage positioning. Child also removed the veil of mystery and elitism that shrouded French cuisine. She said "Phoo" to all that and ran a successful business enterprise educating Americans about French cooking.

Making her mark in French high-gastronomy today is Anne-Sophie Pic, France's only three-Michelin-star female chef. Pic is known for unusual flavor combinations, like pork cooked with a beeswax crust to diffuse "a honey taste without the sweetness."[14] Unlike male chefs in France, who get their Michelin stars through cutting-edge techniques, for Pic it's all about "taste and emotion."

Pic is the third generation to run the Maison Pic in Southern France. Pic's grandfather, father, and brother were all famous chefs who ran the restaurant and cooking school. In the mid-1990s, Pic's brother lost the coveted third Michelin star. In 1998, he handed over the business to his younger sister, who has heralded in a new age of French cuisine.

Sidney Frank's first big hit in the United States was distributing the German beer Jägermeister. To build the brand, he used a squadron of young women—branded Jägerettes—to sell drinks in bars, and he threw parties for high visibility.[15]

After that success, in 1997, at seventy-seven years of age, Frank started to think about vodka. An appealing thing about vodka, Frank realized, is that if you make it today, you can sell it tomorrow. Even Jägermeister is aged for a year.

At the time, the premier vodka in the United States was Swedish Absolut, which was selling for $15 a bottle. To make his vodka exclusive, Frank knew that he would need to charge more. So he decided to price his ultra-premium vodka at $30 a bottle. In a moment of inspiration, he came up with the name Grey Goose.

Frank's only remaining problems were that he had no distiller, no vodka, no bottle, no nothing—just a concept and a name.

Because France is the premier place for food and beverage, Frank approached a French distiller and asked him if he could make vodka. Frank tasted about one hundred vodka samples before selecting one and submitting it to the Beverage Testing Institute, where it won as the best-tasting vodka in the world. That was the basis of his successful branding of Grey Goose: a French vodka ranked at the top of the world for taste.

 BRAINSTORMER: Is there a special heritage you can claim for your business or product?

Positioning Strategy 12: Create Scarcity

Scarcity can be a powerful positioning strategy. For many of us, scarcity fuels desire. Look at the long lines and the stampede to get inside stores offering megadeals on hot items the Friday after Thanksgiving in the United States. Or the faux scarcity created for the launch of Google+ with its "by invitation only" launch.

Luxury handbag manufacturers can artificially limit supplies on the season's "it" bag so that there's a waiting list. They realize that scarcity creates desire. Creating a sense of exclusivity was part of the strategy of Bernie Madoff, the money manager who admitted to running a multibillion-dollar Ponzi scheme. He created the illusion that his investment funds were difficult to get into, which made investors clamor all the more for access. In Madoff's case, to their peril.

The illusion of scarcity and luxury is particularly acute in high-end products and services, where you always have to be ahead of the curve with the freshest, rarest materials and you have to create the sense that only an exclusive group can have access.

Sometimes things really are in scarce supply. Then you can truly create brand exclusivity. One of the toughest problems in business is to keep your brand edge even as everyone copies everything that you do. It's a problem in every industry, none more so than in high fashion, where you always have to be ahead of the curve with the next new look and luxury material.

The Loro Piana family has been in the clothing business for six generations. Today, the company is run by Pier Luigi Loro Piana and his brother, Sergio. The brothers were eager to transform the firm from a high-quality manufacturer of wool and cashmere to something more exclusive. Cashmere used to be an exclusive, rather scarce fabric, but its allure has diminished as cheap Chinese cashmere has become commonplace.

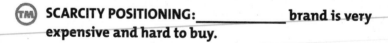 **SCARCITY POSITIONING:**_____ **brand is very expensive and hard to buy.**

To refresh and recharge the brand, the Loro Piana brothers came up with the small idea of moving into vicuña wool, what the Incas called "the fiber of the gods."[16]

To prevent copycats and secure a scarcity positioning, they decided to corner the market on vicuña fleece in Peru, the main country that produces vicuña. Loro Piana buys about 60 to 70 percent of Peru's supply of vicuña fleece. One year it had a contract with the Peruvian government to buy 100 percent.

Vicuña is scarce and difficult to harvest. Vicuñas need space, about two and a half acres per animal, or they won't breed. They can only be sheared once every two years, and even then they don't yield much fleece. That's why Loro Piana suits made from vicuña can cost between $20,000 and $25,000, compared with about $4,000 for suits made from merino wool. To keep its edge, the company is also marketing another rare fiber, "baby cashmere" made from the fleece of infant Hircus goats found in China and Mongolia.

 BRAINSTORMER: How can you use scarcity to create exclusivity for your brand?

Positioning Strategy 13: Go Green and Sustainable

Green can be a powerful brand positioning. The dream of U.K. entrepreneurs Kit and Shireen Morris was to create fine wine from elderflowers.[17] While they were waiting for the vines to mature, they mixed batches of elderberry cordial in their kitchen sink and sold it at farmers markets. People loved the taste, and their sparking elderberry drink developed a cult following for its clean, floral taste similar to that of the lychee.

The husband-and-wife team decided to abandon their wine dream and concentrate on nonalcoholic drinks with a mission of quality without compromise and a commitment to make their products as eco-friendly as possible.

(TM) **GREEN POSITIONING: brand _____ is eco-friendly because _____.**

The Morrises named their company Bottlegreen and created a distinctive green bottle and label to broadcast its green positioning. The sparkling soda is made using a unique, green-friendly bottling process in which recycled water cleans and sterilizes bottles. Bottlegreen tries to source everything locally and is continuously looking for new ways to reduce its carbon footprint.

What could be greener than a farm in your apartment window? A true bootstrapper, Britta Riley initially raised $27,000 for her Windowfarm idea through an online micro-donation site. Her vision? A window farm in every urban dweller's window all made from recycled or inexpensive, easy-to-find materials.

Growing your own food is not only friendly to the environment but it is one of life's simple pleasures. Her website, windowfarm.org, is a crowd-sourcing mecca for urban window farmers to exchange ideas in what Riley calls R&D-I-Y: Research and Develop It Yourself.

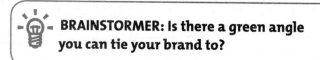

> **BRAINSTORMER: Is there a green angle you can tie your brand to?**

The SWOT Analysis

After you've explored these thirteen positionings, narrow it down to two or three that you think will be most powerful for your brand. To help you decide which one to select, try doing a SWOT analysis, looking at your brand's strengths, weaknesses, opportunities, and threats. It's a good way to look at your business idea in a real-world framework. The SWOT forces you to examine the strengths and weaknesses of your business positioning versus your competitors' positioning and to look at the wider marketplace.

What competitors will you face? What's your differentiator? What are the opportunities? What is going on that could dramatically change things? How might that lead to a fresh positioning of your brand?

The SWOT analysis enables you to figure out quickly whether your business product or service will succeed in the current environment and lead you to the positioning strategy that best takes advantage of your business's strong points, as well as new trends and the competitors you face.

There might be several positionings that could work. Your goal as an entrepreneur is to find the *breakthrough* positioning for your business and for yourself.

When you find the right position:

It will *exploit what's different* about your brand.
It will *be authentic and essential* to customers.
It will *give you leverage* over your competitors.
It will *have staying power* in the marketplace.

EXERCISE: The SWOT Analysis

Strengths: Write down specific ways that your business offers a competitive advantage. What are you really good at?

WEAKNESSES: Write down what you don't do as well as competitors and what you aren't good at.

OPPORTUNITIES: Write down anything that could be an opportunity, such as new trends in the marketplace. A key is to look for unmet or unsatisfied needs. How can you position your brand to take advantage of them? Write down whatever comes to mind.

THREATS: Write down what keeps you awake at night, whether real or imagined, about your business, competitors, and the economy. How can you turn this into a positive positioning of your business?

OPTIONAL: The best ideas often come from the intersection of strength and an opportunity in the market—particularly if the strength is a game-changer in the category. Write down how a key strength of your business meets a unique need in the marketplace. Then, write down how that could be a promise to your customers.

Chapter 4

The Making of a Brand's Verbal Identity

You must have inventiveness, but it must be disciplined. Everything you write, everything on a page, every word, every graphic symbol, every shadow should further the message you're trying to convey.

—Bill Bernbach, Legendary "Mad Man"

In many ways, brands are like people and people are like brands. Just like no two people have the same DNA, no two brands have the same characteristics; you must humanize and give your brand life creatively with a *verbal identity*, *visual identity*, and *brand personality*. For most brands, the creative process begins with a verbal identity for the brand: its name, special words, a brand sentence, a tagline, or a concept statement. Brand identity isn't so different from the movie business, where you have to have a good movie concept and script before you can find a director to visualize it.

The Birth of a Name

Just like with a newborn, your first creative act is to come up with a name for your brand. You have a vision for your brand but now you must name it. In many ways, a brand *is* the name. So you need to come up with a powerful name—one that is different, memorable, and, ideally, positions the brand in the minds of others.

The name is your first and most important strategic and creative decision.

If you've ever named a child, you probably expended a lot of effort in considering lists of names. Almost every parent does, and that's why "baby names" is often a top-ten search phrase when search engines put together their yearly rankings.

This beginning moment in the creative process of branding is full of possibility and fear. How do you get it right?

What Makes a Brand Name Good?

Here's my short list of essentials for creating a great brand name. You should:

▶ **Be different**—It is not at all like the names of your competitors or big-name companies like eBay, Apple, Bugaboo, or Zappos. Quirky names like Spanx for foundation garments and Innocent for fruit drinks stand out and bring attention to your brand.

▶ **Keep it short**—It is easy to remember and spell. Many strong global brands are just four or five letters long, like Nike, Coke, Pepsi, Citi, FedEx, and Tide. Many companies with long names shorten them, like Hewlett Packard did by calling itself HP.

▶ **Evoke meaning**—It doesn't necessarily describe but suggests meaning, like Honest Tea, Vitaminwater, YouTube, Dropbox, and Facebook. Names that have a meaning that relates to your brand are strong because they help lock in your identity and what the business or product is about.

▶ **Make it sound good**—It is easy to pronounce and sounds pleasing or interesting, like M&M, Lululemon, Google, Shake Shack, and Twitter. The Colbert Report is pronounced in the French fashion with both t's silent, giving it linguistic cache. Familiar-sounding names have *cognitive fluency* because people find them easy to pronounce, easy to think about, and easy to prefer, even leading to better stock performance.[1]

▶ **Be sure it's ownable**—If you can't own the name legally or on the Internet, it doesn't have much value.

BRAINSTORMER: Do the names you're considering for your brand meet these criteria?

Naming Wizardry

If you have a catchy business name, you get a big branding boost. Strong names are names, not descriptions of the product or service. They often convey something about the brand—a positive attribute or an inkling of what the brand is about—but they're not a description. National stores, for example, is a description and has an unemotional, bland feeling, while Target is a name for a national chain of stores.

Strong names are different, even quirky, making them easy to remember. Strong names sound different, too. Google has the "g" sound at the beginning and the end, and the double-o in the middle, giving it a friendly sound and feel. Nintendo's Wii has a double-i, which gives it an original look and feel, and is pronounced "we" so it underscores the group dynamics of the game compared to other video games.

American entrepreneur Sara Blakely chose the name Spanx for her new line of shapewear partly for its "virgin-whore tension" and partly for the "k" sound.[2] According to the Spanx website:

> Blakely recognized the value of the "k" sound. Kodak and Coca-Cola are two of the most recognized brand names in the world and in comedy. It is a trade secret that "k" words make people laugh and feel good."[3] Blakely should know: she was a part-time stand-up comedian before she started her business.
>
> So Sara felt that the "k" was good luck and had to be in her product's name. SPANKS hit her one day like a lightning bolt and eventually became SPANX with an "X" because she also knew that made-up names were more successful than real names. We feel the name is edgy, fun, extremely catchy, and for a moment it makes your mind wander (admit it). Plus, it's all about making women's butts look better, so why not?

In the early days, Blakely held her breath every time she said her company name on the phone. Some retailers were so offended that they often hung up the phone when Blakely called to make a sale. When the Spanx website was launched, Blakely's mother accidentally steered her lunch guests to Spanks.com, a porn site!

When Spanx finally found distribution in retail stores, women loved the saucy brand name and trendy shapewear that helped them cover up their saddlebags, stomach rolls, and upper arm jiggles.

As your brand empire grows, you may need to create sub-brands for your company that reflect the sensibility of your umbrella brand. Spanx's Blakely also showed her naming chops in sub-brand names. She calls her lightweight girdle Power Panties, her activewear In It to Slim It, her legwear Tight-End Tights, her casual separates Bod a Bing!, and her lightweight undershorts Skinny Britches.

Mastering the Name Game

Having a name that's different, memorable, meaningful, and conveys your brand's personality is critical in today's competitive marketplace. In 2005, entrepreneur Julie Flakstad came up with a new concept in hair salons called "blow dry bars." Rather than focusing on the typical hair-care services like haircuts and colorings, Flakstad's salon focuses on blow dries. Typically, women just come in for a blow dry for a special occasion, but Flakstad's goal is to change that and make a professional blow dry part of a professional woman's weekly routine.

Flakstad's business idea was to increase the number of times a woman comes into a salon by positioning the business as a *masstige* brand, with salon services and hair products priced between mass and premium brands.[4]

Flakstad named her salon and product line Blow, a hip name that captures the essence of the brand idea and maybe some other associations too. Blow calls its volumizing shampoo Blow Up, its express blow dry lotion Ready Set Blow, and its texturing mist Beach Blow.

It appears that Flakstad discovered an unmet need in the marketplace for women on the go who want to visit a salon for the more polished look a professional blow dry gives them. Women who patronize Blow salons have many times the frequency of the typical salon customer, who goes to a hair salon around four times a year on average.

Other salons are jumping on the trend for blow dry bars, too. One competitor, Drybar, offers only six styles named after stiff drinks. You can choose the sleek Manhattan, the big hair Southern Comfort, or the sophisticated Straight Up. "Pick your poison," as the Drybar menu says.

 BRAINSTORMER: Explore creating names with unusual words and sounds.

Names That Travel Well

Branders love a single global identity. As a brand entrepreneur who wants to create a big brand, having a single brand name that can go global is powerful. Even if you are just focused on a specific region, you don't want to limit yourself. Why not create a name that will give you international freedom?

For starters, try to choose a name that follows familiar linguistic patterns so that it is easy to say by most people, particularly speakers of common languages like English, Spanish, French, and Chinese.

Look at Jack Ma and Alibaba. An English teacher in China, Jack Ma (Ma Yun in Chinese) came to the United States as a visiting scholar in 1995 and got interested in the Internet and how it might lead to a start-up business idea when he returned.

While in a coffee shop in San Francisco, Ma thought that Alibaba might be a good name. So he asked his waitress, "Do you know about Alibaba?"[5] And she said, "Forty Thieves." Then he asked people in the street from Germany, Japan, and China, and they all knew "Ali Baba and the Forty Thieves."

From Ma's perspective, the name had a lot going for it. His man-on-the-street research had revealed that the name was well known and recognized by people all over the world. It was easy to say and spell. It had the repetition of the "ba" sound, a good linguistic device in naming things.

Plus Alibaba had a meaning that related to Ma's idea for an Internet business-to-business services company. If you know the story, the character Ali Baba is not a thief but a kind, smart businessman who helped the villagers. As Ma relates, "Alibaba opens sesame for small-to-medium sized companies."

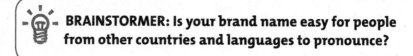

The Internet-Ownable Name

Today, a company or brand name must be especially odd to be one that you can own on the Internet. With over 200 countries on Internet platforms, finding a name that someone else doesn't own already is harder than ever.

It's important to think about, because in today's digital world, you don't have a great name unless you own the dot-com name, _____.com. And if you're a player in global markets, you'll want to own the country code domain name in key countries, too, like _____.co.uk for the United Kingdom or _____.cn for China.

You may have come up with a great name, but if you can't buy the dot-com name or your country's Internet code, you don't have much. It will be harder for people to find you online, and your business will be confused with the party who owns the dot-com name.

Because Internet presence is so crucial, new companies try to come up with made-up names they can own on the Internet and that work in the global business world. One way that can lead to abundant name options is to create a *compound name*. Put two different words together and you'll find there are lots of options for naming. It's best if one or both of the words conveys some idea of your business, like YouTube, Red Bull, PayPal, Zipcar, Netflix, Dropbox, and Facebook.

You can *tweak a word* to create an Internet-ready name. Googol was supposed to be a name that alluded to the vast Internet information that the company was organizing, but the domain name was already taken. So the founders misspelled the name and registered Google instead. Today, both words are in the dictionary, but most people are only familiar with one. Zappos was a tweak of the Spanish word for shoes, *zapatos*. Pierre Omidyar's consulting company was called Echo Bay Technology Group, but when he went to register Echobay.com, it was already taken, so he named his online auction and shopping site eBay.

Another option is to *blend parts of words*. Microsoft blended micro-computer and software, and Skype's name came from sky and peer-to-peer.

Or you can look for a name from a totally *different arena* and apply it to your company or product. There's Apple, Oxygen, and Microsoft's new smartphone, Mango. Many have taken names from Greek mythology, like Pandora or Amazon. Andy Rubin collects robots, a fascination that led him to name his smartphone Android.

You can always opt for a totally *made-up name* to get a name that you can own like Lululemon, which has alliteration too, or Zynga, which was named after CEO Mark Pinkus' dog.

 BRAINSTORMER: Explore creating a name you can own on the Internet.

Create a compound name by putting together two words (Example: JetBlue):

Tweak the spelling of an existing word (Example: Zappos):

Blend parts of words (Example: Skype):

Take a name from a different arena (Example: Mango):

Make up a name (Example: Lululemon):

Anatomy of a Name

Twitter has gone from bird talk to one of the most-used words in the English language, according to the Global Language Monitor.

The name Twitter was the result of a brainstorming session with a small group of employees in 2006. In developing names, the team looked at what the experience was like when someone received a message via the new concept. What analogy could they make? The closest thing was getting a message on SMS. Your phone would buzz. It would jitter. It would twitch. So the team explored names like Jitter and Twitch.[6]

One member of the team searched words that begin with "tw" and found "twitter." Dorsey looked up the meaning of twitter: "a short burst of inconsequential information" and "chirps for birds." The name was perfect.

The first tweet sent by Dorsey read, "just setting up my twttr." Like other tech firms—Flckr, for example—Dorsey shortened the name by removing the vowels. But the team opted for the full spelling and registered Twitter.

The name turned out to be a rich source of inspiration, leading to other catchy company lingo like "tweet" for a message sent on Twitter and its iconic bird logo.

The Sweetest Name

One of the oldest naming strategies for all types of companies is to use the founder's own name or the founding partners' names. Examples abound: Bang & Olufsen, Ben and Jerry's, Christian Louboutin, McDonald's, and Goldman Sachs.

Using your own name can be a great naming strategy if your name is different and easy to remember. It's a naming strategy that many enterprising designers, architects, lawyers, advertisers, and the like use when they want to tie the intellectual property of the business to their personal brand.

Vidal Sassoon set up his first salon in London in 1954 with a dream of transforming the hair industry, and he named his business after himself, Vidal Sassoon. After experimenting for several years, in 1965 Sassoon came up with a different way of cutting and styling hair that he branded the "Five Point Cut."[7] The geometric bob produced by his Five Point Cut took over London. It's always smart branding to name your ideas and creations so they have importance and can be easily identified. Sassoon became a celebrity.

Building on the momentum, he expanded the Vidal Sassoon brand into a best-selling hair product line as well as launching hair salons around the world. In 1968, he famously cut Mia Farrow's hair for the movie *Rosemary's Baby*. (**Guy:** [about Rosemary's haircut] What the hell is that? **Rosemary:** I've been to Vidal Sassoon. **Guy:** You mean you actually paid for it?) The movie ignited the Sassoon brand even more and helped it expand globally.

This naming strategy works best if your name is easy to spell and connotes the right image. Design duo Jack McCollough and Lazaro Hernandez had an auspicious beginning to their fashion business. They created a joint student project at Parsons The New School for Design and sold their entire collection to Barney's in New York City in 2002. Things happened so quickly that they didn't have a name for the clothing line yet. The designers felt that their last names, Hernandez McCollough, didn't read as upscale, so they went with their mothers' maiden names. It was a naming decision they later regretted. Sure, they could get the domain name, but who can say or spell Proenza Schoeller correctly? (Hint: School-er.)

Even if you don't use your name for your company name, try to secure *yourname*.com. It's an advantage if your name Googles well. As a brand entrepreneur, you want to be in control of your name on the Internet. Have a web presence for Brand You where you can host your blog, or at the very least post your personal profile and your business story. If your name is taken, see if you can own the version with your middle name.

Can It Verb Up?

The high bar in names is being able to verb up, like Google, Xerox, and Digg. In the past, to protect the copyright, corporate legal departments advised marketers not to use brand names as a verb or as a noun, and went after people who used the trade name as a generic word for the category.

Now, marketers realize that when their name is used as a verb, as in "Can you Xerox that?" or "I just Googled you" or as a noun, "Can I get you a Starbucks?" that you are extending the brand's visibility for free and locking in your brand's name for the category.

Names that can become verbs have to be short (generally one or two syllables) and "feel" active and physical. You need to be able to say them in a phrase like, "Let's _____ it." Of course, marketers and lawyers can be at odds over this tactic. Lawyers fear that using your brand name as a noun or a verb could lead to your brand name becoming a generic term and thus losing it's trademark protection. So it's a fine line you need to tread, legally protecting your trademark but branding-wise hoping that it will catch on. In fact, verb potential as well as global appeal was a key reason that Microsoft chose the name Bing for its search engine in 2009.

European entrepreneur Niklas Zennstrom's original concept for his Internet phone service was Sky Peer-to-Peer and the name morphed into Skyper. It was later shortened to Skype, giving it an active verb sensibility ("Can you Skype me around 10 a.m.?").

American entrepreneur Kevin Rose originally considered the name Diggnation for his social news company, but he wanted a shorter name. He went with Digg because users can "dig" stories and send them up to the front page of the Digg website. Plus there was a problem with the name Dig. Walt Disney Internet group owned "Dig.com." Digg turned out to be a better choice because the double "g" gives the brand personality, and the name also has verb-up potential that it has exploited.

Dropbox Me

One of the newest brands to verb up is Dropbox as in "Dropbox me." The idea for Dropbox came to Drew Houston on a bus trip to New York.[8] He forgot his USB memory stick, so he couldn't work on the four-hour drive from Boston. So Houston immediately started building technology to synch and store files over the web.

Dropbox solves a new problem people carrying multiple devices like phones, tablets, and laptops face. And others were soon realizing how hot Dropbox could be. It's not many entrepreneurs who are cocky enough to turn down an overture from tech legend Steve Jobs. But that's what Houston did.

He was determined to turn his small idea into a big brand with his co-founder, Arash Ferdowsi. And the duo are on track. In its first six years, Dropbox has over 50 million users, and, unlike other tech companies, it doesn't have a "freemium" problem. Revenues are projected at $240 million in 2011 even though 96 percent of users opt for its free 2-gigabyte service. The freebie users are putting so much stuff into Dropbox, they will likely have to opt for the paid service in the future.

Banning the "The"

In the movie *The Social Network*, Sean Parker famously advised Mark Zuckerberg to lop the word "the" or the "awkward article" before the name Facebook. While "the" is the most commonly used word in English, many marketers, particularly in Silicon Valley, are lopping it off product names. So, it's not the Kindle or the Wii or the BlackBerry, but Kindle, Wii, and BlackBerry.

Apple appears to have launched the trend in 1984 by saying in ads that it would "introduce Macintosh."[9] Research in Motion, BlackBerry's parent, even made it official in its style catalog, stating that BlackBerry is "an adjective not a noun or a verb" and lists as unacceptable calling it "the BlackBerry."

So what's the advantage of an article-less name? Branders believe that removing the "the" makes the brand more iconic and important. It makes a brand less a lowly object and gives it a loftier, bigger feel. Some creative directors feel that dropping the article from the name also makes the brand more immediate and connected to the consumer. Grammarians may cringe, but creative people involved in branding have always been notorious for breaking the rules of grammar and simplifying language to connect with consumers.

Identity Clues

Names that suggest meaning are powerful for a brand because they contain clues to the brand's identity and personality, and that can help lock in your brand in the minds of consumers.

Jonathan Kaplan first came on the entrepreneurial scene as the creator of Flip Video, the simple, pocket-size video camcorder. He gave it a great name and it became a fast hit. Kaplan sold Flip to Cisco Systems in 2009, and two years later Cisco fazed out the popular Flip video camera.

Like his first start-up, Kaplan's new business takes an existing idea and completely transforms it for the modern era. This time Kaplan is not going into the familiar tech space but tackling the humble grilled cheese sandwich, a familiar staple for many American families, though not usually a part of many restaurant menus. His small idea is a chain of fast casual eateries that serve nothing but this unpretentious American comfort food— grilled cheese with soup.

Kaplan came up with a clever name for his restaurants, The Melt. It's a four-letter word like Flip. It's different, memorable, and says something about the brand. It's a great name from a branding perspective.

But Kaplan did something different in his business recipe. He put in a generous helping of high-tech, giving The Melt a different DNA than other fast, casual restaurants.[10] He teamed with Swedish appliance maker Electrolux to develop a special oven—part microwave and part induction burner—that cooks the grilled cheese perfectly in less than a minute.

Kaplan is also developing smartphone apps so that customers can order a sandwich online and The Melt can track customers and have the meal piping hot right when they arrive.

 BRAINSTORMER: Is there a good four- or five-letter name for your brand?

Find a Breakthrough Name in the Category

In breakthrough branding, you want to find a name that's different than your competitors. Of course, fitting in to your category can be hard to resist. Initially even tech legends like Steve Jobs and Steve Wozniak were exploring tech-sounding names like Executex and Matrix Electronics in the vein of then competitors like IBM and Digital Equipment.[11]

In Walter Isaacson's biography of Steve Jobs, Jobs clears up the mystery around the Apple name. Jobs told Isaacson he was "on one of my fruitarian diets" and had just come back from an apple orchard and thought the name Apple sounded "fun, spirited, and not intimidating." It sure didn't sound like a computer company name, either, giving it a breakthrough personality.

 BRAINSTORMER: Is your name completely different from competitors' names?

What Was That Name?

Sometimes breakthrough names come about accidentally. In 2008, Swedish entrepreneurs Daniel Ek and Martin Lorentzon saw a problem in the music marketplace. The choice was between buying legitimate music from iTunes and others for ninety-nine cents or stealing a file that cost nothing, had no restrictions, and sounded better. No wonder so many people were breaking the law. So, they thought, "How do we create a better product than piracy?"

Their small idea was radio meets iTunes. They created affordable, great-quality music for the masses that you can access with iTunes-like simplicity.[12]

Brainstorming about the name for the company one day, the duo were shouting different names back and forth to each other from different rooms. They were even using jargon generators to help them come up with names.[13]

Ek thought he heard his partner say "Spotify" and immediately Googled it. There was not one hit for the word on Google. So Ek quickly registered it. Who knows what name his partner was really shouting, but Spotify was the name they went with. When the media seems disappointed by the name's true origins, Ek has been known to create an after-construction, saying that the name was based on "Spot" and "Identify." For the logo and website design, they went with a distinctive lush green color and hip, designer look.

Rather than selling individual tracks like iTunes, Spotify offers a subscription service with access to a vast catalogue of music and songs that can be played on your computer or mobile phone. What has made Spotify so popular with music lovers is its speed, ease of use, and sound quality. Its speed comes from its peer-to-peer network and is a major advantage over competitors. Spotify has a three-tier plan: a free ad-supported service, a basic ad-free service, and a premium service that allows access via mobile phone. With its Facebook connection, it's easy to share songs with friends and drop and drag playlists.

In a few years, Spotify has grown into the world's most celebrated new digital music service, popular in Europe and introduced to the United States in 2011.

Names Are Forever...

For most entrepreneurs, the name you give your brand is a forever decision. Marketing campaigns and advertising slogans may come and go, but the brand name should be timeless. It should be something that you will stick with throughout the life of your business. You lose the equity you built in the old name when you change names, not to mention the cost involved.

Of course, there are exceptions to every principle, even the equity of the name, if you come up with a much better name. For fourteen years, entrepreneurs Phil Knight and Bill Bowerman called their athletic shoe company

Blue Ribbon Sports. Then a friend suggested they name the company after the Greek goddess of victory. And Nike was born.

Nike was a better name: it was short, different, and meaningful. The new name set up a better positioning for the brand around the promise that a winning attitude leads to victory. The new positioning led to highly inspirational advertising featuring celebrity athletes like Michael Jordan, which gave the name emotional power.

Would the brand have become a global icon and business success story if entrepreneurs Knight and Bowerman had kept the original name, Blue Ribbon Sports? Maybe not. A great name like Nike can help your brand be remembered and liked, just as a bad name can hurt your brand or just not help it much.

What's Your Line?

There's not a lot of demand for sales messages. That's why branders disguise them as entertainment and stories in television commercials. They try to anchor the brand benefit with a tagline or catchphrase. When you write a tagline for your brand, you want to touch the truthful chord, but you need to make it fascinating.

Branders try to capture the brand promise and its personality in a short phrase or tagline. They are trying to create a handle that makes it easy for people to connect the name and what the brand is about. The best lines connect on an emotional level so that people feel something about the brand and want to fulfill the prophecy of the tagline message.

The creators of two of the most successful taglines, "Just Do It" and "Got Milk," said that they didn't realize that the slogans would take off. Dan Wieden, the creator of the Nike line, thought "Just Do It" would work, but he was as surprised as anyone that the expression entered the cultural zeitgeist. Imagine how much extra product sales that generated!

Taglines should be short, direct, and lock in something important about the brand. MasterCard's tagline is just one word, "Priceless," and the company sets it up by preceding it with the slogan, "There are some things money can't buy. For everything else, there's MasterCard."

 Touching the truthful chord is the root of good lines. Tell the truth but make it interesting.

Like naming your brand, creating a tagline is more art than science. You want a tagline that works in your market and connects with your customers, and ideally can translate globally. Great taglines can be catchy and memorable, like Verizon's "Can you hear me now?" or Las Vegas's "What happens in Vegas, stays in Vegas."

Apple's famous "Think Different" tagline is on most lists for the best taglines of all times, and it breaks the rules of grammar since different should have an "-ly" as an adverb. In Walter Isaacson's biography of Steve Jobs, Jobs said he wanted "different" to be used as a noun as in "think victory." Says Jobs, "It's not think *the same*, it's think *different*. Think a little different, think a lot different, think different. Think *differently* wouldn't hit the meaning for me."

Often, marketers try to drill in the brand promise, like BMW's "The Ultimate Driving Machine," the Chinese company Alibaba's "There's no hard business," or Uniqlo's "Made for All." Toms Shoes' line is "One for One," to underscore that a free pair of shoes will be given to a poor child with each purchase. Target's promise is "Expect More. Pay Less," and FedEx's is "The World on Time." Your tagline can position your brand versus its competitors, like Avis rental car's "We try harder."

You want your brand name to be easy to remember. Alliteration or repetition can help lock in the brand tagline, like Spotify's "All the music, all the time" or Jaguar's "Don't dream it. Drive it." A pun can make the tagline sticky, like IKEA's "Make yourself at home" or Weight Watchers' frozen meals tagline, "Taste. Not waist."

One sure way to connect the slogan and the brand is to use the brand name in the slogan, like John Deere tractors' "Nothing runs like a Deere" or Citibank's "Because the Citi never sleeps" or Mumm champagne's "One word captures the moment. Mumm's the word."

Rhyme can make a tagline easy to remember, such as "Takes a licking and keeps on ticking" for Timex and "Nothing sucks like an Electrolux." Some studies show that rhyming phrases are viewed as more accurate and believable, a *rhyme-as-reason* effect.[14]

Intellectual Property

Don't just name your physical products; name your ideas, processes, and services, too. Names make them "products" with name power that can help sell your ideas and services. At Facebook, you can "friend" someone or "unfriend" them. At Twitter, you can "tweet" and "retweet."

Starbucks broke the price barrier for premium coffee by changing the name of a small cup and naming it "tall." It didn't seem so bad to pay so much if you were getting a tall size. And they have their "baristas" and "whip skinny caramel macchiatos" and other interestingly named concoctions.

Politicians can be good at the naming and sound bite game. A twenty-three-year-old congressional aide came up with the name PATRIOT Act, from "Providing Appropriate Tools Required to Intercept and Obstruct Terrorism." Naming the bill the PATRIOT Act obviously makes the bill's opponents seem unpatriotic, which is unfair, but from a branding perspective, the name was powerful and memorable.

If you're a consultant, don't sell your services on an hourly basis. Sell the package of services as a product and name it. Your clients aren't in the market for hours. They are in the market for solutions to their problems. Package your consulting services as solutions and give them a name that makes your brand different. For example, my company, SelfBrand, doesn't work with entrepreneurs on an hourly basis, rather we market individual products like our "SelfBrand Strategy and Marketing Plan."

When you come up with a great name for an idea or concept, you can even trademark the name or expression, like ESPN did with "March Madness."

A Marriage of Business and Personal Brand

As a brand entrepreneur, you'll want to develop a strong verbal identity for your business brand with a distinctive name and tagline and a distinctive voice in your communications, as well as a distinctive verbal identity for Brand You.

Japanese entrepreneur Tadashi Yanai is the design genius and mastermind behind the Japanese brand Uniqlo. Yanai started with one store in Japan called The Unique Clothing Warehouse. He shortened the name to Uniqlo, a distinctive name and spelling. The logo features a strong graphic design with two squares, one with the name in *katakana*, the phonetic alphabet used in Japan for foreign words, and the other square with the name spelled using the Western alphabet: Uniqlo. Both names are rendered in four syllables over two lines, giving it a strong graphic feel that complements the words. The tagline for the brand on its ads is "Made for All."

Uniqlo has grown to more than 700 stores in its home country and has launched stores across the globe. The Uniqlo brand is known for its strong visual identity. It designs and manufactures all the items sold in its stores and is identified with modern, minimalist design in both fashion, accessories, and store design.

Not only is Uniqlo's product line unique, but the company is run by a leader who's not your typical Japanese businessman. Yanai is outspoken and writes about his views. In a 2011 article in the *McKinsey Quarterly*, titled "Dare to Err," Yanai says that "Japan is losing the economic game. Why can't the country learn from its mistakes?"[15] He feels that the Japanese tend to be strong at home and weak away, and that is a major problem in today's global world.

Yanai feels that leadership means understanding the global sales force and that the natural Japanese standoffishness will hinder business success and its efforts toward globalization. It's a tendency that Yanai is determined to avoid as he expands the Uniqlo brand.

What's remarkable is that Uniqlo's recent overseas expansion has come at a time when Japan's economy and many Japanese companies have hit the wall financially and psychologically. To make sure that his company is tuned in to the global world of business, at Uniqlo English is spoken at business meetings with foreigners, and Yanai wants all e-mails to be in English in a few years.

Uniqlo has set up a system to assemble information and collective intelligence from its hundreds of stores in Japan and around the world. Until recently, Uniqlo mainly collected information at its twice-yearly conferences for store managers. In 2006, Uniqlo launched an internal blog content management system so that all floor staff can communicate in real time through their smartphones.

Before the feedback system, headquarters would design ad inserts, but it had no ability to get feedback on the inserts from the local stores. Now headquarters posts the ads and gets comments immediately.

The Creation Story

As an entrepreneur, you'll find that people will ask you again and again, "Why did you start this business?" To answer that question well you'll need to craft a *creation story*, an important part of your verbal identity as a brand entrepreneur.

The creation story is about how you became who you are and how and why you started your business. It's a great story format to use in promoting your business with customers, the media, employees, and the general public.

The creation story not only tells who you are and why you started the business, but it highlights specific aspects of your business—its purpose and values, key products, culture, and customers.

(TM) **The creation story is the who-you-are-and-how-you-started-your-business story.**

Yu Minhong (called Michael Yu in English) grew up poor on a farm in rural China. After high school, Yu had two choices: go to work as a farmer or take the university exams. For poor children living on farms in China, the dream of going to university is a fantasy. Yet Yu was determined. He took the exams and failed. Then he took them again. And he failed again.[16]

Three's the charm, they say, so Yu took the exams a third time. This time he was admitted to Beijing University, though initially he was put in remedial classes. Later, after graduation, he set his goals on going to study at a graduate school in the United States and he took the GRE exams. He got a low score. So he took them again and again got a low score. This time, the third try wasn't lucky, and he didn't get a high enough score to be competitive.

Yu never did make it to the United States as a graduate student. But his epic journey to pass standardized exams made him determined to help other Chinese pass the exams. In 1993, Yu launched New Oriental Language and Technology Group, the leading test preparation company in China. At his company, Yu has perfected a method of passing the exams for Chinese students. Now, Chinese students regularly trounce the rest of the world on international standardized tests.

In China today, Yu promotes his company by telling his creation story in speeches to college students all around the country. His speeches have been a tremendous recruitment and PR tool for Yu and his company. Yu's quest to pass the exams has given him a strong purpose, and he continues to inspire China's youth. Here's a line from one of his famous speeches: "Hew a stone of hope from a mountain of despair and you can make your life a splendid one."

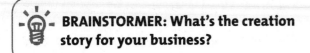

BRAINSTORMER: What's the creation story for your business?

The Purpose Story

As a brand entrepreneur, you need to attract investors, employees, customers, and others to your vision. A powerful way to do that is with the *purpose story*. It's your deeper story—the purpose and meaning behind your life journey. It's the story behind your creation story.

 The purpose story is the why-you-are-here story. It's about an ideal that ties together your business, your values, and your philosophy about serving your customers.

Your purpose story is fundamental to who you are as a person, at your core, and what you want others to believe about you. It's about how and why you want to make meaning in the world. But it's also a universal story that everyone can relate to. We all have a desire to understand how we came to be who we are, to know other people's backstories, and to see a larger purpose in life.

Your purpose is what made you want to lead. It gives context to where you and your company came from and where you are heading. A purpose story isn't about making a lot of money. It's about an ideal—wanting to make a better product or create a service that will serve people better.

This story often involves transformation, a *defining moment* that led you to your purpose in life. It gives people a sense of where you've come from and where you're heading and ties together your business, your philosophy, and the contribution that you want to make as a leader. Ultimately, your purpose is not about you but about how you want to make a difference in your customers' lives.

Suze Orman is a personal finance guru with an in-your-face style on her cable television show and nine consecutive *New York Times* best-selling personal finance books. (You know she's a personal brand by the quirky spelling of her first name.) Orman's purpose story involves her family's precarious financial condition during her childhood in Chicago. A defining moment came when a fire engulfed her father's chicken takeout store, and he rushed back in to recover the cash register, leaving him with third-degree burns. That's when Orman learned that "money was more important than life." Later she worked as a waitress at the Buttercup Bakery in Berkeley, California, before she took charge of her career and financial life. Orman describes her purpose as her desire "to change the way Americans think, talk, and act about money."

Howard Schultz of Starbucks famously wanted to create the "third place"—after home and the office—to hang out, but he also had a deeper purpose story. His defining moment was when his father lost his job and the family lost its health insurance when he was a kid. So part of Schultz's leadership purpose is to provide health insurance, even for part-time workers at Starbucks.

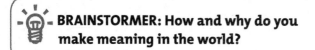

> **BRAINSTORMER: How and why do you make meaning in the world?**

Wrap Your Brand in Your Purpose

Your purpose is a unifying principle for your brand. It sets up your values and beliefs, why these beliefs are important, and why you belong in people's lives. Your purpose can even become your mantra, like Google's, "Don't be evil."

Hot sauce and burritos wrapped in a socially responsible message have made Chipotle a super-hot company. Entrepreneur Steve Ells is committed to only serving animal products from humane providers because he thinks it's the right thing to do.

Ells is an animal lover, a CEO who brings his dog, Bailey, with him to work. He became interested in humane animal treatment after he saw the conditions of animals on a trip to suppliers.[17] Ells is determined to find and sell as much of what he calls the "good stuff" as possible. It's already bringing about change in the industry, as other fast food restaurants start to explore humane meat options.

At Chipotle, every burrito is handmade individually for each customer. Sure, it can slow things down, but customers feel that what Chipotle stands for is worth the wait.

Study the Masters

Entrepreneurs sometimes ask me, "How can I use the power of words to build my brand?" Study the new brand names, ad copy, taglines, and popular expressions that enter the public consciousness. Read the stories that other entrepreneurs tell about starting their businesses. Listen for interesting ways of phrasing things that you hear on television business shows or read in business magazines. But, if you're looking for real inspiration with words, phrases, and messages, read great literature.

For me and many others, William Shakespeare is the writer who continues to offer inspiration. He never ceases to astonish with the power of words. And so many of his words and expressions are timeless. That's the ultimate in breakthrough branding.

Shakespeare achieved the ultimate in verbal branding power. His words speak to all people, regardless of their status in life, just as they did when he wrote them 400 years ago.

As a brand entrepreneur, it's powerful to be good with language so you can tap into the branding power of words. When you have the right name or tagline or catchphrase, you'll know it because:

It will cause people to *linger and want to know more.*
It will *sound like your brand's personality.*
It will be *different from competitors'.*
It will be *something that you can own.*

Chapter 5

Creating Your Brand's
Look and Feel

> "I warn you against believing that advertising is a science. Artistry
> is what counts. The business is filled with great technicians, and
> unfortunately they talk the best game…but there's one little
> problem. Advertising happens to be an art, not a science."
>
> —Bill Bernbach, Legendary "Mad Man"

You've got to come up with something that visually defines the brand: a logo, a shape, a color, or a design. What's the brand going to look like? What's the logo? What's the packaging? What's the website design? What's the store experience like? What's the brand personality?

All these are aspects of a brand's *look and feel*. Look and feel covers all the traditional areas of graphic design, but it's also about creating a special sensory experience for your brand, beginning with the product, the logo, and the product's actual packaging, as well as digital communications, marketing materials, and store experience.

 LOOK AND FEEL cover all aspects of brand design.

LOOK: designed elements like color, images, shape, layout, and type fonts.

FEEL: dynamic sensory elements like digital interactivity and personality.

A Second or Less

Why should looks matter so much? After all, we're all told, "Don't judge on appearances." But we do it all the time. We often decide whether to buy a product based on its design or packaging, particularly if it looks cool or it's a category we don't know very well. We can even decide to do business with a service company because we are impressed with its "packaging"—its website, office, or marketing materials.

Visual identity is very powerful in brand selection. And to make things worse, *less than a second* may be all you have! That's how quickly a first impression registers. What registers is largely a snap visual and sensory impression.

These quick, blink-of-an-eye impressions are what psychologists call *thin slicing*. We see a thin slice of a product, person, event, or experience and we take it all in rapidly.

Our minds want to categorize our experience. Do we like it or not? What's interesting is that these first impressions tend to be surprisingly accurate assessments and stay with us over time.

As a brand entrepreneur, you can't discount the power of first impressions. You need to package your products, package your business, and package yourself in the best way possible. You need to get these quick impressions working in your favor. If your brand is admired because of its name and the way it looks, you have an edge in breakthrough branding, just as when you click with another person when you first meet her and she quickly concludes that you are exceptional.

Look and Feel = Brand Equity

The look and feel of your brand is an important part of its *brand equity*, its value as a brand. There are so many brands to consider online and offline, both for tangible products and for services. The vast number of choices on a global scale makes creative design and packaging of products important as a differentiator.

The average supermarket has almost 40,000 items, and Internet shopping opens up many thousands more. Years ago, packaging made self-service retailing possible, and now with online shopping, packaging is more important than ever.

Product design and packaging help consumers make a decision about whether to buy a product or not. This is true whether it's actual product packaging that they can see in a store or on the web or it's the way you "packaged" your website, yourself, your pitch, and your office.

Great packages get an emotional reaction. That's why the big brands use neuromarketing techniques to find out what packaging, images, names, and messages get the strongest emotional response. In the tests, consumers wear special vests with sensors that track skin moisture levels, heart rate, breathing, and eye movements.

With these new techniques, researchers don't have to rely on what you say in a survey, which is often misleading; they can track when and how you react to something emotionally. While current neuromarketing techniques can't tell researchers what emotions subjects are experiencing, they can tell if the person is emotionally engaged with a brand or not. With some brands, brain circuits light up like fireworks. It's similar to the reaction that researchers get when someone is engaging with a loved one. That's how connected the person is to the brand!

Not Innocent about Branding

Having a great product is key, but having breakthrough branding will help you get noticed. Great branding can be a big, even the major, factor in a new business's success. Innocent was launched by three Cambridge University graduates in 1998. The trio set up a stall at a music festival to test the fruit smoothie drinks they had concocted. They put two bins in front with a sign that asked customers to vote by casting their empties in the Yes bin if they thought the group should start a business and quit their jobs. Only a few empty containers ended up in the No bin, so the three friends resigned the next day.

The small idea behind Innocent is authenticity—healthy fruit drinks made of 100 percent fresh ingredients. The focus on authenticity and naturalness led to the name innocent with a small "i." The logo is a quirky apple shape, almost like a child's drawing, with two eyes and a halo above to underscore the honesty and playfulness of the brand along with its promise of pure ingredients.

A unifying element for the brand, according to Innocent Creative Director Dan Germain, is being "useful and interesting."[1] Innocent puts a heavy emphasis on being amusing in all its branding. It calls its London headquarters Fruit Towers. Innocent experimented with labels that listed ingredients such as "banana, orange, and a lawnmower." When they did a label that listed "plump nuns" among the ingredients, Innocent got some controversial publicity. It also received a reprimand from the United Kingdom's Advertising Standards Authority asking them to change the labels or "start putting said items in your drinks." Nonetheless, it all makes for a great creation story and fun breakthrough branding that connects with its target audience, young, trendy twentysomethings.

Innocent has been a wild growth story. After a few short years, it became the leading smoothie brand in the United Kingdom, has been on the *Sunday Times Fast Track 100* list of fastest-growing companies five years running, and now is expanding into Europe. Recently, Innocent sold a significant stake to Coca-Cola. It's a successful start-up that's even got its own book, *Innocent: A Book About Innocent*.

Logos Work Hard

From a branding standpoint, the logo is an important visual expression of what a company, product, or service is about. A logo can have a mark, a graphic element like the Pepsi logo followed by the product name, or it can be an all-type logo, like Coca-Cola's. Whatever the design, the logo needs to convey the brand personality and ideally something about the brand promise.

Logos have to be a quick read, so you need to brand boldly. Logos need to work large on a sign or storefront and small on a business card. That's why simple graphic designs, strong colors, and contrasting shapes work best. Complicated designs don't translate well in different uses, particularly on the web and on business cards.

Don't go for the design trend *du jour*. Aim for timeless. Like your brand name, your logo should transcend time. You want a logo for the long haul that will work when you're a small business and when you're a big brand.

Your logo may need minor visual tweaking over time to keep it contemporary, but it should evolve rather than change dramatically.

Of course, there are exceptions to every rule. Google's a rule breaker and doodles with its multicolored logo regularly throughout the year to commemorate different holidays and seasonal events. It's a whimsical trend that started in 1998 when the cofounders inserted a drawing into the logo to commemorate their participation in the Burning Man Festival in Nevada.

Your logo should communicate visually. A logo should be an icon, not an illustration. It's better to suggest than describe. It's best to have an idea behind the graphics that conveys something essential about your brand, even if only in an abstract or emotional way.

Lindon Leader, the Landor Associates designer behind FedEx's famous orange and purple logo, noticed a hidden arrow shape in the negative space between the capital E and the lowercase x. Leader began to play with the concept of an embedded arrow between the two letters to represent the speed and precision of the delivery service. The two typefaces he was using didn't quite work, so he experimented and created a type font that was a hybrid of the two, allowing him to embed the arrow in a way that seemed natural in shape and location.[2]

twitter 🐦

With a name like Twitter and a communication service based on short messages, using a bird for the logo seems a natural. Mindful of money in the start-up phase, the founders originally used a graphic from iStockphoto that they paid $15 or less for. The logo has been tweaked through the years by cofounder Biz Stone and other designers and is available for download as part of Twitter's open-platform philosophy.

The Making of a Great Logo

One of the best logos of all time is the "I Love NY" logo designed by Milton Glaser. It's become an icon recognized around the world and one that has inspired countless knockoffs of the I ♥ _____ format.

New York's logo has all the elements of a breakthrough logo design:

▶ **Simple:** Glaser simplified "New York" to two initials and simplified "love" to a heart symbol.

▶ **Bold:** Using a bright red heart icon rather than the word love was a stroke of design and communication genius, because now the logo speaks a universal language.

▶ **Charismatic:** The hip font, the bright red color, and the heart graphic work together to convey the passion, energy, and openness of New York and its people.

▶ **Different:** Influenced by the iconography of pop art and comic books, Glaser created a truly unique logo, not just one that was different from the logos of other tourism destinations; it was different from any logo.

▶ **Timeless:** It's a logo that transcends time and place. It's still as popular today as it was when Glaser designed it in the 1970s.

Anatomy of a Logo

When Michael Bierut of design company Pentagram first presented his logo concepts for the New World Symphony in Miami, his clients weren't thrilled, and neither was he.[3]

Feeling stuck, Bierut looked at the rough sketches that Michael Tilson Thomas, the symphony's founder and artistic director, had done of the symphony's monogram, NWS. The linked letters in the monogram sketches looked eerily similar to the architect Frank Gehry's building sketches for the new symphony building in Miami. The curving shapes of Tilson Thomas's monogram sketches also reminded Bierut of sound waves.

Now Bierut had the concept for a breakthrough logo design: linking the monogram letters, NWS, and the curves of sound waves into one elegant yet energetic symbol. Bierut experimented with proportion, curves, and symmetry. He almost gave up because it was difficult to get the monogram letters to work together fluently in a simple design.

Then it came together: the symphony initials, the sound waves, and the sense of the vibrant music in a single, distinctive logo mark. You can see the initials, NWS. You can see sound waves musically vibrating. But even if you see none of those things, it's still a wonderful abstract design.

Tangibly Intangible

It can be tough to market service businesses because, unlike consumer products, there is no physical brand. Services are not easy for clients to buy, either, because there is nothing tangible to experience. That's why big services brands often use a visual symbol to break through and get noticed and bring their brand promise to life. U.S. insurance giants do this. Travelers has its red umbrella, Geico has its gecko, Prudential has its rock, AllState has its hands, and Afflac has its duck.

As an entrepreneur of a business-to-business or consumer service, you want to have a good name but also a strong visual identity for your company. I worked with entrepreneur Faith Monson when she launched her business as a "success coach" for business executives and entrepreneurs.

Working with a graphic designer for her business logo, Monson knew the business's visual concept was "getting a grip on the excitement of the mind": here's the logo that's kind of a human exclamation point.

Monson also uses doors—beautiful doors—in her website and marketing materials. Some people close doors, Monson is a door opener: doors to possibility, doors to opportunity, and doors to success.

What's the Logo Concept?

For the SelfBrand logo, I wanted to capture the idea of branding your business and branding yourself. The graphic designer came up with this mark, a big red box with a black dot outside it and off-center.

You could look at the mark as an abstract representation of "I" for self or "I brand." Or you could look at it as meaning thinking outside the box, which is essential in good branding. Or the graphic could be a camera, because branding is about identity. Now, of course, the typical person viewing your logo is not going to take the time to analyze it in this way, but having an idea behind your logo design gives it meaning, both consciously and unconsciously, in the minds of others.

In developing the logo, we also played with the idea of the transformative process of branding. So in the name part of the logo, we began with the word "self" in lowercase black letters, representing the idea of the undeveloped potential of a product or person before branding. For the word "brand," on the other hand, we used all uppercase letters, with each letter in a different color, alluding to the transformative power of a branding make-over. (For the full-color version of the logo, visit *www.selfbrand.com*.)

Laura Berkowitz Gilbert is the graphic designer who created the cover of this book and my two previous books. She named her graphic design company Boomerang Studio, because when you have strong branding the benefits will come back to you over time. So the boomerang seemed like a perfect graphic symbol to communicate that message. Besides, boomerang is fun to say.

BRAINSTORMER: How can you make your service business more tangible with a logo and visual symbols?

A Breakthrough Brand Experience

A relatively new area of branding is called *experience design*, creating products, events, and experiences that make contact with the brand memorable and special at every touchpoint. It's particularly important to think about if you are an entrepreneur with a retail store or where customer events are an important part of your marketing strategy.

 EXPERIENCE DESIGN: creating products, events, environments, and processes that enhance the *user experience* or how people experience the brand.

Creating community and a special user experience are integral to the small idea behind Pearl Chen's business. Chen grew up in Houston, Texas, where her family ran a small neighborhood grocery store. The Chens knew everybody in the community. This was a time before credit cards, when kids would come in after school to shop for their moms on credit, and on Fridays the dads would stop by to pay the bill. It was a system of trust.

Chen had to work in the store two hours a day as a kid and she hated it. But years later, when she was married with a family in New York City and thinking about starting a business, she remembered that store and the wonderful community it created.

Her daughter was knitting at the time, and Chen picked up the hobby, too. She started thinking about setting up a yarn store that was the center of a community, like her parents' neighborhood store.

Her business idea was to create a kind of "Cheers bar" for knitters. She envisioned a yarn shop where everyone was welcome, with lots of events and experiences for knitters. She designed her store like an extension of her home, with tables for people to gather for classes or just to knit together.

Located on the Upper West Side of Manhattan, she called her shop Knitty City, and the logo design conveys the idea of knitting, its city location, and the energy of the community.

Chen has created events to attract all different types of communities, and she markets them with pictures of people knitting, connecting, and having fun on her website and on social media. The events range from beginning classes in the store and in local parks to knitting circles for advanced knitters. She has book clubs for literary knitters and hosts talks by well-known fiber artists for those who want to meet the experts. She sells "Stitch and Pitch" tickets for Mets baseball games. She does events for local charities, such as sewing blankets for a local senior center, sponsoring a team for a breast cancer walk, and a 9/11 tie-in event. There's even a men's knitting night!

Chen's inspiration was an old retail idea—her parents' community store—but with some new twists (knitting, special events and experiences, and the Internet).

 BRAINSTORMER: How can you design a special user experience and events for your brand?

A Color, a Shape, a Look

Marketers of breakthrough brands try to own a color, a shape, a visual, something that's a signature of the brand. You should, too.

After a promising first season, things weren't going well for French shoe designer Christian Louboutin.[4] More a creative artist than a businessman, Louboutin lost track of manufacturing timetables in 1993, and his second collection of shoes arrived in stores months late. It was a financial disaster.

But in the tumult of the crisis, Louboutin kept designing shoes. One shoe was inspired by Andy Warhol's *Flowers* and had cloth blossoms on top and a pink stacked heel.

Staring at the prototype, Louboutin felt something was missing. It lacked the punch of his original drawing and Warhol's art. Lost in creative thought, he saw one of his assistants painting her nails bright red. Louboutin confiscated the red nail polish and painted it on the sole of the shoe prototype. The glossy red soles made the whole shoe design pop.

It was a simple, novel idea. Why do anything with the outsoles of shoes? That's the part you walk on! Yet the glossy red soles did something extraordinary from a visual identity standpoint. Louboutin took something that had been ignored and considered of little value and made it visually exciting and valuable financially. Louboutin's red soles project glamour and, no doubt, showy excess.

The red soles are also brilliant breakthrough branding because they are immediately recognizable, and also, according to Louboutin, great for romance. "Men are like bulls," Louboutin says, "they cannot resist the red sole."[5] With the success of the red sole, it's been hard for rivals to resist copying his brand signature.

Louboutin is also known for his iconic shoe shapes and wickedly high heels. His signature shoe is the Very Prive, a shoe he named and first sold in 2006. It has a towering high heel with an extreme hidden platform. Before the Very Prive, Louboutin wasn't as well known as his competitor Manolo Blahnik, but the Very Prive, with its signature heel, sexy shape, and red soles, changed the pecking order in upscale shoe design.

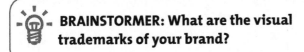

BRAINSTORMER: What are the visual trademarks of your brand?

Good Things Come in Nice Packages

Package design is powerful. Unexpected or unusual packages grab our attention. They even deceive us into thinking there's more inside when the volume is the same as other similarly sized but conventionally designed packages. So you win two ways. People find the package more appealing and believe they are getting more product inside!

That's why it's smart not to derive your brand's visual identity from the same sources everyone else is using. For breakthrough branding, you need to look in a different direction.

Tired of cleaning products that used harsh chemicals, sported ugly packaging, and smelled terrible, Monica Nassif had an idea. What if household cleaners were packaged and marketed like beauty products?

That's the small idea behind Mrs. Meyer's Clean Day line—and it is a big hit at retail stores.[6] Although the line is priced 20 to 30 percent higher than most household cleaners, Mrs. Meyer's is a success because it is considered an affordable luxury.[7] (Undercutting the competition on price isn't the best way to set your brand apart because it's much less profitable on a per unit basis.)

Monica Nassif's small idea had to do with quality and style, not price, and her products appealed to women willing to pay more for cleaning products that looked and smelled beautiful.

Nassif named the line after her mother, Thelma Meyer, an Iowa homemaker and gardener. She talked retailers into displaying the whole line together in stores, in what she calls "brand blocking." So, rather than have one item with the dish soaps and another with the counter cleaners, Mrs. Meyer's products are grouped together for maximum impact with shoppers. It's part of a hot concept called *shopper marketing*, which focuses on effective ways to market your products to shoppers in stores right when they're ready to buy.

The Mrs. Meyer's line has a simple retro look in pastel colors—a contrast to the primary colors and starbursts screaming "New" and "Improved" on typical household products. Rather than a hint of bleach, her products come in fragrances such as geranium, basil, lavender, lemon verbena, and baby blossom. The basil version has "top notes of basil, apricot leaves, parsley, and eucalyptus." That's worth paying a premium price for, don't you think?

 BRAINSTORMER: Are there visual and sensory ideas from a different category that can inspire you?

Lust for Design

In packaging your brand, you want the visual and the verbal to be seamlessly intertwined and distinctive. Look at yoga-wear company Lululemon, developed by Canadian entrepreneur Chip Wilson, who has designed a brand that crackles visually, verbally, and experientially.

Exhilarated by his first yoga class, Wilson got his small idea. Why not marry yoga with his passion for technical athletic fabrics?[8] To come up with a name, Wilson tested twenty names with one hundred people, and the winner was Lululemon. The logo is a stylized A (from Athletically Hip, one of the twenty original names being tested). The stylized A of the logo looks vaguely Greek or Sanskrit and sparks a lot of curious questions about its meaning.

For Lululemon, Wilson created hip yoga designs made from specialty fabrics that he branded and trademarked. One is Vitasea, made with Seacell, a yarn developed from seaweed that is soft and pliable, ideal for exercising. Wilson opened his first store in a suburb of Vancouver, Canada, and created a special brand experience as he expanded in Canada, the United States, and Australia with free yoga classes along with free alterations on yoga pants.

Form as Function and Breakthrough Design

At ten, he made a fifty-foot-long chain of bikes. At twelve, he built a moped. At fourteen, he constructed a motorized cart. Seems that Dutch entrepreneur Max Barenbrug was destined to create an innovative means of transportation.

Barenbrug got the inspiration for his brand idea during his student days, when he was looking out his apartment window. He saw a woman struggling with a bike, a baby, and a stroller. He realized it has to be one movement to fold the stroller.[9] Barenbrug designed a rugged stroller that was tough yet easy to maneuver as one of his final projects at school in 1994. He graduated with honors.

He called his baby buggy the Bugaboo and officially founded the company in 1999. Before Bugaboo, strollers were simple, lightweight, and female-oriented.

Bugaboos are rugged, masculine, and high-tech. They have multiterrain swivel wheels with suspension that can be converted to two-wheel mode for going up hills. They have detachable and reversible seats, adjustable handlebars, and car seats that you can just click in place.

Barenbrug created something people didn't know they wanted until they saw it. Bugaboo has become the stroller of choice with young parents around the world, even with a retail price that is upward of $600. Its design features have forced other stroller manufacturers to try to copy Barenbrug's breakthrough design and functional innovations to be competitive.

Own a Color

Color is powerful. That's why branders think in terms of owning a color, even trademarking a particular color, like some big brands have done. Tiffany has trademarked the particular shade of blue it uses for its boxes, bags, and other marketing. In fact, a lot of people shop at Tiffany to get the turquoise blue box because it is immediately recognizable to the recipient and signals quality and expense.

Trademarking a color is something that entrepreneurial businesses can explore too. Entrepreneurs Stephen and David Mullany trademarked the bright yellow color of their plastic Wiffle Ball bats.

The Mullanys are carrying on the family Wiffle Ball business, started by their grandfather in the 1950s.[10] Unemployed with a family to feed, Mullany senior was watching his eldest son and his friends play baseball with plastic golf balls. Try as they might, they couldn't make the golf balls spin. So father and son started experimenting until they came up with their now iconic design, a white plastic ball around the size of a baseball with eight holes on one hemisphere.

The Mullanys had their small idea, a baseball-like game that kids (and adults) could play indoors or outdoors in small spaces. They named their game Wiffle Ball because David and Stephen's father and his friends called a strikeout a "wiff." The game became a craze in the United States in the '60s and '70s, and in the '80s Wiffle Ball leagues were popular. The game is still played by kids across the U.S. today.

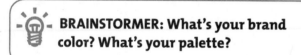

> 💡 **BRAINSTORMER: What's your brand color? What's your palette?**

Designer Sales

Not only are our aesthetics more sophisticated today, but we expect good design in our gadgets as well as our fashions. It's even invaded previously underdesigned arenas.

Look at the common disposable diaper. Birthrates are down in the United States, and the innovations in making disposable diapers more absorbent may have reached their peak, making diaper sales a branding game.

To drive sales, especially in the summer, diaper makers are turning to design. Procter & Gamble puts out limited-edition prints in the summer, including designs by Cynthia Rowley. Huggies has jeans diapers. It's a seasonal impulse that some moms splurge on their babies when it's hot and their baby's fashion statement can be seen.

Almost anything can be part of your breakthrough branding. Design has even come to the lowly bar code that appears on almost every product. Sixpoint Brewery in Brooklyn, New York, launched a new beer in 2011 and did a hip design for the can but felt that the design was marred by the big ugly bar code.[11] So the company designed a custom bar code that incorporates the Statue of Liberty and skyscrapers into the bar-code design. Verdi Italian food has an olive tree rising from its bar code, and Nestlé has a bubble rising from the vertical bar code lines on its Juicy Juice packages.

 **BRAINSTORMER: How can you rev up your brand's design?**

An Indelible Tattoo

Everyone says not to judge a book by its cover, but we do it every day. Today, book cover design is more important than ever. Book sales are down and the cover design has to work postage-stamp size on the Internet as well as pop in the bookstore.

The bright yellow cover with the swirling dragon design on Stieg Larsson's book *The Girl with the Dragon Tattoo* is one of the most memorable book jackets to come out in trade fiction in the United States in recent years. Initially, the book's sales team hated the cover and tried to change Knopf Doubleday Chairman and Editor-in-Chief Sonny Mehta's mind. The salespeople wanted a cover more in the thriller genre, "something darker, bloodier, more Scandinavian."

Mehta had bought the U.S. rights to the book in 2007. The book had been a best seller in Europe, but he thought that the British and other covers that featured provocative women with prominent dragon tattoos were "cheesy" and distasteful.[12]

Knopf designer Peter Mendelsund got the assignment to create something better. He submitted fifty cover designs. One design, a minimalist cover with a white background and little spots of blood, was rejected because it wasn't colorful enough. A fuchsia cover with illuminated letters seemed derivative.

Mehta went with the brilliant yellow jacket and its swirling dragon because it was strikingly different, and he thought it would break through in the marketplace. The words in the jacket title are staggered artfully over the length of the cover, one word to a line. Random plumes of the dragon's flames cross on top of some of the individual letters, so there's a sense of movement and three-dimensionality.

Mehta went with his instincts, and the book has been a runaway best seller, one of the best-selling books of all time. The overall "dragon tattoo" design has been adopted for the two other books in Larsson's Millennium Trilogy, so that all three have a consistent, branded look.

Designer Taste

Pinkberry's combination of taste, design, and store experience has attracted celebrity devotees such as Taylor Swift and Lindsay Lohan, along with legions of devoted fans who refer to the brand as Crackberry. Pinkberry was launched by businesswoman Shelly Hwang and architect Young Lee as a designer brand. "In my stores, I serve you a $5 dessert, and I let you sit in $500 chairs," says Lee of the Philippe Starck Victoria Ghost chairs in every Pinkberry outlet.[13]

Pinkberry started by offering only two flavors, Original and Green Tea. The store and yogurt concept was inspired by mom-and-pop yogurterias of Italy, the source of the dairy-based powder used in Pinkberry yogurt. The store and yogurt concept is also similar to the minimalist design approach and tart yogurt taste of Korean yogurt chain Red Mango, which is also expanding internationally.

Another taste-oriented entrepreneur, Robb Duncan, originally studied industrial engineering at Georgia Tech and installed software for four years. Later, traveling in Buenos Aires, Duncan fell in love with Argentine-style gelato, and in 2004, when he moved to Washington, D.C., he opened a small gelato shop he called Dolcezza (Italian for "sweetness").

Today, Duncan is a top artisanal ice cream maker, and his technical background has spurred his creativity in the kitchen, leading him to search for new ingredients and combinations. His breakthrough brand signature is exotic tastes made from surprising ingredients like lemon with purple basil, lime cilantro, and avocado honey orange.[14]

Duncan is constantly on the lookout for novel flavor creations. Leaping on the cocktail craze of marrying fresh fruits and herbs with alcohol, he created sorbets like Seville orange with whisky and coriander. He keeps tinkering until he gets his concoctions to taste just right, as he did with his blackberry and cream gelato. It started out as a blackberry sorbet, then Duncan tweaked it with ginger and then Cabernet. Still not satisfied, he added cream and kept experimenting with different ratios of blackberries and cream. Finding that the electric mixer destroyed the flavor, Duncan experimented with a strainer to let a little pulp through and give the dessert flavor a distinct tartness and bright purple color. Duncan's taste mantra is "brighten it up, brighten it up."

A Store Is Packaging

If you have a retail store, think of it as part of your packaging. Notice the rise of *experience design* and *choice architects*. It's all about creating a breakthrough store design and layout that lures shoppers in and seduces them into buying.

Entrepreneur Fraser Ross is a master of store layout and design. He owns a chain of specialty stores in California named Kitson, after his middle name. Kitson stores are an eclectic mix of trendy fashion and accessories, but Ross doesn't leave anything to chance.

People can't buy anything unless you get them through the door first. That's why Ross puts novelty items at the front and more expensive items like jewelry and fashion at the back. He lays a path of tempting items throughout his stores, almost like the breadcrumbs in "Hansel and Gretel." In areas where people could veer off, he puts circular tables and shelves that get shoppers moving back to the center of the store.

The holidays are his busiest time, accounting for about 50 percent of his business.[15] Right before Thanksgiving, Ross starts putting out gift items. To get everyone in the holiday mood, about one of every four songs is a holiday song. As the holidays get closer, the mix switches to one of every three songs, and right before Christmas it's every song. He mixes up the selection between contemporary pop and traditional holiday renditions. Music can be powerful branding, so much so that shoppers don't want to leave the store.

Some companies are creating prototypes before they do the hard launch of a new store concept. That way they can fix design flaws before going live. That's what Apple did in a warehouse near its campus. Initially, it organized all its products by category. In the prototype stage, the company discovered that people didn't buy electronic items that way anymore. So it redesigned the store in a hub layout, with computers at the center and spokes for applications like video, music, and the like.

A Total Brand Experience

Think in terms of creating an all-encompassing brand experience at every touchpoint. No one has done that better in the doll and toy arena than entrepreneur Pleasant Rowland.

After a trip to Colonial Williamsburg, Pleasant Rowland began to think about how young girls might become interested in history through dolls. It was a small idea that combined Rowland's love of history with her love of dolls. It's amazing that no one had ever thought of it before, at least not in the way Rowland envisioned her doll brand.

American Girl dolls are not like other dolls, and American Girl stores are not like other toy stores. Unlike other doll brands, where each child makes up her own story, each American Girl doll comes with a story. Each doll has eight or nine books that tell the doll's story and impart a message of empowerment. Because a story and world is created around each doll, it's easy for girls to get immersed and want everything that goes with that world. And that powers sales.

American Girl dolls are also different in terms of image. Rather than the sexy look of Barbie and Bratz, American Girl dolls have a refreshingly wholesome appearance that mothers love.

Initially, Rowland sold the dolls through mail order. To create marketing synergy, Rowland added stores in major cities. Few places will pamper a doll like American Girl stores. They have eat-in cafes where girls, their moms, and their dolls can all eat together, with a mini menu for each doll. There's even a salon where dolls can get their hair done. Every sales professional goes through a weeklong training program on the dolls and the historical stories. Rowland sold American Girl to Mattel, which has added contemporary dolls to keep up the sales momentum.

 BRAINSTORMER: How can you create a special world for your brand?

Have a Trademark Look

Brand-oriented designers aim for a breakthrough brand look that is distinctive and recognizable. Iraqi-British entrepreneur Zaha Hadid is a woman in a very masculine art: architecture. Hadid grew up in Baghdad and later went to the United Kingdom to study architecture. There she became interested in the Russian constructivism and suprematism art movements.[16]

She had her small idea: designing abstract buildings that reflect the soaring curves and asymmetry of Russian avant-garde art. In her first twenty years as an architect, though, Hadid was a paper architect. Her statement buildings with soaring curves and sharp angles garnered awards, but only one was actually built because of the complexity of her designs.

After losing one important project, Hadid made a commitment to herself to pitch more forcefully and have an iron will. (The name Hadid means "iron" in Arabic.)

Then she got lucky. Technology caught up with her art. In 1990, Hadid started using computer-modeling software that made it easier to model her complex biomorphic building designs.

Later, in 2000, Hadid and other architects, including Frank Gehry, started using software designed for the aircraft industry for their building designs. This changed everything. Hadid could send plans directly to fabricators and contractors without going through engineers first. Big structures could be made piecemeal offsite then assembled at the site. Each piece is stamped with a bar code telling contractors exactly where it goes. Now, at very little extra cost, Hadid could indulge her design vision for asymmetry and the kind of sweeping curves associated with birds in flight.

One of her iconic buildings is the BMW building in Leipzig. Part of her mandate was to create communication between the white-collar workers and the factory. So Hadid crafted a breakthrough design: an open space with office desks in ascending tiers, with the assembly line of cars passing overhead on a conveyer belt. It's quite a sight. Hadid was also selected to design the Aquatics Center for the 2012 Olympics in London, her first major building in her adopted homeland.

Complementing her buildings are the aerodynamic curves of the products she's designed, from shoes, jewelry, and flatware to lightweight cars. All have an identifiable Hadid branded look.

BRAINSTORMER: Do you have a consistent, identifiable look? Describe it.

Breaking Through Tradition to the Modern World

Indian designer Rajeev Sethi studied design in Paris and then worked with Pierre Cardin. Today, Sethi brands himself as a scenographer, a German label that he picked up when he won first place for his design exhibit at the 2000 World's Fair in Hanover, Germany.

Despite his early success, Sethi felt unconnected with the world of design. Then he found his life's purpose: reclaiming the value of Indian traditional arts and crafts. Sethi founded the Asian Heritage Foundation, a Delhi-based NGO, and launched Jiyo!, an ambitious project to help struggling local artisans, backed by the World Bank.

Sethi's "small" idea was to forge a partnership between traditional artisans and modern designers to transform local crafts into design products that are appealing to sophisticated buyers. Sethi named the project Jiyo!, which means "live it" in Hindi. For the logo design, Sethi used the handwriting of Mahatma Gandhi, who was a proponent of the "small is beautiful" movement to preserve traditional regional economies and handmade crafts in India.

To launch Jiyo!, Sethi chose several of the poorest provinces in India, and from these regions he selected local craft cooperatives to design new prototypes that were beautiful and sophisticated yet true to traditional techniques and styles. The products include Indian fabrics, wallpaper, home furnishings, lamps, toys, clothes, and other items, all produced by local artisans under the direction of Sethi and his team of designers.

Sethi's goal is to develop a global marketplace for Indian traditional arts and to transform these poor local artisans into entrepreneurial artisans.

BRAINSTORMER: What can you do to make your brand designs up to date?

Sound Advice

Sound can be a powerful branding device. Ad agencies often hire composers to come up with a *sonic logo*, a sound or brief melody that signifies the brand like its logo does visually. Most of us can recognize McDonald's "Ba da ba ba ba" sonic logo or NBC's three-note chime that it's used since 1929. I'm even fond of the bong sound my Mac laptop makes when I restart my computer. It's a C-major chord tone created by an Apple programmer on his Korg synthesizer.

Sonic logos are short and more sophisticated than a jingle, but are very powerful in locking in a brand in the consumer's mind.

Another powerful aspect of a brand's look and feel can be the personification of the brand with a character and voice. It can be a very effective branding tactic for intangible products like financial services. Who hasn't fallen for the charm of Geico's gecko with its cute Cockney accent voiced by the English actor Jake Wood?

The trend in voiceovers is away from the booming "voice of God" sound of announcers in the past to the voices of "real" people done by voiceover artists who can project a range of emotions to engage consumers. The other trend you can't miss is the rise of celebrity voiceovers in commercials and animated films. It used to be that top celebrities wouldn't do voiceovers. It was considered beneath them. But the stigma is gone now that A-List celebrities like George Clooney, Robert Duvall and Jeff Bridges have done voiceovers. It's a great gig—very lucrative and quick to do. And it's great for brands, too. Celebrity voices give a brand cache and engage consumers in the branding as they try to identity the celebrity voice.

The Creative Process

As a brand entrepreneur, you'll want to keep your hand in the creative process. You may even come up with breakthrough creative and marketing ideas yourself.

As you get involved in creative development, write your ideas out by hand and sketch your visual ideas on paper. New research demonstrates the hand's unique relationship to the brain when it comes to composing thoughts and ideas.[17] Handwriting is more powerful than typing in creativity and learning. Writing requires executing sequential strokes to form a letter, whereas keyboarding involves selecting a whole letter by touching a key.

MRI brain studies show that our sequenced finger movements when writing activate brain regions involved in thinking, language, and working memory. Some studies show that people can write more words, write faster, and express more ideas when writing essays by hand than with a keyboard.

My process is to write and sketch by hand first, then go to my laptop and type out my ideas. I print out the ideas and words and then edit by hand and doodle on the sides as I flesh out my ideas. I don't worry about whether an idea makes sense. Drawing pictures can be particularly useful for solving complicated problems that can't be boiled down into a linear story. Often, a picture is the best way to give everyone the same mental image of a problem.

Experiment with words. Build one idea off another. Doodle with illustrations, even if they're crude drawings. Try not to filter your ideas too much early in the process.

If you're having trouble, write down all of your ideas on index cards. Every halfway-interesting idea, line, graphic, or image gets its own card. Then spread all the cards on the office floor or paste them on sticky notes on the wall. It's okay if you have hundreds of cards. Look to see what patterns, visuals, and themes emerge for your brand.

Creativity means breaking away from the norm, making simple changes and putting new imagery and attitude to them. It's using the principles of design to create something that people will love. Sometimes it's as simple as connecting things in a new way.

When you have the breakthrough look and feel for your brand:

It will have a *special design, color, and imagery* that suggest your brand promise.

It will have a distinct *attitude and personality* that suits your brand.

It will have a *different user experience* than competitors.

It will give your brand an *irresistible package* in the marketplace.

It will be *timeless* and something you can evolve rather than redo over time.

Chapter 6

Pimp My Brand!

I realized that the growth of television, along with all the existing media, would result in consumers being bombarded with more messages than they could absorb. So the advertiser would have to deliver his message in a different way—memorably and artfully—if he was going to be "chosen" by the consumer.

—Bill Bernbach, Legendary "Mad Man"

This place might as well be SuperCuts. First of all I was quite unimpressed with the space; it was grungy, with unswept hair on the floor, debris hanging out of closets and on surfaces, and the staff just lolling about in the back. I also had a terrible haircut here. I suppose I shouldn't have expected much for $35, but … the ends came out uneven and riddled with split-ends I didn't have before. Bad cheap haircut! [zero stars]

—Sonia A.

What a pleasant surprise! What a great experience—and so well-priced!!! This salon really exceeded my expectations—from the elegant look of the salon and its cleanliness to the receptionist to the hair guru who cut my hair. I was thrilled with the entire experience, and I will be going back and back again. I totally recommend this salon: I love, love, love it! [five stars]

—Cathy C.

You've just read two reviews of the same business posted on Yelp within the same week. Which one should you believe? As consumers, we live in a time when we can consult one another freely about even the smallest purchasing or hiring decisions. Which neighborhood spot has the best hamburgers? Which car-repair shop or cleaning service is trustworthy? Which nail parlor is hygienic? If we're not sure, we can consult an entire universe of online "instant experts."

We live in a Zagatized world. Knowledge is power, right? And the power belongs to you—the customer!

Now look at the situation from the perspective of the business owner.

You have worked tirelessly to build your business, your reputation, your following—your brand—only to log on to a consumer site like Yelp and discover a scathing review right at the top of the page. Perhaps it was posted by a genuinely unsatisfied customer (we all have them). Or it might have been put there by an unprincipled competitor or disgruntled former employee. There's no way of knowing.

 PIMPING THE BRAND: getting other people to endorse, market, and pass along your content or business information.

What you do know is that in the digital age, your brand is out there whether you like it or not, in ways that you can't always control. Now, with digital media, it's easy for people to endorse your brand and bring in new customers by passing it along or hitting the "Like" button, what I light-heartedly call *pimping your brand*. The trick is to take advantage of all of the benefits of this digital reality while safeguarding against the potential downside.

Promoting Pass-Along

What kind of content do people pass along? And how can you entice them to pimp your content?

It's not what you might think. One researcher studied 7,500 articles that were on the most–e-mailed list in *The New York Times* from August 2008 to February 2009. While the researcher expected to see lots of articles on practical information like the latest diets and gadgets, he found that the most popular stories were the ones that triggered the most arousing emotions, such as awe and anger.[1]

 We "pimp" what moves us emotionally—either positively or negatively.

Turns out we don't want to share facts and practical information as much as stories and emotions. This is true whether we're passing along an article, a video, or an ad.

Why? Research shows that we want to share strong emotions because we want to connect and feel solidarity with a group. We pass along things that surprise or move us because they excite us. Emotional content brings about what social scientists call a state of "high arousal."[2]

When we read or see an article or ad that excites us, our nervous system reacts to these feelings. Our heart starts beating faster, our sweat glands open, and we're ready to do something. We respond in this way whether it's a horror movie or a love story. And when we're in a state of arousal, we're much more likely to pass along and share the news article, ad, or video that aroused these emotions. And the Internet makes it easy to do that. In short, you need to move people if you want to create breakthrough branding.

 BRAINSTORMER: What kind of "emotional" content could you develop for people to pass along?

The Transformation of Media and Brands

Not so long ago, in the 1950s and '60s, life in the business world was relatively simple. Demand was relatively high for goods and services and, compared to today, there was not a vast range and variety of products.

Not only that, but it wasn't difficult to reach your potential customers. If you had the money for television advertising, there were basically three choices, and they all offered programming geared toward the mass market. In those days, network TV programming was tailor-made for advertisers (many of whom sponsored whole series and even got their names above the titles).

If a prime-time program didn't draw millions of viewers, the show was pulled off the air. There were Sunday night and weekday evening series that families watched together and daytime programs that stay-at-home moms watched—dubbed "soap operas" because advertisers such as Procter & Gamble completely underwrote them in exchange for massive exposure of their products.

It was in this robust world for business and brands—more than fifty years ago—that most of the branding models still in use today were developed.

The New Branding

Today's business world—today's world, really—is very different. Both our businesses and our media have moved from a mass-appeal, homogeneous state to a diverse and fragmented one. Since the rise of the Internet, ad-driven mass media, especially television and print, are less powerful as disseminators and gatekeepers of information.

There are many competing products and services and many means for promoting them. We've been freed from the tyranny of ad-supported TV with its mass-market, low–common denominator shows. Now we have variety, with cable, streaming video, and the Internet. You have the freedom to choose.

Creating demand can be difficult, and it's more difficult now to find a way to break through all of the "noise" of the competition and pinpoint your unique market. Today, big brands are putting more money into new media and social media, and Procter & Gamble, the former soap opera sponsor, is leading the way.

These days, media outlets are plentiful, but the audience for each of them is smaller and less diverse. Broadcast television has been joined by cable television. Radio has been augmented by satellite radio. Magazines and newspapers compete with their online counterparts, as do television, cable, and radio. All of these media are looking for new ways to connect with consumers. One innovation is *quick response codes (QRs),* the square matrix-like barcodes on magazine and newspaper ads, billboards, and store shelves that we can scan with our smartphones or tablets for more information. It is a fragmented landscape in which information and selling interrupts other information and selling!

Very few television programs (other than mega-events such as the Super Bowl) can attract a critical mass when there are so many options on the remote—and that means a world of choices and a sense of empowerment on the part of the consumer. So, while traditional media outlets are contracting, the number of viewing (or reading or listening) options is growing, the quality of programming is improving to keep up with competition, and the media audience overall is expanding.

Social Media Is Word of Mouth on Steroids

As much as TV and radio have changed over the past few decades, the real media revolution is taking place in the digital arena of what I call *cyberbranding*. In contrast to tens of thousands of traditional media outlets, there are more than a hundred million new media outlets and counting.

 Cyberbranding takes place in the dynamic digital world, with content created and shared by anyone and accessible to everyone.

The old media was a top-down model, and we viewers, readers, and listeners of television, print, and radio were passive recipients. It's no longer a command-and-control, top-down communication. New media and social media are peer-to-peer communication. We've been transformed from media consumers to media programmers.

New media refers to all the interactive forms of communication that use the Internet, like blogs, websites, social networks, RSS feeds, and the like. One of the hottest areas of new media is *social media*, including Facebook, Twitter, LinkedIn, and others, which provide platforms for a peer-to-peer interactive dialogue and foster the creation and exchange of user-generated content. Social media takes word of mouth to a whole new level, and word of mouth has always been the best (and cheapest) tool for branding!

"Read-Only" to "Read-Write" Media

Digiworld is a democracy. It gives power to the people. Everyone can participate, not just the well placed or well informed. It offers on-demand access to content and information to one and all, anytime.

Indeed, each of us can enter the world of media and develop our own following by launching a website or publishing a blog or creating a profile page on Facebook or Google+. Each of us can talk to many others every time we talk. Unlike traditional media, new media tend to be inexpensive to own and operate. Even kids can do it, and they do!

The big difference between old and new media is interactivity. Books, TV, radio, and print media are *"read-only"* media. Digital media is *"read-write"* media.[3] If you can receive a digital file, you can read it, respond to it, share it, or change it. After all, "we don't make television, we watch it."[4] In digiworld, we can easily make content and distribute it for others to watch or read or change. It gives us a more engaged, collaborative style of media and involvement.

Cyberbranding features interactivity and dialogue with users. We've all got voices, and now we have the means to express ourselves and engage in dialogue with others via social media channels such as Facebook, Twitter, and LinkedIn. For young people, it's nonstop networking every minute of the day via cell phone and social networking websites. Kids are interconnected socially from the minute they get out of bed until they crash at night.

Cyberbranding builds communities. You don't have to have powerful connections to join a group or start your own club. You have as much of an opportunity as anyone else—even big-time competitors—to build your brand and forge bonds with your customers, prospects, friends, coworkers, enthusiasts, you name it.

Social media like Twitter, Facebook, and others helped power the Arab Spring in 2011, providing people with a new way to organize. Plus they could hear the support of people from around the world.

The New Digimedia Arbiters

Mass media made its on-air representatives and off-air editors power brokers who decided who and what gets covered and who and what doesn't. New media is based on networking and sharing, so power can come from all directions. Any one of our blog posts or tweets can become the next *meme* or hot idea on the Internet.

While we have more control in many ways, it's not absolute. Our readers or followers can respond and agree or disagree. They can take our message and pass it along or change it and pass it along.

While we don't have the same powerful arbiters as we did with traditional media, we have arbiters just the same. The digiworld arbiters are less visible. They're the decision makers and programmers who make the software and set up the protocols for search engines, aggregators, and indexers. They may be less visible than the head of CBS, ABC, or NBC, but they determine what counts and what doesn't in more ways than we may realize.

We have to figure out how to score with them so we are visible on the web. We have to figure out search engine optimization (SEO) and how to get selected by the aggregators and indexers so that we get seen and heard. We may need to develop our own software and our own code, so we don't have to follow the protocol set up by others.

The Fish versus the Whale

Cyberbranding is the low-cost way to brand your product or service—to brand yourself—and to connect with your customers and prospects in a genuine way. People want honesty and authenticity, not hype and gloss, and the online world is the place to present your business and yourself as you are, without resorting to "commercials." The fresher your ideas and the better your product or service, the more receptive the digital world will be.

(TM) **Cyberbranding doesn't favor the rich and powerful.**
It favors the new and the nimble.
It favors the human and the real.
It favors those who share.

Unlike traditional media, cyberbranding doesn't reward the important, the famous, and the rich as much as the engaging, the interesting, and the helpful. Sharing is the essential ingredient of digiworld. Cyberbranding rewards those who understand how people use the Internet today to find out about companies and brands and to be a part of those communities.

People and companies that are opaque will have difficulty in the digital age of branding. People and companies that are comfortable in their own skin will succeed. Those who share their personal stories and their business narratives and provide valuable, real, and truthful messages will thrive. Digiworld rewards those who innovate and who make good stuff or offer better services.

Cyberbranding enables you to customize and personalize messages like never before. People want to know your story, so share it with them—the grittier or more truthful, the better. The more you open the curtains to reveal what is going on behind the scenes, the closer and more connected your customers will feel to you. As an example of what I mean, lets look at the story of blogger Heather Armstrong and *Dooce*.

Armstrong began a blog called *Dooce* in 2001, while she was employed as a web designer and graphic artist in Salt Lake City, Utah. In it, she spoke honestly and graphically about her frustrations at home and at work—and she soon found herself out of a job. Whether or not her firing was a direct result of what she wrote in her blog, the term "dooced" has come to mean being fired for one's online activities (something to keep in mind when developing your own web presence!).

No matter—Armstrong chose to see her dismissal as an opportunity. Her loyal readers continued to follow her story through the birth of her two kids, her struggle with depression, her appliance breakdowns, and every detail of her life as a liberal ex-Mormon living in Utah. Her audience grew until, on a typical day, more than 100,000 people visited her site.

Here's the good part. The business part. In 2004, Armstrong began accepting text advertisements on her site, and in 2005, she began accepting graphic ads. She had turned her online "hobby" into a moneymaking proposition, in the process becoming the first personal blogger to derive substantial income from advertising.[5] In 2009, Armstrong was named by *Forbes* magazine as one of the thirty most influential women in media—right alongside Oprah, Diane Sawyer, and Barbara Walters. Estimates of the revenue from ads on her website range from over $300,000 to $1,000,000 a year, and that doesn't include her speaking and endorsement fees and book royalties.

An Antidote to Civilization

While the story of *Dooce* may be exceptional, Armstrong's not the only one-person show who's blogging in the dough. There's no doubt that blogging can be big business if your story and writing connect with readers on an emotional level.

Look at the woman who calls herself The Pioneer Woman, blogger Ree Drummond. She's got a devoted following for her chronicle of daily life on the Oklahoma prairie with her husband, whom she calls Marlboro Man, and their four children.

She's built a lucrative empire with her blog, cookbooks, and media appearances. In her blog, *www.thepioneerwoman.com*, she portrays a life so bucolic and filmic, you just want to jump into the scene and live her life. And many people do, vicariously. The blog receives more than 23 million page views per month and 4.4 million unique visitors, beating out the Huffington Post for Weblog of the Year in 2009.[6]

Connection, Community, and Conversation

Cyberbranding rewards entrepreneurs and companies who give people what they want: *connection*, *community*, and *conversation*. Cyberbranding lets you do something extraordinary: tap into the selling power of friendship. Marketers have always realized that the best way to sell something is to get your friends or other people to sell it for you. That is what denizens of digiworld do every minute on Facebook and other sites, just by clicking the "Like" or "Tweet" buttons next to a particular product or bit of content.

We all seek experiences that enlarge our lives in some way, experiences that touch our emotions and help us grow. The digital world can make your brand a part of that process. People don't need to know your brand well to become interested in your company and products, as long as you create a dynamic presence on the Internet and positive buzz in online forums. This is true of business-to-business companies as well as business-to-consumer ones, as more people research and hire their suppliers online.

Tune In, Reach Out

The Internet is also a cheap source of "market research," helping you keep a finger on the pulse of your customers and what they're thinking about. Jason Kilar, the CEO of Hulu, learned the importance of studying customer behavior when he worked at Amazon. He checks the Hulu site repeatedly, sometimes twenty times a day. That's how he discovered that Hulu users were searching by genre, leading him to add science fiction and comedy channels to the mix.

Indie soda maker Jones Soda uses the web to poll its young customers about new drink flavors, while Dr. Pepper uses its captive "focus group" of over 8.5 million fans on Facebook to test new marketing strategies and messages.[7] Every day, Dr. Pepper posts two messages on its Facebook fan page and monitors the response. Using Facebook tools and other software, the company can quantify how the messages are received, how often they are viewed and shared with other Facebook users, etc.

Not surprisingly, the messages with an overt sales pitch go over less well than those employing edgy one-liners with attitudes the brand's fans can relate to emotionally. One of its most favorably received recent messages was: "If liking you is wrong, we don't want to be right." No hard sell there: just a little something entertaining to think about for a second—brought to you by Dr. Pepper.

Get in a Tweeting Frame of Mind

Blogging and tweeting top executives such as Richard Branson of Virgin and Tony Hsieh of Zappos realize that cyberbranding provides a way to connect with people directly and often. They tell stories and share their points of view. They include you so that you feel a part of their world. You feel that you know their personalities, that you know them.

Sometimes they draw their company's products and services into the storyline, but often they simply write about where they are traveling, who they are meeting, and what they are thinking about. Like any great story, the plot of their tweets and blog posts keeps evolving, offering twists, cliffhangers, and emotion. When Branson or Hsieh's customers choose to "follow" them, they are becoming a part of their story—and that makes those customers feel connected to those brands.

Here's another example of a high-profile tweeter. You might not think of Ashton Kutcher as an "entrepreneur," but he's a businessman, all right, with an acting career, a production company, technology investments, and other business interests to manage. He's also one of the top Twitter users in several categories, with more than 6.6 million followers, prompting *www.wefollow.com* to list him among "The Most Influential Entrepreneur Twitter Users."[8]

Among the Top Ten Entrepreneurs in that category you'll also find entertainer and fashion designer Sean "Diddy" Combs, with more than 3.6 million followers; self-help guru Tony Robbins, who has almost 2 million followers; Tony Hsieh, with more than 1.8 million followers; and Guy Kawasaki, with more than 345,000 followers. (That's as of this writing, of course.)

As a blogging entrepreneur, you've got to be interesting, and guess what? It's not as hard as you think. Share what you know. Tell people what you're doing, even life's little (or big) ups and downs. Remark on something you saw. Explain a complicated idea. Above all, be yourself. It's good to reveal your personality. Don't try to be perfect and corporate.

The more real you are, the more you will draw people in. Be the story-teller for your business and—unlike traditional branding in the old days—your story will be less about the company and its products and more about your customers and their interests and what you're thinking about as entrepreneur-in-chief.

Stay in Touch or Start All Over

Where do your customers touch your brand? What is the experience like? How do prospects find out about you? What do they learn?

Do you know?

As an entrepreneur, it's easy to get so caught up in running the business that you overlook what your brand experience is like for customers. To find out, you need to step into their shoes. When you do that, you'll see there are a lot of contact points, what marketers call *touchpoints*. The obvious ones include the product or service itself; its colors, design, and packaging; the advertisements and tagline; its placement in the store; and the ways that salespeople talk about your brand. If you're a retailer, touchpoints include the store, its location, the retail environment, the music, even the smell of the store.

It's important to make these "real" touchpoints as personal, mean-ingful, and experiential as possible so there's a real contrast with virtual touchpoints and virtual competitors. Your customers don't have to do business with you, the local merchant; they can get everything online, probably even at a lower price. So there has to be a different connection, a feeling of community and a sense that the company is a source of respected advice, as there was with the old market culture of the bazaar or the shops of trusted local merchants.

Today's social media, mobile media, and new technology have created many new touchpoints that are not local but reach a global audience. In addi-tion to Internet vehicles such as your website, e-newsletter, e-mail campaigns, blog, and social media campaigns, there are potentially thousands of new digiworld touchpoints created by others on Facebook, Twitter, LinkedIn, third-party review forums such as Yelp, and the like. These touchpoints are very fluid and mutable because others can take your message and do a mashup or criticize your offering.

Still other touchpoints are more subtle: the way your business telephone is answered, what your customer-service experience is like, even the look and feel of your billing invoice.

Each of these contacts or touchpoints affects the impression your brand makes in the minds of your customers and clients. You want every one of them to convey the right brand impression, be consistent, and be consistently *positive* as much as possible.

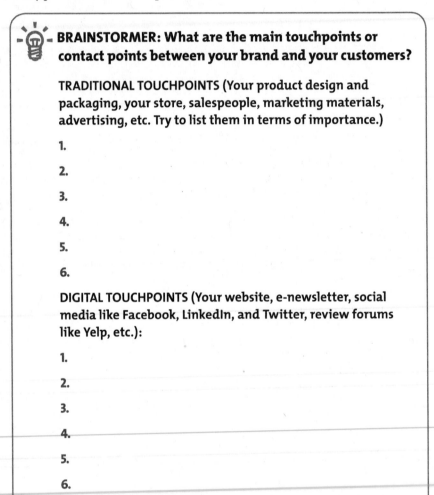

BRAINSTORMER: What are the main touchpoints or contact points between your brand and your customers?

TRADITIONAL TOUCHPOINTS (Your product design and packaging, your store, salespeople, marketing materials, advertising, etc. Try to list them in terms of importance.)

1.

2.

3.

4.

5.

6.

DIGITAL TOUCHPOINTS (Your website, e-newsletter, social media like Facebook, LinkedIn, and Twitter, review forums like Yelp, etc.):

1.

2.

3.

4.

5.

6.

Not All Touchpoints Are Created Equal

For decades, branders looked at consumer touchpoints using the *funnel* metaphor. A funnel, with its wide top and narrow bottom, was a good model for how the buying process for most products used to work. Typically, consumers began with a large array of possibilities (the top end of the funnel) and gradually pared down their choices to a small group, and finally to their purchase choice (the narrow end of the funnel).

Marketers directed most of their money to the two critical touchpoints, the top and bottom ends of the funnel. Big dollars went toward mass-market advertising, including TV commercials and print ads, in an attempt to build brand awareness on the largest scale possible.

Marketing money was also earmarked for promotions and product placement at the other end of the funnel—in stores—because in-store touchpoints are particularly powerful and can change everything. Studies show that up to 40 percent of consumers change their minds because of something they see or learn at the point of sale. The visual experience alone—the way a product looks or the presence of a prominent and intriguing display—can sway the consumer's decision. Shoppers can also be influenced by what a salesperson says or by a great deal offered by one of the brands they are considering.

During the "funnel decades," marketers were in control. Branding was a one-way communication from company to consumer. We call that *push marketing*, because the marketing message was pushed toward consumers. In the "push" era, it wasn't easy for consumers to get comparative information or to voice their opinions directly to a manufacturer. Consumers were forced to rely on the marketing messages pushed at them in advertising, what they experienced at the point of sale, and what they heard from friends and associates.

Most people had little contact with a brand after purchase, other than the experience of using the product (or an interaction with customer service if something went wrong).

All was status quo in the branding and media world until the rise of digiworld.

Listen Before They Yelp

Today, the funnel is an inaccurate metaphor for marketing. The explosion of brands and new digital channels has upended the way consumers buy products and services.

Now, there are thousands of touchpoints, and the consumer's journey isn't a simple one from the wide end of the funnel to the end. Rather, it's an up-and-down, circuitous trip, as the consumer adds and subtracts brands from consideration throughout the decision-making process.[9] The Internet has replaced supply and demand and command and control with a two-way engaged and collaborative style of buying.

Today, people know a lot about brands and are actively involved in the brand conversation. They feel comfortable driving the purchase process themselves. Company-driven branding has been joined (and may soon be overtaken) by consumer-driven branding, because digiworld provides people with an easy way to share their opinions and feelings about brands. And the words of other people are the words that matter.

 Your product isn't what you say it is. It's what others say it is.

No longer passive recipients of marketing messages, your customers are in charge, reaching out to marketers and third-party sources and *pulling* the information they need in order to make buying decisions. This is called *pull marketing*, and it's more powerful than push marketing because potential buyers are initiating the brand contact.

Even though people feel they know brands, they are often overwhelmed by the multitude of choices. A 2009 McKinsey study shows that consumers intentionally start out with a smaller number of brands to consider than in the past.[10] The Internet makes it easier than ever before to study these brands before purchase. People can search, sift, and read reviews. At retail sites such as Amazon.com, they can easily compare product features and read what other purchasers have to say, good and bad.

At sites such as Yelp, they can focus on reviews before they go elsewhere to make a purchase. They have started to rely on (supposedly) unbiased sources—that is, their fellow consumers—rather than trusting what manufacturers say. According to the McKinsey study, fewer than one in ten consumers now go to a company website for information. The opinions of their peers are what matter to them.

But don't give up on the marketing power within brick-and-mortar establishments just yet. People may do a lot of research online first, but most put off their final decisions until they go into a store to see the product. And, as before, they often leave with something other than what they intended to buy, based on what they learn in a store.

What really has changed is that today, many people want a relationship with the brand *after* they buy something—and with other people who have invested in the same brand. Consumers talk about their purchases on social networking sites and post reviews online often for no reason other than to share with a community of fellow users. These consumer reviews become critical touchpoints for your brand because potential purchasers are reading and listening.

Engagement Branding

Denizens of digiworld want interaction and nitty-gritty information. They want two-way communication. They want to be in control as they evaluate brands and pull information that is relevant to them. The McKinsey study has shown that two-thirds of the touchpoints used to evaluate a particular brand were initiated by the people themselves—not companies.

Engagement is the way people do business today, and that has created a new age of customer care. Pioneering Internet-based brands such as Zappos, Netflix, Amazon, and eBay have always thrived on consumer feedback; now, companies in every business category are getting in on the two-way action. As a consumer, when you buy something or have a conversation with a customer service rep online, you are likely to encounter a pop-up screen asking you to rate your customer experience. Then come the regular e-mails with special deals and offers. You are now part of the community of people interested in the company's products or services.

 Five out of six of your customers are passively loyal. They could easily switch to your competitor.

In digiworld, people want to engage with others in their community—and that can become a benefit to you, the owner of the brand. If consumers trust the information you provide and feel that you care about your customer community, they will trust the brand. Remember, McKinsey's study showed that five out of six of your customers are *passively loyal*, meaning that they are loyal only until a better deal comes along. Only your *actively loyal* customers stay with you through thick and thin.

To create active loyalty, you need to create community and to make your community feel special. Your blog, your Facebook page, and your tweets can be focal points. Write them personally and authentically so that your customers feel you are talking directly to them. Don't try to sell them directly—instead, express your own personality and the personality of the brand. By extension, you are expressing the personality of your customers and making it something appealing with which they can identify.

Customers like to be rewarded for their loyalty, so use your Facebook posts, e-mail alerts, and tweets to offer special deals and publicize sales events. Always be connecting with your tribe, drawing them in, and making it easy for them to engage with you by offering feedback, answering questions, participating in drawings or auctions, whatever you can think of.

The Digital Conversation

Today, people want to have a relationship and a conversation with the companies they patronize, and the more direct and personal that conversation is, the better. Authenticity will attract people to what you're selling or advocating.

In the fall of 2009, Conan O'Brien was asked to return to a later time slot after his brief tenure hosting *The Tonight Show*. It was a messy situation and O'Brien was justifiably furious. He stayed up all night composing a letter that began, "People of the Earth." Then he hit the "Send" button.[11]

That same night, unbeknownst to O'Brien, a young graphic designer and die-hard fan named Mike Mitchell also stayed up late—drawing an image of O'Brien standing in front of an American flag featuring the words "I'M WITH COCO" (a nickname given to O'Brien by Tom Hanks when he appeared on his show). Mitchell posted the image on his own site and created an "I'm with Coco" Facebook page and Twitter account.

The next morning, as news of Conan's letter was made public and became widely distributed in the media, the entire digiworld started to rally for Conan. The letter was pitch perfect. He told readers that "no one should waste a second feeling sorry for me." And he built his argument not around his bruised ego but on the legacy of *The Tonight Show*. "I sincerely believe that delaying the *Tonight Show* into the next day to accommodate another comedy program will seriously damage what I consider to be the greatest franchise in the history of broadcasting." The letter was a brilliant example of online reputation management and it moved public sentiment (and brand power) solidly from NBC to Conan.

When graphic artist Mitchell woke up that morning, he found out that he had created a digiworld sensation, too. More than 30,000 people were following his Twitter feed, and thousands more were using his graphic on their own Facebook pages. Just a week after his night-drawing escapade, Mitchell had more than 700,000 followers on Twitter.

Soon, NBC honchos were telling O'Brien to quit the online onslaught. The comedian's response? "Stop what? It's not me."

RSVP or Tweet

At the time that the "I'm with Coco" brouhaha was happening, in late 2009, O'Brien barely knew what Twitter was. He was still in an old media state of mind. But he was starting to get a clue about the power of social media—and starting to think about harnessing it.

His settlement with the network prohibited him from appearing on television for eight months. No matter. Inspired by Mitchell, O'Brien seized upon a new media alternative and started tweeting. His first tweet: *Today I interviewed a squirrel in my backyard and then threw to commercial. Somebody help me.* A colleague retweeted it, and from there, it went viral. Day one on Twitter, O'Brien signed up more than 250,000 followers, setting the single-day record in Twitter history to that point.

Since he didn't have his next gig lined up, O'Brien decided to go on the road, calling his show the "Legally Prohibited from Being Funny on Television Tour." His team booked thirty cities, created a website, got a sponsor, and started to talk about an advertising budget.

Someone on his team suggested holding off on traditional ads. "Why not just tweet about the tour?" Everyone on O'Brien's marketing team laughed. Then they thought, let's give it a shot. They knew they could always purchase conventional advertising later, if necessary. In a few hours, based on Twitter announcements alone, both New York City shows sold out. Soon, cities across the country were selling out. Then the website crashed from an abundance of traffic!

By the time the tour was over, O'Brien's take on old and new media had completely changed. He inhabited a new media body. He realized he had to reach his fans not just by performing for them but by having a conversation with them.

Ouch! A Negative Review

We all believe in freedom of speech in this country, and digiworld gives people a large megaphone. Remember those Yelp reviews at the beginning of this chapter? How do you handle a situation where someone posts a negative or baseless review about your business? Online reviews tend to be anonymous, and it is all too easy for anyone—from a genuinely dissatisfied customer to a devious competitor—to press "Send." Here is where the ease of entering the conversation becomes a double-edged sword.

A bad review can hurt your business, especially if it appears prominently on page one in search results. Online reviews are powerful. According to a 2011 McKinsey study, almost 85 percent of Americans feel that online reviews have a strong impact on their purchasing decisions.

The first step in managing this aspect of your brand is to be tuned in: you have to be aware of what is being said. Start by setting up a Google Alert for your name, your company name, your product names, and the like. There are also tools within Twitter that can help ensure you'll be notified every time a specific name or phrase appears. You should also monitor the most important review forums and local search sites: start by checking out Citysearch, Yahoo! Local, and Yelp, and visit the customer forums on Google Maps, Amazon, Angie's List, and others.

Once you know what is being said about your business, you can respond. The first rule of damage control is to respond quickly and graciously. Don't get angry, even if you feel you've been attacked or slandered. Name-calling will only escalate the situation. Rather, apologize and offer your nemesis a chance to come back and enjoy a better experience with your company, one that is more typical. (To demonstrate that that is the case, you can link them to testimonials or positive reviews on your website.)

Ease-Drop on Yourself

If you feel the review is out-and-out fraudulent, you can try contacting the media outlet where it appeared. Above all, remember O'Brien's lesson in Internet damage control. Use your Internet response to a grievance to rally people to your side by being authentic and sincere. It's the best ad for your business and will win over others to your side.

Another tactic for dealing with bad stories about your business or Brand You is to post frequent content yourself on the Internet. Today, search engines give more weight to real-time updates, so if you're actually engaged with your customers and connect with them frequently, your social media updates will impact organic search results, pushing down the negative reviews in the queue.

Even if you can't completely address the negative review on the site where it's posted, you can respond through social media. Often, you'll find that publicly dealing with customer issues or bad press will attract lifelong customers to your brand.

As a brand entrepreneur, you must play a strong role in creating your own reviews. You can ask happy clients to write short testimonials for your website or online reviews. Most will be happy to do it. If you're encouraging reviews from your loyal customers, soon that pesky one will move far down the line-up and essentially disappear from view. If people do find it, it will look oddly out of place.

Commit to Cyberbranding

What is most effective today isn't one-way, top-down marketing from you, the entrepreneur, to your business prospects. What works is connecting and building a community with your customers, prospects, and like-minded people using multimedia. You need to use all of the traditional and new media touchpoints available in digiworld to do breakthrough branding today.

Cyberbranding is the exciting new media and marketing world with content created, produced, and distributed in real time and accessible to everyone.

Cyberbranding takes place in a new media world that's tailor-made for entrepreneurs:

It's *low cost and democratic*, unlike the old media world.
It's *easy to engage and have a conversation* with your customers.
It favors *transparency and authenticity*, not hype.
It wants *connection* and *entertainment*, so give it to them.

Chapter 7

Brand Big! Boldly Marketing the Brand

A creative man can't jump from nothing to a great idea.
He needs a springboard of information.

—Bill Bernbach, Legendary "Mad Man"

Marketing for your brand can be subtle or heavy-handed, tasteful or obnoxious, outdated or up-to-date, but if you don't participate, you will be left behind.

It is impossible to become a breakthrough brand without visibility, and marketing leads to visibility and engagement. Visibility is behind every product, behind every company, behind every nonprofit, behind every movement, behind every person who does great things.

Visibility pays because visibility has a halo effect. If a company or product is visible and well known, we tend to think it is better than something that is not as well known. We assign familiar things more positive traits and we're more likely to buy them, even if we've just heard the names of the brands and know nothing more about them.

Think about it. When we buy something in a new category, we're likely to choose a brand that we've heard of or one that someone we know is familiar with. That's why, as an entrepreneur, you need to build visibility and engage consumers with your brand through advertising, PR, events,

Internet marketing, digital promotions—whatever works to get your brand tattooed on consumers' brains.

It takes smart marketing thinking to come up with the best ideas and to get everything to work together effectively.

The Creative Brief

Before you start the creative process for your branding, advertising, and marketing programs, take a page from the marketing playbook and develop a *creative brief.* The creative brief is the bible for creative development, whether it's designing the product packaging, creating a website, or doing a digital marketing campaign. The creative brief defines your brand idea and its DNA so that you and the creative people working on a specific marketing project will be inspired to develop the right brand image visually, verbally, and emotionally.

With a creative brief in hand, you'll be able to give good direction, and that in itself will set you apart from other entrepreneurs and most marketers, for that matter. Most business owners and marketers don't give good directions for creative development. They need a logo, a digital marketing campaign, or a new print ad, yet they don't provide much information about the brand or insight about its customers or what the competitive dynamics are like.

As they say in the advertising business, you can only be as good as your client, so if you, as a client, don't give good direction, you won't get good creative work and you won't get breakthrough branding. You can write the creative brief yourself or have one of your marketing people do it for you. But even if you have someone else do it, stay involved to make sure the creative brief and the work is on target and reflects your vision for the brand.

Many people think creativity is a magical process. Yet, the reality is that great creative work comes from great strategic direction, and that is usually a process of reduction. You need to simplify the brand to its essence, to what is crucial and authentic, and doing a creative brief is a great way to force yourself to crystallize your thinking.

You need to give good direction because very few creative people can develop advertising or marketing home runs out of thin air. All good creative work conveys a core truth about the brand, its customers, or the category, and that can only come about through clear prepping and good direction.

On the other hand, you don't want to give creative people a one-hundred-page research report and say, "This will tell you everything about the brand and the industry." (It's happened to me more than once.) Nor do you want to give creative people too many rules about what can and cannot be done creatively for the brand.

You need to inspire creative people with good insight and direction but not provide so much that they feel stifled creatively. And you need to get everyone on the same page so that all your branding, marketing, and communication are unified around your brand idea, and your promise statement captures what's different and relevant about your brand for its customers. No matter what people see or where they see it, everything about your brand must be in sync.

The Good Brief

The creative brief is short. One to two pages is it. Distilling your brand's essence into succinct nuggets of information will force you to think and make choices. Just the act of writing things down can make a big difference in fine-tuning your thinking.

What does this brand want to be? What does it want to look like? What kind of voice does it have? What you're looking for is a clear brand concept from brand idea to support points, from brand personality to consumer insight. Everything needs to work together to create a breakthrough brand.

Most advertising, marketing, and design agencies have their own version of the creative brief. The goal of all of them is to provide clear, concise, and insightful direction that will bring your brand to life for the creative people working on marketing projects for the brand.

Here are the key elements of a creative brief and how each section might be written for a fictitious "green" household cleaner that I'm calling "Spearmint Spray."

> ► **Business snapshot:** This is an in-a-nutshell overview of your
> industry, its key players, and its dynamics—all in three to five
> sentences. Remember, creative people don't know your business,

and they don't need to know it well, but they do need to have a CliffNotes understanding of what's driving things and who the key competitors are.

Pick an "enemy," the key competitor that you want to beat or dislodge in consumers' minds. Tension is important in branding. It's not about trying to destroy the enemy as much as it's about being different. You want to create a brand that people like better, is more memorable, conveys superior attributes, or just grabs more people emotionally.

EXAMPLE: SPEARMINT SPRAY SNAPSHOT: ECO-FRIENDLY HOUSEHOLD CLEANERS

Eco-friendly household cleaners are expected to double in market share in the United States by 2014. This dynamic growth is being driven by consumers who are interested in greener and more sustainable lifestyles and who also value design and the product experience. The white-hot center of growth and profitability are eco-friendly products that fill the emotional desire for beauty—cleaners that do the job but look and smell good, too. Spearmint Spray's biggest competitor is Brand Z, a brand that's eco-friendly yet lacks the style and sensuality of the Spearmint Spray product line.

▶ **Brand promise/reasons to believe:** Define your *brand promise*—the positioning of your brand—in a sentence. This is your dominant selling idea, the most compelling reason that people should use your business and not a competitor's. This is the statement that you've been working on. Under the brand promise, list two or three crisp *reasons to believe* the promise statement. For example, FedEx's brand promise is "Your package will get there overnight. Guaranteed." Why should people believe this promise? FedEx could include in its reasons to believe its money-back guarantee on next-day delivery and its remarkable on-time delivery record.

EXAMPLE: HERE'S THE BRAND PROMISE AND REASONS TO BELIEVE FOR SPEARMINT SPRAY:

Spearmint Spray Promise*: Beautiful, eco-friendly cleaning products that work*

Reasons to Believe:

▶ *Fights dirt in a healthy way.*

▶ *Products come in innovative natural fragrances like Spearmint with Honey Cardamom and Spearmint Strawberry Curry.*

▶ *Our beautiful designer containers are made from sustainable materials.*

▶ **Brand personality:** Write down a series of adjectives or phrases that describes the brand's personality. It may seem odd, ridiculous even. Why bother creating a personality for the brand? Shouldn't you be focusing on more important things? The reality is that consumers want to relate to brands, and marketers help them do that by accentuating people-like qualities such as brand personality. If people find your brand appealing or similar to their own personality, they are more likely to buy the brand.

Brand personality brings emotions, likeability, and depth into the relationship between a brand and consumers. Most people are complex, nuanced, and multidimensional, and brands need to be, too. For example, if you describe your brand's personality as "carefree, trendy, and lively," you get a very different image than if you described it as "rugged, tough, and athletic" or "sophisticated, elegant, and private." Each set of personality characteristics sends you in a very different direction in creating a name, a logo, a website, or a store for the brand.

EXAMPLE: SPEARMINT SPRAY BRAND PERSONALITY:

Stylish and fragrant with a minimalist sensibility: Clean, simple, strong, modern, lovely, fun, interesting, slightly irreverent.

▶ **Customer persona:** The *customer persona* is a portrait of your ideal or typical customer. Write it like a casting call description of your ideal customer so that anyone would have a clear sense of the person—his lifestyle, mindset, and preferences. Creative people will find it much easier to develop your marketing messages and images with a clear persona in mind.

EXAMPLE: HERE'S WHAT A CUSTOMER PERSONA FOR SPEARMINT SPRAY MIGHT LOOK LIKE:

Sophie is a thirty-eight-year-old woman: wife, mother, and up-and-coming marketing manager for a large corporation. She's smart and

caring but no pushover. She loves her career and her family and feels har-
ried trying to balance all the pieces in her life. Most days, Sophie is rushing
to get the children to school, do her job, and keep her house running. She's
very interested in healthy eating and living and cares deeply about green,
environmental, and social issues. She tries to stay on top of the issues by
reading news, self-improvement, and business books on her Kindle.

▶ **Consumer insight:** Convey in a short sentence an important
or surprising insight about the product or business and its customers. This is your flash of understanding about the product,
its customers, or tensions in the marketplace that can inspire a
breakthrough creative idea for your brand.

EXAMPLE: SPEARMINT SPRAY CONSUMER INSIGHT:

▶ *Spearmint Spray is an affordable pleasure for women and their fami-*
lies that can transform household drudgery into an emotionally and
sensually pleasurable experience.

On Strategy and True to the Brand

With your creative brief in hand, you're ready to tackle just about any creative or marketing project for your brand, keeping everything consistent
and true to the brand, with the goal of creating breakthrough branding.
Some marketing opportunities won't be right for your brand. You may
be presented with creative work that is too provocative for the consumer
persona in the brief, or it may not be provocative enough. Or it might not
capture the brand promise or personality just right.

With your creative brief, it will be clear if messages, concepts, images,
and designs are right or not. It's either on strategy with the creative brief or
it isn't. You built your business and product on authenticity and built a sense
of trust with your customers. You want to keep that trust through all of your
communications. If consumers trust the information you provide and feel
that you care about the customer community, they will trust the brand.

Image versus Engagement

Most advertising falls into two camps: *image* or *engagement* campaigns.
Both are part of the equation in breakthrough branding. Image ads are
about the big picture and are designed to build an identity for your brand.

They wrap a story around your brand and its customers that connects emotionally with your target audience. They're designed to lock an image in the mind about your brand and to draw a mental link between the brand and desirable qualities like attractiveness, success, family, or security.

Image ads can do this subtly or not so subtly with imagery and messages. The story the ads tell implicitly appeals to our identity and our emotions. The product is desirable because it is used by desirable people, people who fit with your image of yourself.

Story + Emotion + Identity = Image

Image ads can run in traditional media, such as commercials on television or print ads in magazines. Banner ads and pop-up "commercials" on popular Internet sites have taken their place alongside traditional television commercials and play a similar image-building role. They're not designed to sell specifically—there's no phone number, coupon, or clickthrough button—but to build awareness, familiarity, and preference with a broad audience.

Brand managers think (and measure) in terms of *reach and frequency* of an ad: how many people are in the target audience and how many times did they see a particular message or promotion? They look at total *impressions*: how many times is an ad seen by individual people?

In buying media for an advertising campaign, brand managers think in terms of *reach and frequency*, how much of your target audience does the message reach, and how often does the message reach them? They also measure ad *impressions*, the number of times an ad is seen by someone and the *cost per impression* (CPI) or *cost per thousand impressions* (CPM).

Because there is no interactive component in image advertising, there is no hard measure of ROI or return on your investment. Marketers can measure their effectiveness somewhat by doing a benchmark awareness study of the brand and then following up with a tracking study after an advertising campaign has run for six months or so. This way, marketers can see if the needle moved on key measures such as awareness, messages, and preference for the brand.

With image ads and other marketing programs, marketers try to build *mindshare*, awareness of your brand versus its competitors. One of the key measures in mindshare is *top of mind (TOM) awareness*. Market researchers ask people something like, "When you think of category X, which brand first comes to mind?" Being top of mind, or the first brand mentioned by the target market, is powerful. It translates into sales leadership and gives you pricing power over your competitors. Branders try to build *mindshare momentum* because being the dominant, more well-known brand in a category gives you strategic control.

Engagement Is the New Black

In the past five years, there has been a distinct shift from traditional advertising, corporate websites, and blast e-mails and the passive receiving of ads toward digital campaigns on Facebook, Twitter, YouTube, and other new media options that are two-way, collaborative ways of relating to ads.

In digiworld, people are looking for what marketers call *engagement*. They are looking to interact with a brand, and they can do that by linking, clicking, blogging, referring, friending, following, resending, or subscribing, to name just a few of the engagement measures out there.

All media channels—television, print, online, events—are realizing that engagement is what counts today and are adopting approaches to promote interaction, community, and emotional branding. There's more communication and interaction up, down, and all around. Humans are social animals, and now, as a business owner, you can foster communities with your customers.

For the brand entrepreneur, it's a world of opportunity for marketing, but you also have to think of unique ways to engage customers and get them to participate in your digital promotions for your branding to break through. And that's not so easy, with all the other messages vying for their attention. So many of the new media and digital options demand more advanced and high-tech solutions. It isn't necessarily the purview of a graphic artist and writer as much as technology experts who know how to capture the potential of the new tools. And there are new digital and technology marketing options coming about every day.

With engagement marketing, you need to socially engage customers and prospects with campaigns that are more open, interactive, and directed personally to them and their communities. Streaming video, social media, and mobile apps give people the ability to communicate, respond, and be involved.

 Interaction + Emotion + Community = Engagement

Engagement campaigns can be highly emotional, too. They can surprise, move, delight, and connect with people. The goal of breakthrough engagement branding is to get people to react and participate in the brand community and its marketing.

As a brand entrepreneur, you want to be adept at image and brand engagement. They're two different ends of the spectrum—the big picture versus interaction—and both will contribute to building your brand. You need to master both in breakthrough branding.

Of course, these days, the dividing line between the two can be hazy, since the best image ads trigger brand engagement or connection to the brand. There are new tools that allow you to click on print ads and outdoor billboards from your smartphone to get more information or a special deal. The best digital and engagement campaigns help to build brand image, too. In all your branding and marketing, you need to weave your brand throughout with a powerful identity and a different customer experience that's on strategy for your brand for breakthrough branding.

The Sincerest Form of Flattery

Marketers have always known that the best way to sell a brand is to get others to do it for you. Today, with the Internet and electronic tools, it's easy for people to pass along information about your brand. But first, you need to find stories and images that people like so much that they want share them.

Look at the breakthrough branding campaign of Chinese Internet retailer Vancl—a campaign that was so engaging it went viral. Entrepreneur Chen Nian came up with the idea of an Internet fashion brand, kind of the Gap of China, except it has no physical stores. Chen named his e-retailer Vancl. The Chinese characters for Vancl literally mean "ordinary people," so the concept is stylish, inexpensive clothes that ordinary people can afford.

To represent the brand in ads on outdoor posters and on the Internet, Vancl chose two of China's most well-known celebrities, Wang Luodan, a popular television actress, and Han Han, the counterculture intellectual, race car driver, and blogger. The ads feature a simple, strong graphic picture of the celebrity with evocative copy.

Here's the copy from Han Han's ad.

I love the Internet. I love freedom.
I love getting up late. I love eating at street stalls in the evening.

I love racing. I also love T-shirts priced at 29 RMB.
I'm not a flag bearer.
I don't represent anything either.
I'm Han Han.
I represent myself. I'm the same as you.
I'm Vancl.

There's a double entendre at the end of the ad with the store's name, Vancl, and its literal meaning, "ordinary people."

Young Chinese loved the ad and its message, and many did mashups on the Internet with their own copy lines or substituting their favorite celebrity in their ad. Yes, maybe the viral campaign got a head start from people at Vancl's marketing agency seeding the effort, but the Vancl campaign took off nonetheless, with consumers creating their own Vancl ads that blanketed the Internet and got lots of PR for the brand in China.

People Like to Laugh

People like to be surprised. They like to connect with others. When you create marketing content that's entertaining or tugs at the emotions, you have a much better chance of your video going viral and getting a lot of viewers. So, don't make your online content about selling the product. The more salesy you are, the less effectively you will connect emotionally or amuse people.

In the United Kingdom, a fun T-Mobile video spoof of Prince William and Kate Middleton's big day became a viral hit on YouTube, as wedding fever intensified in the days before the April 29, 2011, event. More than 23 million people viewed the online video ad, which featured uncanny look-alikes of the royal family boogying down the church aisle.

It wasn't until the very end of the video that the T-Mobile name appeared. Most people who encountered it didn't even realize it was an ad until it was over—and at that point, the brand was associated in their minds with a few minutes of absolute fun. T-Mobile's audience is a broad consumer audience, and here was an entertaining marketing video about an event that just about everyone was interested in, but they treated it in a fun, playful way that portrays T-Mobile as a fun, likeable brand.

Make the Brand Resonate

How many ads have you liked but then later couldn't remember which brand the ad was for? Or you mistakenly thought it was by a competitor? It happens all the time, and it's money down the drain for the company that paid for the campaign.

That's why, as an entrepreneur, you want to tie your brand and its brand promise into the marketing so people make the right connection, as Honest Tea did so successfully with its "Honest Cities" brand engagement campaign. The social experiment was about measuring the honesty of people to see if they would pay $1 for the drink they picked up. So I ask you, if you saw a rack of refreshing beverages on the corner of a street with only a sign that said to drop a dollar into a box if you take a drink, would you pay?

The brand set up small, unmanned drink stands in some of the largest cities in the United States: San Francisco, Los Angeles, Washington, Chicago, Atlanta, Boston, and New York. They had a hidden camera film the results and produced short videos on YouTube about the Most Honest Cities in America.

The campaign was a brilliant success, creating buzz around the brand. Honest Tea was able to compute Honesty Rankings for the various cities. It had great footage of people debating whether to pay or not because no one was around. They got lots of local PR in each city. The "Honesty" campaign tied in the brand's name, Honest Tea, and its honest positioning as having high-quality, pure ingredients with the "Honesty" promotion. It would be hard to misidentify the sponsor of the marketing campaign.

The campaign received over 280 million total impressions, 160 press stories, $2.79 million in earned media. Best of all, the brand had double-digit growth in each target market; San Francisco was the largest, with 56.31 percent growth. Pretty good for a campaign that probably didn't cost that much to produce. Just in case you're wondering, Seattle is currently winning, with 97 percent of the folks being honest, while Los Angeles is the most dishonest, with 87 percent.

 BRAINSTORMER: Going viral
How can you enchant customers so much
that they pass along your content?

Local, Social, and Mobile

One of the hottest areas in digimarketing is local, mobile, and social marketing campaigns. Not surprising, since smartphones are everywhere and more than 1.6 billion mobile phones were sold in 2010. People are using their mobile phones for search on the go, and they are looking for something local a third of the time.[1] If you have a retail business, local, social, and mobile marketing are important avenues to explore, and experimentation is a good way to learn how to use them best to create breakthrough branding for your business.

 **95% of consumer spending
takes place at local businesses.[2]**

In 2009, entrepreneur Joe Sorge launched AJ Bombers, a small restaurant chain specializing in "P-nuts, burgers, and beer" in Milwaukee.[3] Sorge has been successfully experimenting with Foursquare, a leader in local social marketing on mobile devices, one of the hottest trends in digimarketing today.

Foursquare allows users to connect with friends and update their current whereabouts right on their mobile devices. By tapping into it, local businesses such as AJ Bombers can reach out and offer special deals to those who have "checked in" nearby.

One of the restaurant's promotions included the offer of a free burger for the "Mayor." (That's Foursquare talk for the person with the most check-ins at a particular destination.) AJ Bombers also gave a free cookie for anyone who added a "tip" about the restaurant on the Foursquare site and showed it to her server.

Initially, Sorge's local mobile promotions brought in a lot of new customers, then check-ins slumped. Sorge discovered that many customers felt they couldn't compete with the "Mayor," who piled up lots of check-ins, so they didn't bother to try. Sorge responded by creating a loyalty club for high-ranking Foursquare users, not just the number-one player, with a special menu deal.

Sorge has done fun promotional ideas with Foursquare, like the "I'm on a Boat Special." Sorge put a kayak outside the restaurant so that Foursquare members could come, sit in it, take a picture, and get an "I'm on a Boat" badge from Foursquare. It ended up attracting his best tie-in and busiest lunch crowd to date.

Sorge has also held successful fundraisers for community causes and parties by soliciting Foursquare members, driving traffic into his burger joints and building community at the same time. Sorge has even published a free e-book on how to use Foursquare to drum up business.[4] Plus, he's gotten a lot of local PR that's built buzz for his burger joints.

Brand Your Mobile App

Before you get involved with mobile social media promotions like Foursquare offers, make sure that you have optimized your website for mobile viewers, and you might even want to consider a mobile app. Where should you start, with a mobile website or an app?

In a test done by InterContinental Hotels in Europe, the mobile website won hands down. It's more valuable as a marketing tool because mobile websites are more flexible across different platforms. But apps have their apps. InterContinental developed an app, the Priority Club Reward App, that lets customers book rooms, check rewards points, and view reservations.

New ways to use mobile devices are being devised every minute. Google is offering visual search through a new product called Google Goggles (great name!). You can use a smartphone to take a picture of an ad that has a QR code and you're connected with the company website for more information. Google Goggles is still in beta, but initial tests by marketers demonstrate its promise for engaging customers in your brand in a radically new way. Another hot idea is web advertising called *phototagging*. It's like tagging friends on Facebook applied to photos on the Internet. So if a viewer sees an item of clothing a celebrity is wearing or an interesting product in a photo on the web, viewers can put their cursor over the item, and the brand and price appear. As more of these inventive ways to advertise come about, the challenge is to execute them creatively without cluttering the Internet.

 BRAINSTORMER: Are you mobile?
How can you use local, mobile, and social
tools to build your business?

Branding from the People

When your brand connects with customers so much that they get involved in designing your brand's marketing and packaging, then you've got something pretty powerful, as former Canadian ski instructor Peter van Stolk found out.

Van Stolk feels a big part of brand success as an entrepreneur is *fluid branding*, learning branding and business rules and then breaking them to better connect with customers.[5] Van Stolk's small idea was an indie soda for people like himself who were drawn to alternative sports. He originally wanted to name it Smith Soda because the name had a populist feel, but the name was taken so he went with Jones Soda. In keeping with its populist leanings, the company's slogan is "Run with the little guy."

Van Stolk had a small budget, so he couldn't afford a custom bottle, which can cost upward of $250,000 for the mold alone. So he opted for clear glass and a stock shape. But he used the standard-issue clear glass bottle with a long neck (similar to the Corona bottle) to his advantage, spotlighting the colorful drinks inside, like the bright blue of its Blue Bubble Gum flavor. Even the labels are in black-and-white, to keep the attention on the drink inside.

One day a photographer friend suggested using his pictures as labels. Van Stolk loved the idea, but in keeping with his populist leanings, he wanted to open the photo op to everyone. So Jones Soda urged fans to send in their photographs to use as bottle labels. So far, the company has received more than a million submissions, and more than 4,000 customer photos have appeared as labels. Van Stolk also gets customers involved in sending in ideas for new soda flavors.

To build a market for Jones Soda with people interested in alternative sports, van Stolk started out selling with an "alternative distribution strategy" at skate, surf, and snowboarding shops; at tattoo parlors; and in clothing and music stores. Only later did he move into grocery and corner stores. Rather than pricey ad campaigns, Jones Soda focuses its marketing on its website and the indie sports events it sponsors.

 BRAINSTORMER: How can you get customers involved in creating your branding and marketing?

Do You Care?

Digiworld has created a new age of customer care. Pioneering Internet-based brands such as Zappos, Netflix, Amazon, and eBay have always thrived on consumer feedback; now, companies in every business category are getting in on the two-way action with pop-up screens or follow-up e-mails asking you to rate your customer experience.

To create active loyalty, you need to create community and to make your community feel special. Your blog, your Facebook page, and your tweets can be focal points. Write them personally and authentically, so that your customers feel you are talking directly to them. Don't try to sell them directly—instead, express your own personality. By extension, you are expressing the personality of your customers and making your brand something appealing with which they can identify.

Customers like to be rewarded for their loyalty, so offer special deals and publicize sales events. Always be connecting with your tribe, drawing them in and making it easy for them to engage with you by offering feedback, answering questions, participating in drawings or auctions—whatever you can think of.

Another way to reward customers is to provide them with hard-to-find information. The most-read section of Virgin Atlantic's Facebook page is its travel tips from crew members. The tidbits are casual, believable, and, above all, useful. After all, who knows better than airline crew members how to travel safely, comfortably, and efficiently? The lesson: be generous about the information you provide about your product or service. Don't use jargon; make it real and easy to understand.

Satisfy the drive we all have to get a great deal and be appreciated, and reward your most valued customers with the best offers you can come up with—or even just advance notice of general sales. You can reward them for referring new customers to you. You'll be making your loyal customers feel special, and that makes them more likely to spend money and recommend you to others.

 BRAINSTORMER: What special treatment can you offer your customers? Your best customers?

Brand Ambassadors with a New Prescription

Another marketing strategy for getting others to sell your brand for you is to find high-profile people to be *brand ambassadors*; these are people willing to endorse or sponsor your brand. But how do you pull it off if you don't have a budget to pay people to represent your brand? It takes some improvising, especially if you're still in school, like the four enterprising M.B.A. students at the University of Pennsylvania's Wharton School who launched Warby Parker.

In 2008, the quartet was brainstorming business ideas. One topic they explored was eyeglasses. They figured out that it was less expensive to buy an iPhone than a pair of prescription glasses. "Why are they so expensive?" they wondered.

One of the team, Neil Blumenthal, who had worked at a nonprofit that gives away glasses in developing countries, thought he knew why. The optical industry was dominated by a few players, so it is not a free market but an oligarchy making incredible margins.[6]

Bingo. The quartet had their small idea: an indie, antibrand eyeglass brand with good prices and hip designs. They named their business Warby Parker, two names they found in unpublished writings of Jack Kerouac that the New York Public Library had just discovered.

The team branded the look "modern vintage" and charged just under $100 for a pair of glasses, prescription lenses included. The four found that school was the ideal incubator for their start-up because their 820 Wharton classmates were their target consumers. To sell the glasses, they recruited brand ambassadors from their classmates. After they graduated, they enlisted department store buyers, restaurant maître d's, and other people who come into contact with lots of potential customers as brand ambassadors. The deal? They get a free pair of glasses and a discount code for their friends.

The cofounders developed a company culture and customer program that is "modern vintage," too. Warby has a showroom in downtown Manhattan, but most of its business is done virtually, through its website. You can try on eyeglass styles through Warby's free home try-on program, which lets you try out five frames at once. Or you can try them on online by uploading a headshot of yourself and "trying on" frames virtually.

When founders started the business, Warby Parker was the only stylish, affordably priced online eyeglass business around. They created a new subcategory, the first to offer stylish, affordable online eyeglasses. But their success has attracted copycats who are duplicating their business model. It's a problem that every entrepreneur faces, and it's particularly acute for Internet businesses, where cloning can be easier, making marketing and category domination critical. Warby Parker is working hard to keep its first-mover advantage.

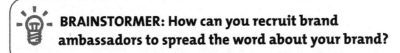

> **BRAINSTORMER: How can you recruit brand ambassadors to spread the word about your brand?**

Low-Key Branding

Many professionals like architects, designers, and chefs have long realized the value of building a strong business brand and personal brand. Even pure business-to-business professionals like major architects and designers are expanding into consumer products to build their brands, and the visibility pays off with more assignments for big commercial projects.

But for many professionals—lawyers, accountants, consultants, psychologists, and the like—bold branding may not be the way to go. Some industries, like law, have traditionally shunned advertising and marketing.

In fact, for years many state bar associations prohibited legal advertising. Even passing out your business card could be regarded as illegally soliciting clients! New business was done the old-fashioned way, through reputation and word of mouth. Branding and promotion were viewed as unseemly.

Now we're seeing lawyers and law offices advertise, blog, and tweet, as these proscriptions have become things of the past. Lawyers, like so many other professionals, are finding social media and the Internet a low-cost way to market their expertise and attract new clients.

Lawyers are using Facebook, Twitter, and business blogs to reach out and comment on high-profile legal cases in the news, to showcase their knowledge of the law and to add context and meaning to these legal cases. They are pitching local news stations, newspapers, and radio stations as expert commentators on legal stories in the news, and having a website, blog, published articles online, or a book are additional credentials that offer a strong marketing platform with the media as well as with prospects.

Being quoted in the news or featured on television is powerful because people will perceive you to be an expert. Why else are you being quoted?

Don't think that digital assets are just for consumer businesses. Even if you are in the B2B world, new business prospects will check you out online before they meet with you or consider a business relationship. Like it or not, this is the way business operates today, and you might as well get on board and use the Internet and new media to your advantage.

You can post a short promo reel on your website, YouTube, and other venues. Or post video highlights of a talk or a short interview that show-cases your area of expertise. Publish an e-newsletter and/or a blog in which you comment on trends or pertinent news. Send out e-mail blasts offering special research reports, articles, and white papers to clients and prospects, as well as posting them on your website, on industry sites, in the broader media such as The Huffington Post, and on relevant gathering places such as LinkedIn.

Hook Them with Your PR Pitch

Like everything you do in branding, you want to think *outside-in*. Who is the audience for the publication or broadcast station (the *outside*)? Then think of what you have to say that will appeal to them (the *inside*).

Yet, most businesses do the opposite. They think inside-out and write long press releases about a new office opening or a new service. The problem is, nobody cares. You have to frame your news so that it has appeal for the publication's or show's audience. You need to find a news hook so that the reporter or producer will be interested. Your pitch must have tension. You must have a different mental angle than the consensus.

You also must customize your pitch for a specific audience. To appeal to a tech writer and a sophisticated tech audience, you need a cutting-edge tech angle. For reporters and producers covering the job market and careers, you need fresh tips that will appeal to their readers and viewers.

A good tactic for pitching media is to write a brief *story pitch* that you send to a reporter or producer. Write a short lead paragraph about a story in the news, a new research study, or a new trend. Then, quickly list your credentials and express your point of view about the issue, including three to five bullet points on what you might say in an interview. Reporters and producers tend to follow hot stories, and that way you can be part of the media conversation, position yourself as an expert, and get your brand in the news.

Be a Modern-Day Peter Zenger

New media give you the opportunity to be ubiquitous and spread your message, like early American editor and journalist Peter Zenger, who fought for freedom of the press.

The problem is that the web is a beast hungry for content. How do you manage it, with all the vehicles that you can use to display content, and run your business, too? Not all of us are equipped to be 24-7 marketing machines, tweeting from the car and posting to Facebook at the coffee shop. You need to simplify things and create a content supply chain.

Begin with the most important social media and websites, such as Facebook, YouTube, Twitter, LinkedIn, and your blog. Set up your profile on each and set up a system to reuse and repurpose everything that you possibly can. If you do a video for marketing, post it on your website, YouTube, and other digital channels as well. Then write about it and link to it on your blog, send out a link in a blast e-mail, tweet about it (with a link included), and feature it on your Facebook page. Pick individual lines in the script and tweet them. Get the idea?

Here are pointers on how to make each digital platform work for you:

▶ **Website and blog**
  ▶ Make sure your website and blog have a similar look, feel, and personality—one that is very different from that of your competitors.
  ▶ Update your blog regularly, at least every few days, with interesting content. Reformat interesting bits for Facebook and Twitter.
  ▶ Use widgets, buttons, and links so that your content is easy to distribute, pass along, and comment on.
  ▶ Make special mobile versions so that your content is legible on smartphones and tablets and so things like Flash don't gum up the works.

- **Broad social media like Facebook and Google+**
  - Create personal and business profiles and fan pages that tell a story about yourself and your business.
  - Do a launching tab like big brands do on Facebook, with special graphics for your business, that ties in with your website look.
- **Business social media like LinkedIn**
  - Start a group around your business area (mine is SelfBrand on LinkedIn groups), or get involved in the discussion on other groups.
  - Don't just list your career history but tell an interesting story about yourself and your business in the profile.
- **YouTube**
  - Keep your videos short—one to two minutes—except for a special demo reel.
  - Put relevant keywords on all your videos to aid search.
  - Make your videos entertaining or enlightening rather than sales pitches. At the very least, they should inform or educate.

You don't need to and shouldn't try to do it all yourself. While cyber-branding may not cost a lot of money, it can be very labor intensive creating the media content and promotions that break through. Once you set up your overall brand marketing plan, you can bring in other people to help you out if you don't have the time or the inclination to run the digital show. (Communicating via digital means is second nature to anyone under a certain age—and many young people are looking for full- or part-time work.)

Invite customers to write guest posts on your blog. Encourage them to share videos, pictures, or other original material on your website, blog, or Facebook page. Ford Fiesta created FiestaMovement.com to encourage just that, and it has become a content creation factory for the carmaker. Fiesta fans share original videos, pictures, and stories that in turn attract new members to the Ford Fiesta community.

It's Not a Sin to Repeat

It's not a sin to repeat tweets or other digital messages. The entrepreneur Guy Kawasaki repeats each of his tweets four times and gets an average of 600 clickthroughs each time, effectively expanding the views of each tweet from 600 to 2,400.

Consider repeating some of your messages, just as old-school branders rerun their TV commercials many times. (In the history of TV advertising, there is only one well-known instance of a commercial that ran once: Apple's infamous "1984" commercial—but, of course, in that case, the single airing was part of the concept.) People aren't watching TV every minute of the day, so marketers run commercials repeatedly until they effectively reach the target audience multiple times. News programs repeat the top news stories throughout the day so it reaches a wider group.

Advertising works cumulatively. People have to see a commercial or read a marketing message multiple times—an average of seven times, according to various studies on traditional media—before they remember it. It's what media people call *net effective reach*. Once a consumer has seen your message more than seven times, your marketing communication has achieved *wear-out* and it's time to change the message. The reality is that most of our messages aren't remembered because people don't see them enough times to remember the brand and its message.

Automate Your Cyberbranding

Digital technology can also help you manage your digital communications by automating certain processes. For example, you can arrange your Twitter settings so that everything you tweet automatically appears on your Facebook page.

Other sites, such as Hoot Suite and Social Oomph, help you feed material from one social media site to another, as well as helping you schedule your tweets to go out at specific intervals (one minute, one hour, one day, etc). That way, you can create the appearance of tweeting regularly, whether you do so or not. You can use Flickr to manager your photos and bring them online and SlideShare for your presentations. No doubt there are entrepreneurs out there right now devising additional ways to help small businesses manage and optimize their digital assets.

If imitation is the sincerest form of flattery, appropriation isn't far behind. Make it easy for people to pass along your content or your company information, whether it's an interesting story, third-party endorsement, or thought for the day. Twitter's "Tweet" and Facebook's "Like" are two of the most powerful buttons on the web—add them to your website, blog, and other digital properties so that people can easily spread the buzz about your business. And keep your ear to the ground for new ways to optimize your online presence—new things are happening every day.

You can get an idea of what's working on video and viral videos through advertising and marketing websites. Visible Measures does a weekly Top 10 Viral Ads Chart so you can keep up to date on the viral campaigns with the largest viewers. Visible Measures tracks what they call "True Reach," the number of viewers who saw the video that was posted by the company (brand driven) and the viewers who saw it because it was forwarded by a friend (viewer driven).

Playing to Win

Today, people are bombarded with more messages than they can absorb, and you're bombarded with more marketing options than you've ever dreamed of. As an entrepreneur, you'll need to make decisions and set goals for what you want your marketing to accomplish. The creative brief will keep you on track in developing all the creative elements of your branding and marketing programs. The *marketing plan* can help you keep on track for the various efforts you've launched for the brand.

Because I believe in simplicity, I favor a short, five-to-ten-page mini marketing plan rather than a twenty- or fifty-page document. If you've followed along in the book, you'll pretty much have all of the pieces together. You just need to add specific programs you're testing or implementing for your brand. Most marketers draw up a yearly marketing plan for each of their brands. It's a good habit to copy.

Here are the key sections of the marketing plan:

▶ **The challenge:** What is the key challenge you face as an entrepreneur at this time?
▶ **Goals:** What are the major goals you want your marketing to achieve? You can tie it to a specific revenue, new business, or customer goal. Your challenge could be related to dislodging a key competitor and improving your brand identity in the marketplace.
▶ **Situation analysis:** Write down key thoughts on the current situation of your company and products, key competitors, and customers.

- ▶ **SWOT analysis:** Use the SWOT analysis you did in chapter 1.
- ▶ **Key market segments:** Define a primary target market for your business or product, as well as secondary and tertiary target audiences if you have them. Include a few sentences that describe each target market.
- ▶ **Marketing programs:** List each marketing program you plan to launch, continue, or test this year with a time frame, creative development plan, budget, and, if possible, metrics for how you plan to evaluate the program's success.

The challenge is to develop marketing programs that people are going to want to view or read and respond to and that are on strategy for what your product is and can be. To do that, you can't play it too safe. Safe marketing programs are usually boring marketing programs.

To be a great marketer with breakthrough branding, you have to put yourself in your *customers' shoes*, people who are bombarded each day with more messages than they can absorb. Ask yourself:

Would I *stop what I'm doing* to learn more?
Would I *want to read* this ad?
Does it make me *smile*?
Does it offer *something new*?
Would I want to *send it to a friend*?

Chapter 8

Company Culture:
One Team with One Dream

An idea can turn to dust or magic,
depending on the talent that rubs against it.

—Bill Bernbach, Legendary "Mad Man"

A hot new area of branding today is internal branding, the brand you build inside your company with employees. Successful entrepreneurs and big companies alike realize that it's not just a race to attract customers, but you also need to attract the best talent and create a strong company culture. A key audience for breakthrough branding comes through the door into your company each day.

You will be more successful if you have a strong *employer brand*, a culture that thrives on growth and where there is a dream team at every level of the organization.

 EMPLOYER BRAND: the culture and work experience your company offers its internal "customers"—its employees.

In internal branding, the "product" you're selling to employees and prospects is your company's work culture and work experience. The perception that people have of your company as a place to work is your *employer*

brand.[1] Your employees and the talent you are trying to attract are the "customers" of your employer brand.

Casting Is Everything

Job number one as an entrepreneur is landing the first ten or so core employees. You need to have a clear idea of the kind of talent you want to attract, because this core group sets up your *employee brand* and your start-up's DNA. As a start-up, you're unproven. You need to have a clear sense of the different types of people you need in the company and how to unify them under a common culture with its own customs, beliefs, and procedures. You also need to be a leader who's easy to follow, with a clear mission and a strong sense of the results you want to achieve.

 EMPLOYEE BRAND: the kind of people who represent your company's values, work style, and personality.

Thinking in terms of employer brand and employee brand can be a powerful strategy for creating a culture that champions its people and helps them flourish. Having a strong internal brand can help grow your business, because you're more likely to attract the best talent and everyone will feel challenged.

In this model, don't think of yourself as above your people but as representing the employee brand yourself. One entrepreneur I worked with created a special culture at her consumer product company. When she talks about the company's growth, she often shares what she is working on personally for her own development rather than just talking in an impersonal way about revenue forecasts. She shows her employees that it's okay to be human, and they feel a special bond to her and the company.

Creating a Growth Culture

You're not trying to run a social club. Your goal is to win in the market. But to do that you need to create a special culture.

Make sure that you hire people who have skills, resources, and knowledge that you don't have. Even the most well-rounded entrepreneur isn't good at everything. You've got to figure out your shortcomings and fill the gaps with team members who have those aptitudes. Otherwise, it is unlikely that you'll be around after the start-up phase. Make sure that you have people who can help you land business and bring in revenue—critical tasks in the start-up phase.

You need to create a workplace with the right amount of challenge and expectations, the right amount of freedom and control. You want everyone to be a growth agent empowered to do her job and help grow the business. Studies show that the worst work environments are those in which people have little say over their day and always have to follow someone else's orders. They feel like a cog in a slow-moving corporate machine and consequently don't do as well as those who work in companies where people have more freedom to decide how to handle projects and assignments. According to these studies, money isn't the key driver for most people. It's working in an environment where people have the ability to grow and develop their potential.

You need to create a culture where everyone is on a shared mission, where people understand that they don't have jobs, they have responsibilities. And where there is a shared culture that celebrates victories, even minor victories, along the way. Come up with creative ways to reward people. These can be monetary rewards or tickets for a movie or ball game. You want to create a sense of fun and a shared culture.

As your business grows, your people will start to watch your every move and decision. You may even be perceived as having some "secret sauce," superior intelligence or salesmanship or innovativeness. You might even become a symbol of the group and its purpose, a source of inspiration that represents something greater than who you are. World leaders like Nelson Mandela, business leaders like Jack Welch, and religious figures like Mother Teresa can appear superhuman and represent an ideal that we strive for.

 BRAINSTORMER: What skills and aptitudes do you lack? Are they covered by other team members?

Radical Creativity

How do you create a dynamic, innovative culture where it's everyone's job to come up with ideas and grow the business?

First, create a culture where it's okay to fail. The most innovative people are the ones with the most ideas. Most of them are bad ideas that fail. Some companies are even rewarding risk-taking that fails with employee-recognition bonuses and trophies, or setting aside time in the week for new idea generation.[2]

Second, set up the offices and common areas so that there is lots of mingling in the workplace. Contrary to the image most people have of the solitary inventor or entrepreneur, it turns out that most breakout ideas don't come from loners. Innovative ideas aren't solitary things. Most successful ideas come from people interacting with each other in environments where ideas are discussed and shared.

That's why there is a long history of simultaneous inventions. Transformational ideas like the electric battery, the telephone, and the radio were all made by several people who came up with the same idea at practically the same time. Most of them didn't even know each other, but they were plugged into what was happening in their industry and influenced by similar ideas, what some researchers call the *hive mind*. That's the kind of culture you want to create for your business, with all your people, not just the senior people, reaching for innovative ideas.

 Create a company that champions people and ideas, and watch the leaders and innovations come forth.

You need to encourage a culture where ideas and innovation are organic, not part of a programmed process. Most corporate off-sites are not good for generating ideas because they are scheduled events. You can pack up all of your most creative people and drop them off in Timbuktu, but you're unlikely to get great insights, studies show.[3] The mind has time to predict and that stifles creativity.

So many breakthrough ideas come about through serendipity, in fluid environments where it's easy for people and ideas to collide and not a lot of rules or protocols. As Thomas Edison famously said, "Hell, there ain't no rules around here. We're trying to accomplish something."

What you should do is encourage an organic environment where your people intermingle with new ideas and environments. The more radical, the better. Even though we're in the virtual age, being in close physical proximity where you can have face-to-face meetings is as important as ever.

One Harvard study showed that scientists who worked in close proximity to other scientists produced higher-quality papers than those who didn't. And the best research was done by scientists working within about thirty feet of each other, where they could easily meet in person and not through the Internet.[4]

Of course, for a brand entrepreneur it's also important to recognize a good idea and jump on it. Neither the mouse, the iPod, nor iTunes was Steve Jobs's idea. He got the ideas from others, recognized them as something important, and took them to the next level.

Ideally, you want to create a culture in which all employees are encouraged to dream and innovate, to make suggestions on process improvements, new products, and services and not be greeted with, "That's not the way it's done here" or "That won't work." Smart entrepreneurs create a culture where innovation, professional development, and personal empowerment are part of the culture for everyone, not just the senior people or those with marketing, R&D, or engineering backgrounds.

You want to create a company where people are dying to work because it's not just work—it's fun and things are happening. To win the war on talent, many Silicon Valley companies offer elevated perks like free gourmet lunches and on-site haircuts and dry cleaning. You can take your pet to work at some companies; game-maker Zynga will even pay for pet insurance. (The company is named after the CEO's dog after all.)

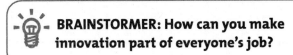

> **BRAINSTORMER: How can you make innovation part of everyone's job?**

"Hire for Smarts, Rent Experience"

A penchant for risk-taking, unrelenting drive, and innovation are pretty standard fare for the typical entrepreneur. But how do you hire the right people and create a culture that drives these qualities throughout your organization?

Let employees choose their own creative job titles, for starters. At Cranium Control, Scottish-born entrepreneur Richard Tait called himself the Grand Poo Bah. His partner was the Chief Noodler and the CFO was Professor Profit.

Tait's talent philosophy was to "hire for smarts and rent experience."[5] He was looking for smart people who fit culturally into the dynamic, innovative, and fun culture he cultivated—not necessarily those with a lot of experience in the game business. Sure, in operations and finance, he made sure to find people who knew their stuff, because missteps in those areas can destroy a business, particularly a start-up, fast. Tait also believed that you should "fire for style," because if someone isn't right, he will fragment and destroy your culture.

Tait created a decision-making space at Cranium that he called the Red Dot Room. To promote focus and short meetings, there were no chairs and no distractions except for the red dots in the carpet design.

Not being bound by traditional thinking in the game business led to distribution breakthroughs. Rather than just selling its intelligent games in toy stores, Cranium went where its target customers hung out. Cranium was the first game sold at Amazon, the first game to be sold at Barnes & Noble, and the first noncoffee product sold at Starbucks. Tait sold his business to Hasbro in 2008.

 BRAINSTORMER: What's your employee brand and employer brand?

We've Got Talent

To promote a thriving employee brand, McDonald's launched an American Idol–like talent competition called Voice of McDonald's. Employees from around the world submit audition videos and sixteen semifinalists are selected to compete at McDonald's annual trade show in April, where they get vocal coaching and a chance to win the $25,000 top prize and three runners-up prizes.[6]

The competition has been a colossal success, attracting more than 10,000 singing employees. McDonald's uses social media like Facebook, Twitter, YouTube, and international social media to promote the competition and asks the public to vote on the finalists. In 2009, more than 685,000 people voted for their favorite singer.

McDonald's says its employer brand stands for opportunity. Twenty of the company's top fifty executives, including the CEO James Skinner, began as restaurant workers. And the Voice of McDonald's competition reinforces the opportunity positioning with employees and customers.

The singing competition is a highlight of the Orlando gathering, a mega tradeshow with more than 15,000 franchisees, employees, and vendors in attendance. People from around the world come to network, check out the menus in other countries, and share the latest branding and operations tips.

 BRAINSTORMER: Is there a fun way to promote your employee brand?

Buy a Loud, Red Telephone

How do you create an internal culture where the customer is king? Kayak. com cofounder Paul English bought a red telephone with a very annoying ring for the office. And he made it part of the job of his software engineers to answer the phone at his popular travel search engine, Kayak.com.

Initially, the engineers complained about the phone. And frankly, many would rather have had a call center deal with customers than do it themselves. But now everyone knows how important English feels it is to answer the phone. (He often answers it himself.) And when engineers hear the same complaint about the site a couple of times, they fix the code to stop the calls!

English's philosophy is simple: do what you need to in order to make the customer happy. English loves talking to customers himself because it gives him a lot of ideas about how to make the site easier to use. And customers are amazed when English thanks them at the end of the call and identifies himself as the cofounder and Chief Technology Officer.

English's goal is to build a dream team of customer-focused super-smart people. So he's constantly asking people, "Who's the smartest person you ever met?" And then he tries to find and recruit that person.[7]

At Kayak.com, the company has four monitors that display real-time information about the site—number of visitors, clickthroughs, and the like. It also shows the last customer e-mail and a picture of the employee who answered it. Kayak.com also developed software to randomly select a customer response each day and blast it out to the entire company and its investors. "It keeps us on our toes," muses English.

English gets about 400 to 500 e-mails a day and sends out about 120 himself. Even with all this e-mail traffic, his philosophy is to keep his inbox lean, at around ten e-mails at any one time. When an e-mail comes in, he deals with it—delete, reply, or delegate.

 BRAINSTORMER: How can you create a culture of customer service?

Make Me an Offer

How do you find out if new hires are really committed to making the company great or are just in it for the money? Put them to a test, says Zappos CEO Tony Hsieh.

Customer service is the Zappos credo, so every new hire at Zappos goes through the same training as its call-center reps. Every new hire learns the Zappos story. Each gets trained in customer service, Zappos style. Then everyone starts taking calls. According to Hsieh, "If we are serious about customer service, then it shouldn't just be a department. It should be the whole company."

Then Zappos makes each employee an offer that is hard to refuse. It offers each trainee $4,000 to quit after completing training. Why does Zappos do that? As Hsieh says, "We don't want employees that are just there for a paycheck. We want employees who are there because the culture is the right fit for them."

Once employees start working at Zappos, the company encourages community. There's an open environment, so employees don't feel isolated. Plus, there's only one entrance to the building, so they're likely to bump into each other coming and going.

For employees not at main headquarters, Zappos has installed community into its computer system. When employees sign in each day, up pops a picture of a random coworker, and they can take a short quiz to identify the person. Then they are introduced online through their profiles.

 BRAINSTORMER: How can you weed out uncommitted employees?

I'm Feeling Lucky

What questions do you ask to recruit people who are right for the culture you're creating? In the early days at Google, cofounder Sergey Brin did a lot of the interviews himself, and they could be unnerving for the prospective employee.

In 1999, Douglas Edwards was interviewing to be Google's first brand manager. He had worked at ad agencies and had held corporate branding jobs, so he felt unusually confident that the meeting would go well. Plus, he had spent six months living in Siberia so he spoke a little Russian. "Perhaps I would become his mentor and we would toast each other's health with fine Siberian vodka," Edwards mused as he waited for Brin to appear.[8]

Brin showed up in gym shorts, a T-shirt, and in-line hockey skates, and immediately started peppering Edwards with questions. After that detailed line of questioning seemed to go well, Brin switched to Russian to see how much Edwards had picked up in Siberia.

According to Edwards, "Finally, leaning forward, Brin fired what he called 'the hard question.' 'I'm going to give you five minutes,' he told me. 'When I come back, I want you to explain to me something complicated that I don't already know.' He then rolled out of the room toward the snack area."[9]

Edwards decided to go with the theory of marketing, since his current boss was a Harvard M.B.A. and had encouraged him to bone up on marketing and had even lent him her marketing books. "By the time Sergey came back, I had enough to talk for 10 minutes and was confident I could fill any holes with the three Bs (Buckets of Baffling Bullsh--). I went to the whiteboard and began drawing circles and squares and lots of arrows. I was nervous, but not very. Sergey bounced on a ball and asked questions that required me to make up things on the spot."[10]

Douglas Edwards became employee number fifty-nine.

 BRAINSTORMER: What are the hard questions and interview techniques you will use to find the right people for your company?

Ask the Frontline Workers

Forget the pricey consultants and operations experts—try asking your frontline workers for innovative ideas. Even small suggestions from frontline employees can give you an advantage in a tough economy.

Just ask U.S. entrepreneur Andrew Schuman, who bought Hammond's Candies in 2007. It was a ninety-year-old business, but Schuman didn't know anything about the candy business when he bought Hammond's.

Schuman learned that the idea for the company's successful ribbon snowflake candy came from an assembly-line worker, not from an executive in marketing or operations. It gave Schuman an idea. Why not tap into the talent of his employees? After all, they all knew more about candy manufacturing than he knew at the time.

Schuman launched a cash-bonus program—small cash rewards for ideas about how to do things more efficiently. And it's had a sweet payoff for Schuman's business. One employee suggested an adjustment to a machine gear that enabled Hammond's to cut the number of people on the assembly line from five to four people. Another worker suggested a new way to pack candy canes that cut breakage 4 percent.[11] It's been a win-win, especially since frontline employees feel valued for their ideas, not just their physical labor.

 BRAINSTORMER: How can you set up a rewards program for innovative ideas for your business?

Paint the Walls

How do you transport the company culture when you are expanding, particularly when you're setting up offices in new countries? Facebook does it with a "landing team." The job of the landing team is not just to transfer knowledge but to make sure the Facebook vibe is also imported: its energy, risk-taking, and sense of fun.

Job one of the landing team is to set up the physical markers of the Facebook culture, such as its open space and cubicleless room layout. The team may even paint the walls with Facebook values, like "focus on impact," "move fast," and "break things."[12]

The landing team brings Facebook's Palo Alto culture to its global outposts but personalizes it to the local culture. For example, at corporate headquarters in Palo Alto, Facebook's conference rooms have funny names given in honor of Internet memes. In one wing, called the Hall of Bad Ideas, conference rooms have names like "Subprime Mortgages" and "Land War in Asia." In the Facebook offices in Hyderabad, India, the conference rooms are named after Hindi films, so they're dubbed "Dostana" and "Umrao Jaan," while in the London offices, they're named after London landmarks, so bear names like "Oxford Circus" and "Liverpool Street."

The landing team also imports Facebook traditions, like its Friday "All Hands" meeting (from "all hands on deck"), where everyone shares what he is working on. In India, they call it the *Gupshup* (chit-chat) meeting. They also export the company's "Hackathons," its informal partylike gatherings where people get together to take on thorny problems after hours. The landing team is a great way to keep alive the culture that makes the company strong as it expands across geographic borders.

 BRAINSTORMER: What are the key markers of your company culture that you would want to transport to new locations?

Resist the Copycat Syndrome

Groupthink is when everyone in a group starts thinking alike, and it's alive and well in the business world. Most entrepreneurs generally resist groupthink and the copycat syndrome, but they can creep in as your company expands. People in the same company share so many of the same influences and belong to so many of the same clubs and organizations that they can even start to dress alike.

Don't try to copy the competition's culture no matter how successful they are. You want to stay on top of what your competitors are doing to be competitive, but you need to create your own company customs and ways of staying in the lead. The best way to be a leadership brand is to harness the creativity and business thinking of every member of your diverse organization. That can only happen when you encourage and reward out-of-the-box thinking and new ideas for making the business more competitive.

The business world is dynamic, so you have to be strong with your external customers and with your internal customers (your employees, if you want to do breakthrough branding). Don't leave an opening for a new entrepreneur to gallop on the scene with something new and steal away your best talent. You want your company to be the one everyone is clamoring to join. To do that, you need to:

Make everyone a *corporate entrepreneur who is a growth agent* for the company.

Encourage *innovation and ideas at every level*, especially the frontlines.

Create a culture with *customs and rituals* that are special to your company.

Make sure all employees know their *objectives and key results* (*O.K.R.s*).

Be *easy to follow as a leader.*

Chapter 9

What's Your Pitch?

*You can say the right thing about a product and nobody will listen,
but you've got to say it in such a way that people will feel it in their gut.
Because if they don't feel it, nothing will happen. The more intellectual
you grow, the more you lose the great intuitive skills that really touch and
move people.*

—Bill Bernbach, Legendary "Mad Man"

Every day, entrepreneurs make tens of thousands of business presentations and business pitches, all around the world.

Most of them are very boring, with way too much information.

That's a lot of misery—on a global scale.

Yet despite the evidence, the blank eyes and fidgeting movements, most business presenters turn on the PowerPoint, dim the lights, and put slides with tons of words on the screen. There is no emotion in lots of bullet-point facts, just too much information. It's not the way to promote a breakthrough brand idea.

Of course, we all like to believe that presenting lots of information is effective in business. We think it proves that we're serious players. We're presenting all the data, after all. The reality is that logic and analysis don't sell as much as emotion does, and too much complication confuses and unsells people.

We also like to believe that a great business idea should speak for itself. The reality is that no one can recognize a good idea unless it is presented by a good salesperson.

Every Talk Is a Pitch

The words you use and the talks you give can be persuasive and stick in the minds of others, or they can scatter in the wind like packing peanuts in a hurricane. Your job with every talk is to connect with your audience and persuade people of something, not to give out information.

Every speech, presentation, or business dialogue is a pitch, really. Whether it's a new business pitch or a meeting with your team or an interview with the media or a possible new hire, each is an opportunity to connect and persuade.

As the entrepreneur behind your business, you have got to be the persuader-in-chief.

The secret that persuasive people know is that, as the presenter, you've got to become one with your audience. You have to understand their concerns so you can connect emotionally with them, alleviate their concerns, and solve their problem.

You'll find, as people who have mastered pitching and selling know, that the best way to sell and connect with others is through four things:

▶ Warmth
▶ Emotions
▶ Clicking
▶ Stories

Every presentation, every pitch, every important talk should tell a story about your business or yourself that takes your listeners on a journey—a journey that persuades them to your way of thinking or that leads them to your product. You don't have a big brand yet, so you have to learn how to tell stories about your business and to tell them with a passion that wins everyone over.

Warmth versus Competence

It takes less than a second for another person to take you in and decide whether they like you or not. It's all based on a visual impression—how you use your facial features and whether you project warmth—that provides the other person with a *spontaneous trait inference*. While you might think projecting competence is paramount, it's really warmth, hands down, followed by competence.[1]

So how do you project warmth? It always helps to smile naturally, what social scientists call a Duchenne smile. It's the kind of smile that lights up your whole face and uses the muscles around the mouth and the eyes, too. It's the smile that's an invitation for others to connect. When you smile, others are likely to smile, and that will help everyone relax and enjoy the pitch.

Certain body movements project warmth, such as leaning forward and being on the same plane as the other person. That's why it is good to move to a chair next to someone rather than sitting behind your desk and why moving down from the dais to the same level as the group is always a welcome gesture.

Projecting power can also help you sell your ideas and yourself in a pitch. There are two poses universally linked with power—taking up more space and openness.[2]

Expansive postures such as open arms project power. Closed, contracted poses such as crossing your arms in front of your body communicate low power. It's very hard to pitch well if you're pushing people away from you.

Emotions versus Logic

In the business world, we like to believe that logic and reason prevail. It's a myth. Emotions prevail. Studies show that people use the emotional part of the brain to make business or other decisions.[3] Most decisions are made on autopilot. They are quick emotional responses and are not made through analysis.

So get wise and don't make your presentations, pitches, and talks about lots of facts, data, and analysis. Sure, make an argument for your product or service and include figures that will create interest and give reasons that tie in with your audience's values and purpose. People need reasons to defend their decisions to others as well.

But first think, what does your audience want emotionally, and how can you satisfy that need? Then tell stories and anecdotes that will connect with them emotionally. All of your stories, points, and reasons have to mean something to them on an emotional level. Advertising people tend to be great at emotional pitches, so for inspiration check out Don Draper's nostalgic pitch for the Kodak Carousel business from the popular show *Mad Men* on YouTube.[4]

The Passion of the Pitchmaker

Don't be afraid to be passionate about the ideas you believe in. People will be more likely to respond to your ideas if you talk about them with passion and emphasis.

The use and control of your voice, as well as expansive body movement, can be very powerful in conveying passions and your emotions, and in selling and persuading.

You can take your voice from high to low, from forceful to soft, depending on the emotions you want to express. You can make a dramatic pause before an important point or story. In terms of voice, most men have an advantage because they have deeper voices, and that projects power, dominance, and competence.[5] A high-pitched voice can suggest nervousness. It's important to use inflection, varying the pitch from high to low and switching the volume from soft to loud, and that's something everyone can learn.

Before you get in front of a group, mentally prepare yourself with positive self-talk so that you will give a passionate, persuasive performance. Here's the incantation that mega-speaker Tony Robbins has used since he was seventeen:

> *I now command my subconscious mind to direct me in helping as many people as possible today by giving me the strength, the emotional persuasion, the humor, the brevity, whatever it takes to get them to change their lives now!"[6]*

If you have a prop, use it. If you have a new product, act like a maestro and, with a flourish of the hands, give a demo. You want to use whatever devices you can to pull people into your message.

Click with Your Audience

Great speakers and business leaders connect with their audience whether they are talking to one or a thousand. People who engage others quickly are what social scientists call *clickers*.[7] Either consciously or intuitively, clickers tap into the social and emotional rhythm of the other person or the group.

When two people have a good conversation, they feel that they have clicked. In large groups, for listeners who enjoyed the stories and personality of the speaker, a similar clicking takes place. A kind of mutual syncing happens, studies show, so there is a kind of *mind meld*. Often, this effect goes beyond the areas of the brain and people even start to imitate each other.

One group we tend to click with is people we see a lot, people who work near us or who we bump into a lot in business. So as an entrepreneur, you want to be out and about and to master what I call the *comfort connection*, finding areas of shared interest or passion. If you believe that most people are more similar than different (and they are), you will easily be able to find connections.

Another way to speed up clicking is being open and revealing who you are as a person. We're used to being formal and trying to appear flawless in a business setting, but in reality it's self-disclosure and vulnerability that are most powerful in jump-starting a relationship with other people.[8] That's why a lot of sales leaders tell self-deprecating stories. It cements the bond. In terms of quickly connecting with others, vulnerability is a strength, not a weakness.

Like it or not, one of the best ways to click with others and get into their rhythm is through the power of imitation. Quick social bonding comes from mimicry. It's usually unconscious, but you'll need to start out consciously at first, until it becomes second nature.

 To "click," express similar interests and use similar words, similar movements, similar facial expressions, and even similar breathing patterns.

Of course, clicking is easiest to do in small meetings or in one-on-one conversations. Clickers use similar words, gestures, and movements when they are with others, and that creates a vibe of goodwill. Here's how it works. If another person is concentrating his eyes on you, do the same. If he is fidgeting and glancing around, do a little of that after a one- or two-second pause. If the person is laid back, take the meeting slowly and casually. If the person is brusque, get to the point efficiently. Expert clickers even take on the breathing rhythms of the other person, studies show.

To be effective, you have to do your mimicry slowly and imprecisely. Most people who are natural clickers do it unconsciously. For them, it's a way to relate to the other person.

Studies found that people who mirror other people when they meet with them or give a pitch get cooperation and a positive response, even from complete strangers, within minutes.[9] It may seem contrived, but clicking can help you connect with others and be more persuasive through the power of similarity.

It also helps to be similar to your audience in the way you dress. You don't want to come in a bespoke suit from Savile Row for your pitch to a corporation in most parts of the United States outside New York City. Nor do you want to underdress, since that shows a lack of respect. You want to be yourself but appropriate.

Clicking and Persuasion

One reason subtle mimicry works is that it activates the part of the brain connected with feelings of empathy. It's the same thing that successful salespeople activate when they relate a challenge similar to that of the client they are pitching.

Each of us has mirror neurons in the brain that enable us to understand and connect with others through simulation. We have emotional and audio mirror neurons and many mirror neurons for modeling physical behavior. When people tune in to others in this way, they feel a strong sense of connection.

When you practice the secret of clickers, you'll find it easier to establish rapport with others. You're in tune with each other. And the more comfortable someone feels around you, the likelier it is she will agree with what you're proposing.

Most super salespeople are clickers. And to make sure they click, they often do research before important client meetings to try to figure out what's going on with a particular client. They try to determine the client's business problems. Then, when they go to the meeting, they weave in a story about having a very similar problem, to create rapport.

It may seem calculated, but why define it with that word? You can define it as smart emotional branding. The tactic creates a mutual feeling of empathy and rapport. Creating this sort of quick connection by mutual shared experience is a tactic of people who click with others in business. It's a tactic that you need to learn.

Clicking with a Large Group

Of course, when you are speaking to a large group, you can't practice physical mimicry, but you can click with them nonetheless. Arrive early so that you can mingle with the crowd and start building a bond with individuals in the group, which has a surprising impact on your ability to connect with the audience.

In your talk, you'll want to select different, specific people in the audience that you are talking to, beginning perhaps with someone in the lower right quadrant of the audience, then moving to the back left quadrant, and so forth.

Actors talk of becoming one with the audience, and you should try to forget yourself and engage with your audience. You want to create a mutual rhythm and energy. You need to use your whole body, your kinesthetics, to connect, and you need your feelings and emotions to be read by the audience.

Like a stage actor, you'll have to use bigger gestures and facial expressions. Try to engage all the senses, so your audience hears what you say, sees what you say, and feels what you say. Include intelligent bits for the left brain and emotional and visual bits for the right brain.

Come up with ways to involve your audience in your talk. You can move through the group. You can ask questions. You can set up competitions that get volunteers on the stage to participate in solving a problem you propose in your talk.

The Persuasive Power of Story

Story is the ancient secret of communication. And it's a universal language. Cultures and religions from the earliest times use story. Story gives meaning to the facts and the figures, to people and events. People remember things better when they are presented in a narrative rather than as a list or in an expository paragraph.

Stories persuade in a subtle way, because the listener gets involved in the story, what is taking place, and what the underlying meaning is. It's best to show, not tell, so that your listeners come to the conclusion themselves. You don't tell a prospect that your product is better; you tell a story that leads her to that conclusion herself so that she owns the decision.

You've got to become a good communicator to be a good leader, a storyteller who can build a narrative around your vision and goals. Strategic storytelling is at the heart of any great pitch, presentation, or meeting. You've got to develop and tell stories that sell your business, your products, and yourself to investors, to customers, and to the media.

Stories allow you to say what you want to say in a memorable way. In a story well told, listeners can be transported to a different state of awareness. That's why the creative teams and executives at advertising agencies are not only master storytellers for their brands, they are master presenters who use stories to sell their creative marketing ideas to their corporate clients.

Story Pulls People In

Language is a uniquely human ability, and story gives language emotional power. And emotion is the short route to the brain. Stories create movies in the mind that we can see, feel, and remember.

Stories are powerful because they involve the left brain and the right brain. Most presentations, with their facts and support points, just connect with the left brain—our rational side. Story pierces the right hemisphere and makes us visualize and feel what we hear as well as think about what we hear.

Story is a lesson from the Madison Avenue advertising playbook. Marketers are master storytellers who wrap their brands in myths and stories relayed in their advertising and promotions.

Story is a *pull* strategy. It attracts and pulls you in. Stories are not passive. They get the listener involved in connecting the dots, figuring out the meaning behind the story, and reacting.

Great storytellers transform their audience, and that should be your goal with every talk and story you tell. Great storytellers make people feel the story and react. You don't come out the same as when you went in. You are a changed person. You learned something new. You get a new perspective. You see things differently. You are moved. You see things the way the presenter intended. You are persuaded.

Become One with the Audience

Great storytellers find the right pitch and the right story to connect with a particular audience. To do that, begin by thinking *outside-in*, as you would in branding.

Outside is the audience. Who are you pitching? What is their problem? What reaction do you want to get? How do you want to change them? What is the one thing you want them to remember from the pitch?

 What is the *one thing* you want your audience to remember?

Then think *inside*: inside is you. What is your purpose in this talk? How can you solve your audience's problem? What is the key message you want them to remember from the talk? What is the best story to tell to connect with them and solve their problem? What emotions do you want them to feel?

The goal of your talk is to get the audience to remember one thing, and your presentation should show how you can solve their specific issue or problem. If you're talking to potential investors, their problem might be determining whether getting involved in your business is a good investment. If you're talking to customers, their problem might be deciding whether to switch to your product or company. For potential employees, their problem is deciding whether they should join your company. And your problem is deciding if they are right for the company.

Once you figure out the audience's problem, what is the key *takeaway message* you want them to remember that solves their problem? The takeaway message is your *meta-narrative*, the story behind the story.

When you're clear about what their problem is and what your takeaway message is, then you can brainstorm about the right story to tell. It helps to think in terms of writing your talk to one specific person so that it is personal, engaging, and conversational. You want people to feel that you are speaking to them.

Have a Story Meeting with Yourself

In Hollywood, studio executives have story meetings to review scripts for possible movies. You need to have a story meeting, too. You're not looking for made-up stories or stories from a book; you are looking for stories inside you. You're looking for stories from your own experience in business or in life. You're looking for stories that employees on the frontlines tell you.

You want your stories to reflect your values and your experience. You're probably thinking, "My life is so ordinary." But that's why people will relate to it. Your stories will connect with them and remind them of their stories. People will only remember a few things, so tell the story that says the most about your brand or the story that will be most persuasive for a particular audience.

As a brand entrepreneur, you want to create a company culture that creates more stories and memories. And you want to make sure that you connect with employees at all levels who have stories to tell or to set up a mechanism so that you find out about their stories.

Each year, Zappos asks its people to write a few paragraphs about what Zappos's culture means to them. Employees are encouraged to share thoughts, stories, and photos about their personal experiences. Zappos Culture Book not only is a rich source of employee, vendor, and customer stories, but the book itself is a great business story that Zappos's CEO tells about his company in talks and interviews.

 BRAINSTORMER: How can you find out about interesting stories about your company culture, customers, and vendors?

How to Tell Your Story

In crafting a tale, you need to set the stage with a place and time so that your listeners understand the context. You can even begin with the question that needs to be answered or the problem that needs to be solved. Most stories are told in chronological order, with a beginning, a middle, and an end, with excitement building slowly and steadily.

Keep your business stories short, about one minute to two and a half minutes, depending on their importance in your overall presentation. So, you'll have to be a good editor, eliminating extraneous details and minor characters that make the narrative too confusing.

You need a hero, a likeable hero who your audience can relate to and who gives them a point of view. The hero of your story could be you. He could be a client. She could be a colleague or the team lead on a project.

Good stories have tension. There needs to be something important at risk, a conflict, an antagonist, an unexpected change, something that sets up drama and excitement in the story. These are the obstacles that the hero must overcome and that give the story meaning. Most good stories are ultimately about human nature, too, so there is a sense of universality, of situations and experiences we can all relate to.

Dialogue can help people hear a scene. If someone is decisive, don't say it, demonstrate his character by describing something that he did.

Good stories are visual, allowing us to see and feel the story. Visuals and emotions are critical for memory, and emotions are the key component in business decisions, more than facts. You should show your emotions, too, as you tell your story.

 You want a story that people can see.
Tell it like you were filming it in a movie.

In a story, we travel with our hero until there is a turning point. Often the turning point is in the form of a test for our hero—a test that transforms the hero—and the results of the test determine whether the story ends happily or tragically.

Most stories follow a simple three-part structure like a three-act play:

The catalyst: You want to begin with what Alfred Hitchcock called the MacGuffin—the problem, decision, situation, or person that changes life for the hero and sets everything in motion.

Obstacles: We go through the obstacles that the hero must overcome before she can reach her goal or regain her life back.

The turning point: When the problems reach their high point, the hero faces a test of her true character. It's the turning point in the story.

Good stories have complications and problems that have to be solved. Often there's a reversal of fortune, twists and turns that take us somewhere we weren't expecting to go and that make the story exciting and interesting. For the same reason we like reversals in murder mysteries, we respond to reversals in business stories: they introduce the element of surprise. We like happy endings, so most stories end with the hero surmounting the obstacles, passing the test, and achieving the goal.

 BRAINSTORMER: When you write down a story, highlight the visual parts that you could easily film in a movie.

The Power of Three

The power of threes is an important thing to remember when putting together a talk or story. Stories usually have a three-act structure. Classic stories and fables have three obstacles that must be overcome, three wishes that are granted, or three main characters. There are "The Three Little Pigs," "Three Blind Mice," "Goldilocks and the Three Bears," "We Three Kings," *The Three Musketeers*, and, in more contemporary times, The Three Stooges. Even today, how many stories have you heard about the rabbi, the priest, and the minister?

When you're presenting options in a pitch, three is the right number, not five or ten or twenty. One or two is too few, yet four or more will lead to confusion and the lack of a decision. Studies show that it is easy to grasp three points or three elements, but when you throw the fourth one in the mind gets confused and begins to wander. Make it easy on your audience and stick to three.

Three is often a good internal structure to use in a talk for expressing an idea or to simplify the logic around an argument or point of view. The U.S. Declaration of Independence speaks of "Life, liberty, and the pursuit of happiness," and France's motto is "Liberty, Equality, Fraternity." Three has a sense of completeness that is powerful.

The Business Pitch

The *business pitch* is about what makes your business unique, special, and needed. It is your pitch story that you use with clients, investors, the media, and employees that describes the essence of what your business is all about.

It is a story of drive, brains, and pluck. The ruling emotions are passion and confidence.

(TM) **The business pitch sells what's special about your business and shows why it's a winner.**

Your business pitch incorporates your "small idea," the brand sentence that defines the essence of your business idea. The brand sentence must communicate your brand positioning, your value proposition about how you are better than your competitors. Fill in the blanks: We're the number-one choice for your business because _____ and _____.

Even though a key use for the business pitch is pitching a prospect for business, don't make it a bragathon about "We're the leader in X" or "We innovated Y." It isn't about you and your genius. Nobody cares about that. What they do care about is how great you'll make them. What can you do for them that nobody else does? Keep the focus on them and their problems and needs.

Here's a good way to structure the new business pitch:

1. **Grab them at hello.** Begin with a story, anecdote, or topical comment that disarms the group, such as a self-deprecating story about being in front of such an important audience given the small size of your company. Then segue into a story that defines the problem the client has, ideally framing the problem in a new way.
2. **Tell your company story.** Keep this section about your company story short. Make your business story as compelling and visual as possible and define the advantages your company and its approach offers. Share some client stories and your customer satisfaction reports.
3. **Throw in "magic dust."** Spend most of your pitch on the prospect's problems and solutions. Rather than taking them on a journey to one solution, win over their trust by presenting three options. Express the advantages of the decision you want them to make, even its shortcomings. Then throw in some "magic dust." The magic dust moment is something compelling about your business idea or solution that makes the audience want to know more. If you have a prototype, give a demo. Ask questions to get them talking and

involved in the conversation and solution you are proposing. Suggest a small step that they can take to move things along in the path you are recommending.

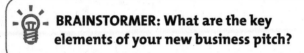

BRAINSTORMER: What are the key elements of your new business pitch?

The Investor Pitch

When you are pitching investors or venture capitalists, you want to give a version of your pitch that I call the *business pitch on steroids*. You have to be succinct and passionate, and you need to make it clear why you need money, what you're going to do with the investment, and how your business will make money, not just why it's a cool business idea.

Investors and VCs have a short attention span. The may not have ADHD, but it sure seems like it sometimes. So, be prepared with some super-quick speed branding.

Prepare three pitch lengths:

▶ The brand in a sentence pitch: five seconds
▶ The elevator pitch: sixty seconds
▶ The full pitch: fifteen minutes

Have your five-second *brand in a sentence pitch*, which we discussed earlier, ready, as well as a sixty-second *elevator pitch* that offers an in-a-nutshell description of how your business idea will succeed and some tangible proofs of why that is so.

If all goes well, segue into your ten- to fifteen-minute *investor pitch*. Keep your slides and bullet points to a minimum. A product demo may be a key part of your presentation. You want to connect with and wow this group with your project using your confidence, passion, and strength.

Here's how to structure your business pitch to investors and VCs:

1. **Grab them at hello.** Launch your talk with your brand in a sentence—how your product is different, special, and relevant. It should be a memorable sound bite that clicks with investors.

2. **Use stories that demonstrate a need in the market.** Follow your catchy opening with stories that demonstrate why the brand will be successful: how it's different from competitors' brands, the research studies that support your idea, and your knowledge of the industry. Demonstrate demand by showing who's been buying the brand and orders in the pipeline. Use visuals—slides or props—to bring your business idea to life.

3. **Show why *you* are the person to lead this company.** Include a short top-line bio about your experience and accomplishments.

4. **Explain how you plan to spend the capital you raise.** Be very specific about how you plan to spend the funds. Here you might want to throw in a little humor to get a conversation going.

 BRAINSTORMER: What is your five-second pitch? What are your sixty-second and your full fifteen-minute investor pitches?

Persistence Wins the Day

When an investor, client, or prospect you're pitching says no, pretend that you can't hear him.

Look surprised. Say, "What about...?" Suggest a new option.

Ask questions. Keep the conversation going.

 A good rule of thumb in business is to act strong when weak and act weak when strong.

Everyone talks about persistence, but the truth is that most people give up too soon. The winning entrepreneur keeps on going. You need to keep knocking on doors and telling your business story until you knock one of those doors down.

Michelle Madhok pitched her idea for a women's internet shopping site to her boss at AOL and was turned down. She pitched it to the editor of Hearst's *Shop, Etc. Magazine,* and the editor told her that she didn't like internet shopping and suspected that Madhok was a marketer who wanted to be an editor.

So Madhok started the business shefinds.com, a name she bought from a porno site for cash and a large box of beauty products Madhok had received to review on her site.

But Madhok didn't stop pitching. In 2007, Madhok went to a Make Mine a Million $ Business (M3) event for female entrepreneurs in New York. Each entrepreneur was given three minutes to make her pitch to an audience of investors and media.

Knowing from experience that investors don't like a lot of words, Madhok prepared slides with interesting visuals to wow the audience and told a passionate story about her journey as an entrepreneur and why she was the right person to grow the business.

Afterward, a reporter from *Inc. Magazine* who was in the audience contacted Madhok and did a two-page spread on Madhok for its "Business Pitch" column. An investor from Vancouver picked up a copy to read on a flight to London. He came across Madhok's pitch, was impressed, and called her when he landed. Within two months, Madhok had a million+ dollar investment in her business. And it all happened from Madhok's persistence and showing up at the M3 event with a short, compelling investor pitch.

As a brand entrepreneur, you'll want to have a lot of "for example" business stories and anecdotes, short subplots that demonstrate why your business rocks. It can be a story about getting your first big client. It can be about a letter you received from a particular customer that demonstrates your company's deep connection with its customers. You want to have a roster of stories that show what you're all about. You want to have the capability to come up with rejoinders and examples quickly, and never, ever give up.

David versus Goliath Story

David versus Goliath is the entrepreneur's tale. In the biblical tale, David, when told that Saul would reward any man who defeats Goliath, accepts the challenge. David's initial plan was to fight a conventional battle with swords against Goliath. So he prepared to go into battle by putting on a coat of mail, a brass helmet, and a sword. No one believes that David can succeed against such a strong opponent.

David versus Goliath is the classic story of the underdog succeeding against a bigger, established opponent.

Then, somehow, David realizes that he can't win against Goliath using conventional methods and armament. "I cannot walk in these, for I am unused to it," he says. David then takes a secret weapon, a slingshot, and five smooth stones from a brook.

Against the odds, our hero defeats the giant. He hurls a stone from his sling that hits the giant squarely on the forehead. David takes his sword and cuts off the giant's head.

Goliath is the big, established brand that everyone fears. It has seemingly insurmountable resources—superior size and market clout, along with thousands of supporters and a decades-long head start. Yet, our hero, through pluck and inventiveness, defeats the giant. The mood is one of courage, innovation and suspense.

In essence, the story is about a small upstart with a secret weapon fighting a much bigger foe and winning. It's an excellent format to use for your creation story or new business pitch, where you developed a new product with superior performance or a new technology that solves an old problem, and you had to fight an established competitor to succeed. You don't battle the industry leader conventionally, but as a small company you use guerrilla tactics to succeed in the marketplace. This could mean doing a stealth rollout of your new product in small stores or small markets and building critical mass under the radar.

The David and Goliath story is one of bravery in spite of conventional wisdom that says there is no way that you, the underdog, can succeed. A powerful aspect of the story casts the giant as not just big and dominant but evil, and you, "David," as the force of good saving the day for the broader society. The story of Apple's rise against established competitors with vastly superior market share is a classic example.

A good example from the movies is the Harry Potter series, particularly *Harry Potter and the Deathly Hallows Part 2*, in which Harry defeats the evil wizard Lord Voldemort.

It's a great story format to use when you are the small upstart who has developed a different approach than the market leader, which is pretty much always the case if you're a brand entrepreneur.

BRAINSTORMER: How have you had to battle giants in your industry?

The Quest Story

The quest is the hero's journey. It is an ancient format and the most common story format. Many stories from around the world, like *Ulysses*, feature a hero who goes out from his normal world on a journey into the larger world. He is tested with obstacles and hardships. The hero wins a decisive victory and comes back stronger and wiser as a result of his journey. Often, the townspeople applaud the hero when he returns from the heroic journey.

 The quest story is about overcoming obstacles *to achieve a hard-fought goal*.

Business is all about setting and reaching goals. So the quest is a great format to use when you talk about achieving any goal, such as starting your business, landing an important client, fending off a new competitor, and the like.[10]

Your creation story is most likely a quest story. An example from the movies is *The King's Speech*. The hero (Bertie, the second son of King George V) is in a particular life situation (he stutters). Then something disrupts his life (his older brother abdicates the throne and Bertie becomes King George VI). Now, the hero must embark on a journey: in Bertie's case, a quest to find his voice. There is often a person who serves as the hero's mentor, like the speech therapist Lionel Logue in *The King's Speech*.

 BRAINSTORMER: What's your quest story about achieving a goal?

The Lost in a Strange Land Story

The *lost in a strange land story* is about dealing with change and new terrain that we don't know well and how to master this new world.[11]

The lost in a strange land format is about mastering change or a new environment.

In essence, it's a story about self-discovery and growth as you (or your group) master the strange land. In the end, you're not lost anymore because you've learned how to succeed in this strange world. What's more, it's not strange anymore because you understand it now.

In business, the lost in a strange land story is a great format for talking about launching your brand in a new market or for a new demographic or fighting off a new competitor. The format is great for any situation where the world that you once knew has been totally upended by a new environment that's different from the one you've known. It's about learning how to succeed in that strange new world.

It's a format you can use in describing the early years of being an entrepreneur and learning how to get financing, set up the business, attract customers and clients, and make money on your own. The strange land story works for changing careers or mastering any new environment where you must learn a new set of rules, customs, and procedures.

I use the strange land story when I talk about how I moved from the nonprofit world into the branding world early in my career. In job interview after job interview, I was rejected because of my academic credentials and nonprofit background. Then, I realized that I had to brand myself so that I fit into the for-profit world. I changed my resumé and my elevator speech to emphasize the parts of my background that were marketing oriented. I jettisoned the parts that were overly academic and were leading people to view me as someone who didn't belong. I learned the lingo of the new world I wanted to enter. I still told a true story. Your story has to be true. But now it was a story that fit into the new world.

Mastering a New Environment

High-powered Hollywood producer Jerry Weintraub told a lost-in-a-strange-land story in his autobiography to describe his first meeting with the legendary Walt Disney when Weintraub was starting out as a talent agent.[12]

Disney flew Weintraub to Los Angeles first class and had a limo take him to the Beverly Hills Hotel. Sounds great so far, right? Every day, Disney had a chauffer drive Weintraub to a private office on the Disney lot. Every day, Weintraub was told, "Mr. Disney is not ready to see you yet."

After five days, Weintraub was finally summoned to meet the legendary Mr. Disney himself. He walked down a long hall with Disney's Oscars displayed on both sides. Finally, Weintraub reached the maestro's office at the end of the hall.

"I was intimidated, parched. I felt like I had come through the desert," said Weintraub. Mr. Disney was at his desk drawing. Weintraub imagined he was drawing a picture of Mickey (Disney) pounding Goofy (Weintraub).

Weintraub quickly agreed to everything Disney proposed. He reminisced later about how much he learned from this trip, such as feeling out of place and intimidated by a creative legend surrounded by all of those Oscars. He learned the importance of home field advantage and the cost of letting others establish their authority while you are passive. Weintraub went on to conquer the world of Hollywood, becoming a maestro himself as a dealmaker, producer, and agent to many celebrities.

Before he left Disney's office that day, Weintraub asked Disney what he was drawing. It was a design for the bathing suit of a supporting actress in his upcoming movie *Bon Voyage*. Weintraub couldn't believe it. Disney didn't have a costume designer design it. The maestro was drawing it himself. He realized that Disney hadn't lost the intensity of the brand entrepreneur.

In the movies, a great example of the lost-in-a-strange-land story is *Avatar*. The movie takes place 200 years in the future on the planet Pandora, a lush planet with a native people who have a rich culture and language. Jake, a wounded former U.S. Marine, is sent by planet Earth to exploit the planet's abundant biodiversity. It's a very strange land that Jake is drawn into, but gradually he masters the people and their culture. In the end, Jake realizes that the strange land of Pandora isn't so strange after all, and he crosses over to lead the indigenous race in a battle for survival.

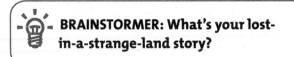 **BRAINSTORMER: What's your lost-in-a-strange-land story?**

The Redemption Story

The sexiest story around is the story of someone on the way down who has a sudden reversal and is on the way back up again. Redemption is an age-old theme about falling and rising again. These stories are exciting because of the dramatic reversal of the hero's fate. The redemption story is perfect for entrepreneurs who have a comeback story. (And most of us have a failure or two in our background.) It's a great story because we all love how-did-they-recover-from-that-train-wreck turnarounds.

The redemption story is about the person who's been maligned or rejected by the business world, who failed in a business, who was shown the door, who wasn't valued, or who was decimated in some way. Your fall could be because of your own doing, such as a business failure, personal demons, or a ruinous business decision.

 The redemption story is about achieving success *after a big fall in status*.

A variation of the redemption story is the revenge story. The revenge story is about getting even after a wrong has been done. The best way to frame this story is to make it not about getting revenge by hurting the person who did the wrong but about proving yourself to be superior. You best the person or organization that underestimated you by achieving more fame and success than your opponent has. In short, you end up on top.

A classic example of the revenge story is Steve Jobs and Apple. Jobs was famously thrown out of Apple, the company that he founded. Like a phoenix rising from the ashes, he came back during Apple's darkest time and completely revitalized the company, reaching a level of fame, fortune, and success that few achieve.

Another example is Jamie Dimon, once the heir apparent to then-CEO Sandy Weill at Citigroup. Dimon was banished and ended up starting over at Bank One. He then spearheaded a merger with JPMorgan Chase, one that left Dimon in charge. Today, Dimon works hard to manage his brand, and JPMorgan Chase's market cap is now larger than Citigroup's or Bank of America's.

> **BRAINSTORMER: Do you have a redemption story to tell?**

The Rags-to-Riches Story

Everyone likes a good *rags-to-riches story*. After all, if someone can go from living on the street to being CEO of a successful business, we can too.

> (TM) **The rags-to-riches story is about rising from poverty to great success.**

There's a lot of pluck involved and sometimes a dose of luck, too. It's a great storyline to use for talking about the secrets of your success, like U.K. retailer Chris Dawson does with his rags-to-riches story from poor barrow boy to CEO of the Range chain of stores.

U.S. entrepreneur Chris Gardner never knew his real father and fled his home because of his abusive stepfather. Later, Gardner was really down on his luck; separated from his wife and with no money, he was homeless, living with his young son in subway station bathrooms, flophouses, and city parks.

Then, Gardner had a lucky encounter with a man in a Ferrari, a stockbroker named Bob Bridges. Bridges introduced Gardner to the world of finance.

Gardner's saga takes other twists and turns before he succeeds as a stockbroker and later sets up his own financial services company. You probably recognize this homeless salesperson-turned-stockbroker story from the movie *In Pursuit of Happyness*, based on Gardner's memoir of his rags-to-riches journey and how he harnessed his passion to succeed.

> **BRAINSTORMER: Do you have a rags-to-riches story? What are the lessons you learned?**

The Love Story

The *love story* is a partnership story, but, just like in life when two people fall in love, it's ultimately about change.[13] After the infatuation phase, different expectations and emotions on each side come into play.

The love story is about being transformed by the merger or partnership. Neither side is the same as before. A plus B equals C. In happy love stories, the combination is stronger and better than each individual component. The two parties come together and are transformed in an important way. It's a great plotline for discussing a merger, partnership, or joint venture.

 The love story is about being transformed by a partnership or alliance.

Here's an example. In 2005, Andy Rubin gave a talk at Stanford about his new start-up. Larry Page, the cofounder of Google, was in the audience. *Bloomberg Businessweek* magazine described Page as "smitten" with Rubin and his company after hearing his talk. Before long, papers were signed and Rubin's small company, Android, merged with deep-pocketed Google.

Almost immediately after the partnership, Rubin's feelings began to change. Rubin quickly discovered that, despite his previous success as an entrepreneur and support from the Google founders, he was nobody at Google because he didn't ship anything.[14]

At first, he worried that Google wouldn't give him enough resources. He knew he had to prove his worth. Rubin and his Android team spent three years of incubation at Google, working long hours to continually refine the software and develop different versions of Android. Rubin's team named the different versions of Android after desserts, like Cupcake, Éclair, and Donut.

Finally, Google recognized Rubin and his team's work and responded by increasing Rubin's group from eight to seventy-nine engineers at the first release of Android in 2008.

Google agreed to follow Rubin's vision of giving away Android and the software development kit to app makers. Motorola, HTC, Samsung, LG, and others adopted Android as their mobile operating system. In a short few months, Android had a 35 percent share of new smartphone shipments.

By July 2011, Android powered more than 100 million gadgets. And that number is expanding rapidly, to the tune of more than 400,000 Android devices being activated every day.

As you can see, this is a love story that transformed both sides through a successful partnership. One plus one equals three.

The love story has distinct phases, just as it does with people: there's the excitement of wooing the other partner, the dreams about the future, and the inevitable problems that complicate the relationship. For variations on the plotline, think of the movies *Titanic* and *Gone with the Wind*.

 BRAINSTORMER: Do you have a business love story you could tell?

The Parable

As a brand entrepreneur, you need to have several different stories in your story library. You don't have to craft them from scratch: there are ancient story formats that can guide you in constructing your stories.

The *parable* is a teaching story that you can use to motivate employees or teach a valuable lesson. The parable is a short story that has a teachable moment.

 The *parable* is a teaching story with a specific nugget of wisdom from your experience.

When Joseph J. Plumeri, CEO of the insurance brokerage Willis Group, gave the commencement address to the new 2011 graduates of the College of William & Mary, he asked the students if they had heard of the Sears Tower, the tallest building in the Western Hemisphere. Plumeri told the graduates that he had wanted to rename the Sears Tower after his company, Willis, but everyone told him that it couldn't be done. The tower had had the Sears name since 1973, even though Sears hasn't been in the building in decades.

Plumeri described how he met the owner of the building and negotiated a contract to take 2 percent of the office space—the building was 20 percent vacant at the time. After Plumeri negotiated a good price per square foot, the owner asked if they had a deal.

"Not exactly," Plumeri said... "The problem with the Sears Tower is the name. It's a jinx. I said you need a new name, a vibrant name, a name that signifies the future, not the past."

Later, when Plumeri was on the evening news with Brian Williams after the dedication, Williams asked him, "How, Joe, after so many years that it was called the Sears Tower, did you get them to change the name to Willis?"

Plumeri looked into the camera and he said, "I asked."[15]

Think of how much more successful this use of story was in driving home its message than an exhortation to new graduates to reach for the stars and ask for things.

 BRAINSTORMER: Can you develop a short business story that has a teachable moment?

The Metaphor

A dramatic metaphor or analogy works like a photo snapshot—it's quick, visual, and it gets the listener to engage.

 A METAPHOR: compares two things that are not alike in most ways but are similar in one important way.

Famous U.S. defense lawyer Clarence Darrow was known for the *visual metaphor* that turned his defense into a prosecution. In 1898, Darrow represented striking workers who worked at Paine Lumber in Oshkosh, Wisconsin. Mr. Paine owned the town of Oshkosh in those days; even the police captain was on his payroll.

Speaking to the jury, Darrow told a story about how workers were locked in the factory at 6:45 a.m., once they had all arrived, and kept locked in, except for a lunch break, until the guards turned the key when it started to get dark.

Then Darrow created a dramatic visual metaphor for the jury: "Why, gentlemen the only difference that I can see between the state prison and George M. Paine's factory is that Paine's men are not allowed to sleep on the premises."[16] Mr. Darrow won the case for the strikers.

Taming a Hostile Crowd

If you know that a presentation is going to be tough, then you can prepare for it. The best tactic is to disarm the audience by talking to them straight. Begin with a smile and say, "Hello, it's great to be here." Then make eye contact with one or two people in the audience.

Then confront the problem head-on. A good way to disarm a crowd is by agreeing with them and their frustration. Then explain what happened and how things will be dealt with in the future.

If you get a trick or hostile question, don't make the rookie's mistake and try to answer the question. Learn to master the pivot like politicians do so well. The technique is to begin to answer the question with a nod to the questioner, almost as if you agree with that person.

Say a couple of sentences that summarize their criticism and point of view. Then you pivot to your point of view and outline the reasons why you feel as you do or how you have set up better procedures for the future.

Speaking Is a Conversation

By using a story, you'll have interesting, persuasive content that people will remember. But there are two other ingredients to being a great speaker, storyteller, and pitch maker: passion and connecting to the audience.

When you start watching, you'll notice that great speakers have a conversation with the audience. There's an energy and openness that feels natural, not staged. They reach out, sometimes quite literally, to the audience. That's why it's smart—no, essential—to not only develop the script of your story but to hone your stage presence in delivering it, just as an actor would, through careful preparation and practice. The Internet can be a wonderful tool in this process.

Watch speaker videos posted online on YouTube and other sites to get ideas about how to move your audience. Great speakers are smart *and* emotional. They open up and invite the audience in, becoming one with their listeners.

Political speeches are a great place to start your research—check out how winning candidates captivate voters. Take a look at some religious leaders too. They can be powerful at appealing to people's hearts and spirits, changing their minds and behaviors—making them believe in something new or validating what they already believe.

Effective public speakers engage their audiences much as stand-up comedians do. When you learn to express yourself well and harness the power of your passion and charisma, you will motivate your listeners, whether they are clients, investors, or your own employees. If no one listens to you because you are a boring presenter, or no one can understand you because you speak business jargon, you can't be an effective brand entrepreneur. No one will remember what you say or care enough to want to do what you want them to do.

Glory Comes with a Great Beginning

You need to warm up the audience so that they can decide that they like you. Top music groups are preceded by lesser musical acts whose job it is to warm up the audience and set the stage for the main act. It's much easier to give a great performance if the audience is already in the mood and someone has "warmed the boards" as they say in the theater business.

You can do this yourself with a little lighthearted banter to break the ice. You can get ideas when you come to the venue early so that you can mingle with the crowd before your talk. This will help you begin your talk by saying something specific about that particular audience and that location.

Some speakers who give the same speech over and over find ways to connect with each specific group in some way. The late U.S. politician Tip O'Neill used to arrive early so that he could go to a local landmark, and he would talk about that visit in his introduction to connect with each group.

U.S. entrepreneur Guy Kawasaki, who is active as a speaker, takes pictures of the city or the audience and uses them in his introduction to break the ice. Find your way to connect with the audience early in the speech. One U.S. entrepreneur who was introduced in Spanish at a conference in Spain, began, "My Spanish is not very good. Did you say I'm a big woman?"

The Do-Over: What'cha Gonna Do?

What do you do if someone bungles your introduction? Or there is a loud conversation or noise that's penetrated the room? Or a waiter drops a tray of desserts?

You've got to respond to it. You've got to follow your audience to what they are paying attention to and respond to the disturbance.

It can be a unique opportunity to click with the audience. Comedian Mike Welch describes the worst introduction that he ever received. It was early in his career, and the MC said, "We've got some kind of comedian, but I forget his name. Let's bring him on."[17]

Welch knew that he would bomb if he just opened with his act, so he responded with, "Let's do this introduction over again." Then Welch improvised an elaborate introduction gushing with praise, and the audience loved it: "I said, 'Now, when I run off the stage, you're going to cheer like crazy.'" The audience stood up and cheered. It ended up being the best performance of his career.

The key to handling any type of unexpected situation and connecting with the audience is to follow the dictum of improv, "say yes" to whatever is thrown at you. TV entertainers can be a great source of inspiration on handling impromtu surprises. At the beginning of his faux news show, "The Colbert Report," Colbert takes questions from the studio audience to connect with them before he hops on the stage and the cameras start rolling. One time a young Black boy asked him, "Are you my father?" After a short pause, Colbert replied, "Kareem?"

Be Easy to Follow

Now, you need to take your audience on a journey, an exciting journey that weaves in your stories to make your key points. You need to take your audience on a journey from "why" to "how," from "passive" to "active."[18] You need to live the journey as you tell it.

What the audience wants most from you is energy and authenticity. Give it to them! Open up and be yourself. Don't try to memorize your talk. Internalize the story and converse with the audience.

Keep your stories simple and speak from the heart. Try to include a *verbal sweet* on every other page of your talk, a little piece of humor or anecdote that will get the audience to smile.

Most people only remember one thing after a talk, so make that the key message of your most important story, and pause before you tell it. Don't spoil your talk with negative details that mar a story. That's all people will remember afterward.

You want to get so wrapped up in your talk and connection with the audience that you lose your sense of self. You are in the flow. You are one with the audience. You have everything you need to give a great performance.

Let Them Know It's "The End"

I never was a fan of the presentation wisdom that you should "tell them what you're going to tell them, tell them, and then tell them what you told them." That shows no respect for the intelligence of the audience and is way too boring, particularly for an entrepreneur or intrapreneur. You do need to end strong and signal that you're done.

Most speakers and presenters don't know how to end, and the talk ends more with a whimper than a bang. It's been a challenge for me, too. In the movies, we know it's over when the screen fades to black. Many movies used to spell it out: "The End."

The strong way to end is not with a summary of what you told them but with a call to action, something that you want them to do regarding the purpose of your talk. Then, with a flourish of the hands, a bow to the audience, and a hearty thank-you, you signal the end of the journey.

Practice Makes Perfect

Even though I often give the same presentation again and again, I still practice before each one. When I say practice, I don't mean reading through the presentation. And I don't mean pulling up the PowerPoint slides on my laptop and saying, "With this slide I'm going to talk about X," as many people do.

By practice, what I mean is speaking the whole presentation out loud just like you plan to deliver it, with the energy and emotion you plan to use with each story or point you make. You don't have to do it in the mirror or in the room you'll be doing your talk, but if it's an important talk, that's best. You can practice in the car driving to work, even.

Practice the talk as you want to deliver it live, with passion, with your stories and your personal examples. Practice it with intention—the specific reaction you want to get from your audience.

When you've given a breakthrough pitch, talk, or presentation, you'll know it because:

You will have *changed or persuaded* your audience in some way.
You will have *enjoyed it*, and so will your audience.
It will have *stories and anecdotes* that lock in your message.
You will have *clicked* with your audience.
Everyone will have gone on an *unforgettable journey*.

Chapter 10

Take the "Work" out of Networking

Nothing is so powerful as an insight into human nature ... what compulsions drive a man, what instincts dominate his action ... if you know these things about a man you can touch him at the core of his being.

—Bill Bernbach, Legendary "Mad Man"

Traditionally, we have seen the entrepreneur as a lone wolf who creates a big, powerful enterprise on his own. The reality is quite the opposite. Successful entrepreneurs cultivate a network of contacts. Alliances with others will keep you in the know and stimulated, and your business will be more successful as a result.

No matter how great your business idea is and how smart you are, you can't grow a business alone. Of course, we'd all like to believe that business success is based on merit, that the best business idea wins, and that there's a level playing field and all that.

The truth is that a big part of breakthrough branding success is who you know and who knows you. Important alliances and a broad business network will make you richer in terms of options and opportunities and, most likely, financially too. If you aren't part of the in-the-know crowd in your industry, you will be left out of the opportunities and knowledge that others—your competitors—have.

A Social Network for Ideas and Relationships

You'll find networking a lot easier if you take the work out of networking. You make it a chore when your primary goal is making contacts. Make your goal expanding your thinking and getting new ideas for your business and maybe making some lifelong friends in the process.

Just this shift in emphasis can make a big difference. You'll be much more successful in networking if your motive is curiosity and getting to know a wide variety of people rather than hustling contacts or business.

People can sense when you're genuinely interested in discussing ideas and sharing experiences and when you're interested in knowing them because they can help you.

It's a cliché, but offer to help the other person first. Studies show that it's smart because of the *reciprocity principle*. Even just giving someone something of very little financial value, such as an article or lending them a book, usually results in a return favor. So being nice pays off, which is not to say that you shouldn't be nice for its own sake.

The more people you get to know, particularly people from diverse backgrounds and from different areas of the world, the greater the payback to your business, both emotionally and tangibly.

The Networking Economy

Networking involves an economy. It's a hidden economy. You can't check it out in *The Wall Street Journal*, but it's a powerful economy all the same. It's an "economy of favors."

Networking is like a business transaction, a system of informal quid pro quo. The networking transaction works like this: I do you a favor, and there is the unspoken understanding that if there is an opportunity in the future, you will return the favor. An economy only works well if there is active trade back and forth, or everything will come to a halt.

 Like any healthy economy, your network works best when there's active trade back and forth.

Defining networking in terms of an economy might turn you off because it may seem, well, too transactional. It might seem less like a relationship and more like using people—too calculated. It isn't. It's more like being generous, because for it to work well, you need to be generous with your help to others. And like any economy, it works best if real relationships are formed between the players.

Networking is not using people so much as creating an informal support group of business and personal contacts. After all, it isn't like you'll be putting together "I owe yous" for the help you give and get. There is only a subtle expectation of repayment. The "favor" may or may not be called in. (But if you get a reputation for never helping others, you will have a bad credit report in the networking economy and lose out on future opportunities.)

Strategic Networking

You can't meet everybody, so you'll have to do some planning (that is, maneuvering) when you go to business events. Otherwise, the opportunities could come and go and you may not meet as many people doing interesting things in business as you'd hoped. One colleague always makes a point of asking questions and going up to meet the speakers, and many of them have become business contacts. She also leaves enough time to mingle at conference networking events—not frantically running around trying to meet a lot of people but trying to have a conversation and connect with a few new people at each event. Because she follows up afterward, she's even formed business alliances with some where they help each other grow their businesses.

As we all know, there is a hierarchy of networking events and organizations. Some business events will have a stimulating program with interesting people to connect with, while others might not be for you. And it's the same for trade shows and business meet-ups. Then, there are all the online networks and groups that you can be a part of, along with entrepreneur forums, broad business groups, and social networking sites.

How can you keep up?

Make it a point to read the bios of important people and speakers before an event or conference. Look for areas of connection: schools, jobs, interests, or hometown. Google them and check them out on LinkedIn or Facebook to learn more and see if you have friends in common or similar business interests.

If there's a connection or an area of mutual interest, e-mail or call the person to see if you can set up a time for a one-to-one meeting over coffee at the event. Or approach the speaker and comment on her talk. Most people will be flattered, and you're likely to not only learn more, but you might even form a lasting friendship.

A lot of the action takes place in the hallways on break. Reach out and introduce yourself and strike up conversations. Your goal is to meet new people. A good tactic is to go to an event with a friend but split up during breaks to network separately, and if you meet someone interesting, you can bring your new acquaintance over to meet your old friend (and vice versa).

 BRAINSTORMER: What are the key components of your networking game plan?

The Inner Sanctum

At the pinnacle of business meetings are events like the World Economic Forum Annual Meeting in Davos, Switzerland, which attracts top CEOs, hot new entrepreneurs, and leading government figures from around the world. It's not easy to get an invitation, but it's a great place to meet the people who are leading change in the world.

Klaus Schwab, Davos's creator, came up with the idea in 1970 and got a business acquaintance to lend him about $11,000 to launch the first conference the following year. Initially, Davos was a two-week European event to share concerns and knowledge, and the organization went global in the 1970s with the oil crisis.

Schwab has learned to experiment but to control the brand. Some years back, Schwab invited Hollywood celebrities who were involved in the issues to participate at Davos, but the event became all about them rather than the issues, so he hasn't invited celebrities again. With the World Economic Forum, Schwab has created the premier global event attracting the elite from business, politics, and the world of ideas.

Who's Watching Out for You?

While most of your networks will be informal ones, as an entrepreneur, it's wise to put together an advisory board for your business. You can include your lawyer, banker, accountant, business colleagues, or educational professionals.

You'll need to clearly define the commitment you expect, but an advisory board can offer the sounding board that every entrepreneur needs. Some of them may donate their time, while you will have to pay others, such as your accountant and lawyer, at their hourly rate. Pitch your financial advisor, banker, and insurance agent to serve on your board as part of their professional services. You can set up a yearly meeting or do it more often if there are important issues to discuss.

There are other formal groups that can be important, like YPO, Young Presidents' Organization. You can also join a local gathering of entrepreneurs or CEOs that organize discussions led by a facilitator. These smaller groups can be a great way to meet with peers on a regular basis to share best practices and get ideas on how to grow your business.

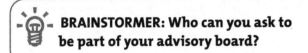 **BRAINSTORMER: Who can you ask to be part of your advisory board?**

Endorsement from the Oracle

Endorsements from important people and business leaders are like the third-party endorsements marketers pay a lot of money to get. And some endorsements can be very powerful indeed, giving your brand instant credibility.

Chinese entrepreneur Wang Chuanfu sure knows how to dream big, market his brand (BYD, or Build Your Dreams, in English), and attract high-profile investors.

Wang is a master storyteller and showman for his brand. He sometimes shows up for media interviews wearing a beige workman's uniform with the badge "Employee No. 1." In 2005, he wooed legendary investor Warren

Buffet as a major investor in BYD. Getting the Oracle of Omaha to endorse your stock—that's salesmanship!

At just twenty-nine years of age, Wang launched BYD in 1995 as a manufacturer of rechargeable batteries. The company grew quickly, and within ten years, BYD had more than half of the world market in mobile phone batteries and was in the top four worldwide in rechargeable batteries.

But Wang's dream for BYD was bigger than batteries. In 2003, Wang catapulted from consumer batteries to cars, becoming a player in the auto industry by acquiring Xi'an Qichuan Auto.

A couple of years later, he captured the attention of Warren Buffet and his partner Charles Munger, who started investing in BYD when it was valued around seven or eight yuan a share. According to Wang, Buffett was attracted to BYD's story: its new technology strategy, its fast growth, the management team, and its work style. With Buffet and his company, Berkshire Hathaway, buying the stock, a lot of other investors did, too.

Today, Wang's BYD is a major player in electric vehicles, energy-storing power plants, and solar energy. The keystone of these three businesses is something that Wang knows better than anyone else, battery technology, and he sees a bright future for all three industries. And Wang is still dreaming big. His goals are to be the largest automaker in China by 2015 and the largest in the world by 2025.

 BRAINSTORMER: Name two influential people who can help you build your brand.

Become a Little Bit Famous

Most of us have low wattage on the visibility spectrum. We are unknown outside a small network of friends and professional contacts. We are not name brands. We are not boldface names.

But visibility and its companion, fame, are things you should think about. We're talking here of fame on *some* level, of being famous in the business world, famous with entrepreneurs, famous in your industry, famous in your town, famous on LinkedIn, famous in your community.

As in the product world, it pays to be visible because visibility has a halo effect. If someone is visible and well known, we tend to think he is better than someone who is not as well known. He must be good, or why would he be so well known, is how the thinking goes. We assign familiar people more positive traits, and we're more likely to click and build relationships with them.

Visibility can be more powerful than hard work. It can be more powerful than smarts. That's why you need to get a little bit famous, too. Here are some of the benefits that visibility gives you and your business:

► Credibility
► Differentiation
► Pricing power
► Business opportunities
► Connections
► Recognition

Of course, it's easy to scoff at visibility as a phony game. But visibility is part and parcel of our culture. It's not just the media machine that thrives on it, either. Business does, too. Your customers do, too.

Is There Room in the Channel?

One thing you need to keep in mind in visibility seeking is whether there is *room in the channel*. PR isn't a limitless thing. There is only so much room or coverage that can be absorbed in any one topic (though there always seems to be room for a juicy scandal).

As a rule, only a certain number of people can dominate each arena. Only a certain number of new faces can be highlighted every year. Some industries are hotter and more glamorous than others.

That's why, ideally, you want to find an arena where the media isn't already dominated by articulate entrepreneurs. If it's dominated by inarticulate entrepreneurs, you're fine!

Is your industry mediagenic? You'll also get more visibility if you're in a hot industry or you can latch on to trends that are in the news. Some industries are inherently of higher interest than others. It will be much easier to generate visibility if you are in a high-profile business area like technology, media and entertainment, pharmaceuticals, and many others where there is constant interest in what's going on. Creating something new is always mediagenic, no matter what field you're in.

Successful media seekers have something fresh to say. Tony Hsieh became well known with the extraordinary success of online shoe store Zappos. But he's achieved even more visibility with his blog, his best-selling book *Delivering Happiness*, his media interviews and articles, and his speaking engagements.

Hsieh is mediagenic because he talks differently than other business leaders. I've already outlined some of his radical ideas about customer service and creating a special company culture. But Hsieh also talks about poker and the important business lessons he was dealt at the poker table. He's also a sort of business philosopher as he ruminates on the topic of happiness. How many CEOs do you know who write and talk about happiness?

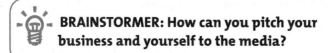

BRAINSTORMER: How can you pitch your business and yourself to the media?

Strategize Your Breakout Story

Think strategically about your *breakout story*. The first story that launches you in the media is your most important story. It will position you first in the minds of others and have lasting consequences.

As an entrepreneur, your breakout story is likely to be your creation story—how and why you started the business. It can include your purpose story, your backstory of who you are and what your values are. You need to be able to tell these stories well, and the more unusual or real the story, the more the impact it will have as a breakout story.

It's hard to top Dal LaMagna's creation story, since he got his business idea from sex. LaMagna, a Harvard Business School graduate, was a serial entrepreneur in his early years, and all the businesses failed. He didn't even have enough money to attend his ten-year HBS reunion. One of his class-mates told the others that LaMagna's low income had caused a drop in the average income for the class. His future did not look bright.

When he was in his early thirties and living in Venice Beach, California, LaMagna saw two neighbors sunbathing in the nude on their deck, and he joined them. The boyfriend of one of the women came by, and soon both couples paired off. Well, one thing led to another.

When LaMagna returned home, he had dozens of redwood splinters in his rear end. The tweezers he had didn't work very well, and he couldn't find quality tweezers at the pharmacy either. Later, when LaMagna was working at an electronics firm that used long-nose tweezers to handle components, he thought of that day in Venice Beach.

He had his small idea, creating a consumer version of those high-quality industrial tweezers. He founded his company, Tweezerman, in 1980 and grew it into a multinational personal care brand. Now LaMagna is a social activist and supporter of small business.

Toot Your Horn (Artfully but in a Breakthrough Fashion)

To succeed at visibility, you need to control how you are perceived. This is true whether your goal is getting more well known in a small pond (your area of the country or your company) or in a big pond (your industry) or the ocean (nationally or internationally).

Today, more than 70 percent of all "news" comes from public relations sources. The media has a tremendous need for content, and as a person interested in promoting your business and your self brand, you'll need to know how to give the media good content and how to create good content in digiworld so it will benefit you and your business.

Here are the most important guidelines for promoting yourself effectively without seeming to promote yourself:

- ▶ **Tell stories.** Dishing up your accomplishments or ideas with a narrative, plot, and dialogue builds suspense and gets people involved in the story so it doesn't seem to be about "you" but "what happened."
- ▶ **Prepare sound bites.** Come prepared with catchphrases and special names for your ideas so that they are memorable. Speak in short sentences on television and avoid long-winded explanations.
- ▶ **Put the spotlight elsewhere.** Don't put the focus on yourself as much as on the problem you were trying to solve or a customer need you wanted to satisfy. Always make the stories you tell to the media about something larger than yourself.

- ▶ **Bring the audience into the story.** Put your audience in the story, to get listeners engaged. ("I wish you could have been there when …")
- ▶ **Prepare a talking points memo.** For important media interviews, write down key questions that you expect to be asked and how you will answer them. Also prepare bullet points on the key points that you want to make, with anecdotes about each so that your point is brought to life.
- ▶ **Role play.** Since it can be unnerving to do a television, cable, or national media interview, get a communications professional or trusted business associate to role play questions and answers with you.
- ▶ **Stay on message.** Even if a question is off track, bring the reporter back to the message you want to give. Reporters are looking for a good story. A good story is when you say something controversial. It's your job to stay in control of the message, no matter what question you are asked. But dress up your message so that it's interesting.
- ▶ **Adopt the right mindset.** A friend told me to prepare for important interviews with this three-part mantra:

  Have the vibe of joy—you are happy for this opportunity.
  Have the vibe of authority—you know what you know.
  Have the vibe of caring—you are concerned about others.
- ▶ **Have a summary line.** Have a final takeaway line that you want to leave the audience with, a summarizing sentence that ties everything together. That way you won't be caught off guard, like I was when a television host said to me, "Catherine, we'll let you wrap this up."

More Valuable Than Money

A reputation is simply defined as when a lot of people have similar perceptions about you. And reputations work differently on the way up than they do on the way down.

Neuroscientists have discovered that we're wired to dwell on the negative over the positive. Good reputations take a long time to build but only a short time to destroy. (Life isn't fair.) That's why you have to *build* a reputation by racking up a lot of achievements and positive perceptions over time, but all that good work can be blown to smithereens with a high-profile fall from grace.

And to make things worse, bad reputations not only spread quickly and erase years of good deeds, but they are hard to shake. Bad reputations are sticky, especially in the digital world, where it's hard to erase Internet content. That's why, as a brand entrepreneur, you'll need to guard your brand's reputation and your own and move quickly to remedy a problem before it gains currency. Contrary to what you might think, we remember the bad over the good. Perceiving a bad event lights up the brain rapidly in MRI scans.[1] That's why we can remember vividly where we were when very bad events like the 9/11 terrorist attacks occurred but not much about what we were up to when a happy event occurred.

 Negative reputations are hard to peel off.

Not that you can't rebuild a brand after a fall. You can, but it isn't so easy, and sometimes the damage is permanent unless you come up with a good redemption story for yourself. Sometimes the best strategy after a negative story is to just ignore it unless the story is very visible. Engaging in a dogfight with someone who criticizes you online often calls more attention to the story. Just ignore it.

What's Your G Score?

Your aim as a brand entrepreneur is to own the real estate on your search results. The Internet and social media can be great avenues for high-visibility real estate for Brand You, through websites, blogs, profile pages, Twitter feeds, video posting, e-zines, and the like. You don't need much to get started. Even vlog stars like Gary Vaynerchuk keep it simple with a bare-bones set and no mic. If you consistently post on a blog and tweet and update your Facebook and Google+ content, you're a mini–media mogul creating media content for others to consume as well as building visibility for yourself and your business.

The game is about building an audience of fans, so you need to carve out a distinct niche for your blog or social media channels so you don't get lost in the noise. In order to enter the media space effectively and build an audience, you need to have a different spin, different content, a different attitude, a different something. And for your blog to be successful, the "news" and views it creates must not seem self-serving (i.e., overly salesy) and it needs to have personality, be entertaining, or have fresh content.

With celebrities and brands, it's easy to tell who the stars are and who is at the red-hot center. Several companies track celebrity and product rankings, but the industry standard is the *Q Score*, which measures familiarity and likeability. A high Q Score means you are a breakthrough brand and translates into money you can take to the bank, since you'll be paid more to star in movies and advertisers will want you for product endorsements.

While we may not have a Q Score yet, we can look up our G score. Google or Bing your name and your business name to see how many results you get. Does your name come up? Explore reputation management tools you can use to track your brand such as, Trackus, Brands Eye, and My Reputation.

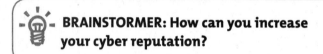

> **BRAINSTORMER: How can you increase your cyber reputation?**

Rub Shoulders with a Celebrity

The celebrity endorsement is a well-known standby in the advertising business. Studies by ad agencies tell us why the celebrity touch is so powerful. It's not that consumers really think that the product will necessarily be "better." It's that they notice and pay attention to more of the sales message and are more likely to buy a product when a celebrity is behind it.

Event planners seek out highly visible people to attend corporate and civic events to draw a big crowd. You should try to invite some "celebrities" to key events for your business. Your celebrities can be high-profile people in your community like local politicians, media personalities, business leaders, and the like.

It gives your brand cachet if you have celebrity pals. Just being touched by a nationally recognized celebrity can burnish your brand, and it's something that we all seek out if we have a chance. Attendees line up to get their pictures taken with the well-known people at business, social, and political events, and many frame the pictures for the office or home. In his book

Enchantment!, author Guy Kawasaki included a picture of himself with Richard Branson, among other pictures.

Take the Hollywood Road

High visibility is often the strategy of choice for celebrities, television personalities, and sports stars, where the worth of their personal brand depends on mega visibility. Sometimes visibility is the only strategy for a celebrity (for example, Paris Hilton).

Celebrity-making involves positioning, image development, packaging, storyline, marketing messages, and PR just like breakthrough branding. Celebrities develop a marketing platform based on their movies, entertainment bookings, TV interviews, and product endorsements. After their prime, aging celebrities often develop new ways to extend their "shelf life" with tell-all books, speaking gigs, political activity, and other means to keep their celebrity brands visible to the public.

Celebrities (or their agents) are constantly on the lookout for opportunities for visibility that would be good for their brand. You should always be on the lookout for ways to increase your visibility that are compatible with your self-brand and your business.

Now, along with the rise of the celebrity CEO, there are the celebrity entrepreneur, celebrity chef, celebrity doctor, celebrity lawyer, celebrity hairdresser, you name it, who have marketing platforms and use high-visibility tactics. Frank Gehry and the Bilbao effect even gave rise to a new term: starchitect.

Build a Marketing Platform

With the expansion of media outlets, the Internet, and social media, businesspeople have lots of avenues for visibility.

Like celebrities, you must think in terms of building a *marketing platform*, a game plan for building and maintaining visibility in traditional and digital media, through important endorsements and alliances, and involvement in high-profile events.

MARKETING PLATFORM: having a range of traditional media, digital media, and other venues for building visibility for Brand You and your business.

You can enhance your visibility through interviews on network and cable television or in consumer and business publications. You can give speeches at industry or outside events. You can provide expert testimony. You can seek board seats at other companies. You can become involved with charities or causes.

Like entertainment and sports celebrities before them, businesspeople are pursuing line extensions outside their areas of expertise to expand their visibility. Buying a sports team, running for political office, or writing a book packs a high-visibility quotient.

Some businesspeople are even trespassing on celebrity turf by launching television shows, fueled by the success of Donald Trump and his reality show, *The Apprentice*. And there are publicity-driven CEOs, like Richard Branson, who have turned PR into an art form. Each is so adept at creating visibility and manipulating PR that he's in a class by himself.

No one is immune these days to the draw of visibility. In the past, academics were not known outside a small circle unless they published a best-selling book. Now, academics appear regularly on talk shows, speak around the country, and have memorable quips that are quoted in the media, not to mention being profiled in the alumni magazine.

Step-by-Step Toward Visibility

Begin with low-visibility tactics to get more visibility with your customers and in your industry. Brush up your presentation skills so that you are an effective speaker and communicator internally at meetings and externally at industry and other gatherings. The better you are at speaking and communicating, the more opportunities will come your way.

Look for ways to make your talks special, or set up a dramatic introduction to someone else. Think about how you enter a meeting. Don't ever rush in. Enter slowly, and if you are in a company where you can pull it off, you can even enter grandly.

When you talk about your ideas and proposals, use the branding techniques discussed earlier, like "naming" your ideas to make them big ideas and coining words and expressions. Look at the different types of story formats we discussed and how to weave in stories, anecdotes, and metaphors to bring your points to life.

Write an article for a trade magazine, or suggest a story idea about new trends or developments in your industry for business magazines and websites. Don't make the story about you or your business but about something broader in the marketplace that you and your company are involved in. Glory will flow back to you, and you won't appear self-promoting.

Visibility and the Intrapreneur

If you are employed in a company, you may not be able to talk about the company or your job to the outside media unless you are a senior executive and have been authorized to do so. You probably can't use high-visibility tactics unless you are involved in something outside your job, such as chairing a fundraising drive for a nonprofit or are active in a cause of personal interest to you.

But you can use a lot of low-visibility tactics to get more visibility within your company and your industry. Start by taking a more active role in volunteering for cross-functional projects at work. Ask to participate in or lead corporate initiatives, where you can make a contribution. Besides learning something new, you will come into contact with executives outside your area of the company. Even something low key, like setting up a monthly brown-bag lunch and inviting senior executives and outside vendors to speak, will help you get noticed outside your department. Social media like LinkedIn and Facebook can be great vehicles for building visibility, though, as with every visibility tactic, you should be very careful what you place on the Internet for general consumption.

Elizabeth is a business development executive at one of the world's leading technology companies, and she works across the converging worlds of Hollywood, Silicon Valley, and Wall Street. On the job, her goals are to execute large-scale business development efforts and high-velocity sales. Because corporate entrepreneurship and women's leadership are lifelong passions, she was appointed U.S. cochair of the Women in Technology group at a major division, where her mission is to attract, develop, and retain top female talent and to develop innovative external partnerships to help reach those goals. Elizabeth Hitchcock conceived and was part of the team that launched a Worldwide Speaker's Bureau to position its female leaders as speakers at conferences to attract women into technology, a growth industry in which women are sorely underrepresented.

Look at the comparison chart in the box below to see a list of high-visibility and low-visibility tactics used by entrepreneurs and intrapreneurs.

High-Visibility Tactics	*Low-Visibility Tactics*
Television show	Speaker/panelist trade shows
Television/cable interviews	Trade media interviews
Book	Trade articles
Keynote talks at business conferences	Local media interviews
Business media feature stories	Blog/website
Blog/website	Chair company initiative
Social media platforms	Social media platforms
High-profile charities	Local charities

Leadership Has Its Rewards

Superlatives rock. If you have a claim to leadership for your brand such as "the first brand to _____" or "the only brand to _____" or "the leading brand in _____," you have something very valuable for PR that can help propel your small business into big brand territory.

Leadership has advantages. As the leader with the biggest market share, you're likely to get more respect with more positive coverage by the media. You'll get more mental shelf space with customers and prospects. Once established, brand leaders are hard to topple.

Being perceived as a leader personally is powerful, too. You'll get more "shelf space" in that you will be on the short list for important projects and business deals. It will be easier to form alliances with important players in your industry and the business community. It's important to seek these relationships and alliances with peers and mentors.

Even if you're running a very small business today, you can brand your business and yourself as a leader by getting involved in leadership roles in professional associations or entrepreneur groups. Or you can begin by submitting articles to trade magazines or online forums or writing a blog that is noticed by your peers and your customers.

Leadership pays off. You're likely to be quoted in the trade press. Your peers will see you differently. A leader is in the inner circle—the winning circle. And the bigger the group you lead or the more influential the business group, the more prominent and valuable you will be. You may be invited to participate in high-profile business panels, give the keynote address at your industry conference, and even be invited to Davos, the ultimate global gabfest for CEOs, star entrepreneurs, and world leaders. Your position will be hard to topple, too.

As in the product world, personal leadership comes with a halo. When people view you as a leader, they bestow you with a host of positive attributes—and that can be a self-fulfilling prophecy. The perception of success actually brings about more success, because, after all, you *must* be better than others—you're a leader!

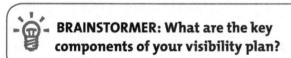

BRAINSTORMER: What are the key components of your visibility plan?

Cast a Role for Lady Luck

Luck is the big white lie behind most entrepreneurial success stores. While I believe that you create your own "luck," that doesn't mean you can't add a dollop of luck to your story. People attribute their success partially to luck, because it goes over much better that way than telling people the truth. Namely, that you have been working 24-7 on building the business and have suffered every hardship known to humankind.

Luck is a key element in most stories of achievement. Luck makes people look like they had not "planned" their success or used PR or managers to promote themselves. Many people think it is "wrong" somehow to go after success. It just isn't "right." Our motives should be more noble, such as changing the world for the better. (And they might be that, too!)

The reality in almost every case is the opposite. Almost no one achieves great things or becomes a well-known brand without wanting it and working very hard toward it. Strategy, creativity, and persistence have more to do with achieving success than luck.

People who achieve great things work smart to achieve what they do, often with the help of business coaches, branding experts, and public relations specialists. But to say you planned your success goes against the grain for most people. It isn't as dramatic as emphasizing those bouts of serendipity you had and compressing all the years of struggle and hard work.

But if you say, "Gee, I just got lucky. They needed an architect to design the new arts center, and I guess I was in the right place at the right time." Or, "I accidentally bumped into an old school chum on the Champs Elysées in Paris, and we got to talking…" Or "I dropped my sandwich into the petri dish and…" Then your story has all the ingredients for success.

Hard to Build and Quick to Ruin

Often, people at the top of their game get a false sense of invulnerability. In fact, they are more vulnerable. Realize that when you become a boldface name, you will be living in a fishbowl. People will be scrutinizing what you say and do more closely than when you were not so well known. Some will be looking for mistakes or questionable activities. Jealous competitors may try to take potshots at you.

And as much as the media likes to build people up, the media likes to take people down. The story of Ms. Big's fall from grace sells. So does the juicy scandal that Mr. Big got caught up in. It appeals to people's *schadenfreude*—delight in the misfortunes of others.

And you have a lot to lose. The name you spent a lifetime building can be tarnished, or even torn down, very quickly. Studies show that it takes a lot of promotion of "good acts" to build a reputation yet only a little promotion of a "bad act" to tarnish it.

That's why it's wise to adopt the mindset that there are no secrets and that people will find out everything. So if you're presented with something that would be truly destructive if it were known, let that "opportunity" pass you by. More than possessions, losing your reputation can severely damage your self-brand identity.

If you are about to get caught in a PR nightmare, try to take control of the story. The old PR saying goes, "Tell them everything and tell them first." If the news gets out in front of you, there are still things you can do, starting with an account of your side of the story. You have to give something up so that the news gets out of the news cycle.

Building visibility and a broad network are areas you need to master for breakthrough branding of your business brand and your self brand, whether your goal is to become well known in a national (or international) arena or a little bit famous in your industry and community.

When you have the right networking and visibility plan in place, you'll know it because:

You will be *known for something*, not as a self-promoter.
You'll be doing *favors for others* in the networking economy.
Many new networking acquaintances will *become friends*.
You will be able to build your *visibility with finesse* because you'll be
    doing it without seeming to be doing it.

Chapter 11

From Small Idea to Big Brand

"We are so busy measuring public opinion that we forget we can mold it. We are so busy listening to statistics we forget we can create them."

—Bill Bernbach, Legendary "Mad Man"

Rarely do things go as planned. The business world is dynamic. Markets change. The economy goes up and down. Customers develop new needs. New competitors spring up and give us the jitters.

Your passion for being an entrepreneur is what drew you in—don't lose sight of it by getting caught up in the minutiae. When you are starting out, it is natural to attend to every little problem. But too many entrepreneurs stay in start-up mode once they are up and running, micromanaging all aspects of the business.

Every day, you need to think of new ways to grow, new tactics to attract customers, and new product offerings to fortify yourself against competitors. You'll never find the time and energy to grow your brand if you've got your fingers in every detail. As a brand entrepreneur, you've got to focus on growth. If you have trouble remembering that, put a big sign over your desk with a dollar sign on it, and ask yourself, is what I'm doing right now leading to growth for the company, or is there something else I should be doing?

Many entrepreneurs get stuck in the small end of small business. A lot of small businesses are even "lifestyle businesses." They may even bring in good income for an individual or a small group of employees, and some small business owners want to keep it that way.

The problem with a lifestyle business is that it is very dependent on you and not on the brand or platforms that you can leverage for growth. You don't have the brand awareness, capital, or systems in place to attract big projects or expand to a larger marketplace. You're not building an asset that's scalable and that you can sell for much if you want to pull out.

If you have the mindset of a brand entrepreneur, you'll want to grow your small business into a big brand, and that will demand every resource you can muster and will require you to focus on growth strategies. It involves trial and error. You need to field test different products, services, messages, partnerships, and sales channels so you can continually expand your customer base. You need to explore both traditional and new media channels for marketing, learn what works, and ditch what doesn't.

The entrepreneurs building breakthrough brands in this book are different in so many ways, but they do have similarities in the way they approached building their small businesses into big brands. Following are the seven key drivers of growth they all share that can help you propel your brand's growth and build a breakthrough brand.

1. Brand Bold—For Your Business and Brand You

If you look at the rapid growth of U.K. beverage brand Innocent, clever breakthrough branding played a key role, from its different name and fresh look and feel, to its cheeky, fun personality in its marketing and its zany creation story. Fresh, indie branding along with a good product made it easy for customers to love the brand, and it drove success quickly. It's a successful indie brand that's even launched a series of books.

Building a business brand in tandem with your personal brand can help you double your impact and break through a cluttered, competitive marketplace, particularly if you have a telegenic personality like entrepreneur Gary Vaynerchuk.

While in college in 1995, Vaynerchuk discovered the Internet in a friend's dorm room and thought there had to be a way to help his dad sell more wine at his liquor store with this new medium.[1]

As a teenager, Vaynerchuk had hated working at his father's liquor store, since he was shunted to the basement to bag ice and do other chores. After a year of begging to go up to the main floor, Vaynerchuk was put on the floor to sell Kenwood Chardonnay over a busy Thanksgiving holiday, when he was only sixteen. Vaynerchuk isn't sure how much wine he sold that day, but he knew that he had found his place in the world—selling.

At the time, the store was called Shopper's Discount Liquors, and the store looked like its name. Vaynerchuk noticed that liquor buyers who came into the store knew exactly what brand they wanted to buy. But the wine buyers seemed lost. They didn't know what they should try. Vaynerchuk started to read *Wine Spectator* and other wine sources. Then, he started telling stories about the wines he liked. Now, he had truly found his calling.

Even in the early days of the Internet, Vaynerchuk saw that it could be a great vehicle for selling wine. He launched WineLibrary.com in 1998, and later his dad changed the name and location of the liquor store, so that it looked more upscale to match the Internet name.

(TM) **Cyberbranding gives you a big microphone, so you can speak to many every time you speak.**

In 2005, Vaynerchuk discovered social media, particularly video, after seeing a *Saturday Night Live* clip. The clip went viral online, and it got Vaynerchuk thinking about how he might use video to build a personal brand online to help grow the family wine business even more.

Vaynerchuk called his video blog *WineLibraryTV* and named the show "The Thunder Show."[2] In 2011, he changed the name of the show to "Daily Grape" and added new bells and whistles to engage viewers and promote wines.

The show's set is simple: a table, Vaynerchuk, and his "big-ass glass." The fifteen- to twenty-minute show is filmed unscripted and uncut to keep costs low and reality high. He doesn't even have a mic. He samples different bottles of wine and shares some historical facts and then talks about whatever comes into his head as he smells, swishes, and tastes the wine. Vaynerchuk comes across as a regular guy, with his plaid shirt and makeshift set. Vaynerchuk's Russian last name is long by naming standards, so his trademark introduction is to say his name slowly, clearly pronouncing each syllable: Vay—ner—chuk.

Vaynerchuk is spontaneous, fun, and has an interesting wine palate. With more than 80,000 viewers a day, the video blog has been a big sales generator for the family's wine business, taking it from $1 million to $2 million dollars a year in sales to $50 million dollars a year, with half of its sales online.

 Breakthrough branding is image building and relationship building.

For Vaynerchuk, the video blog isn't just about selling wine. It's about building his personal brand and a relationship with his customers and viewers. He's branched out from wine to giving business advice to entrepreneurs. He has a multi-book deal, and the first two, *Crush It!* and *The Thank You Economy*, have been business best sellers. As he does on his videos, in his book Vaynerchuk makes sure readers can say and spell his name by breaking it up on the cover as Vay•ner•chuk.

 BRAINSTORMER: How can you use new media and traditional media platforms to build your business and personal brands?

2. Try to Dominate the Category (or Create a New Category You Can Dominate)

Small brands that break through to grow big find a "small" idea that fills a gaping hole—a need in the marketplace that wasn't met before—and they keep filling that need so that they can dominate the market, especially since competitors will come along and try to copy that winning idea.

Sometimes it takes a little tinkering to find the white space, an arena you can dominate. You can always slice and dice to find a niche, a place that your brand can dominate. Think of how you can diverge from the main category to create a subcategory that you can dominate. You may not be able to dominate the whole household cleaner and laundry category, but you can launch a boutique household cleaner like the Mrs. Meyer's Clean Day brand that dominates the aromatheraputic household cleaner and laundry category, where ingredients come from the garden, not the chemistry lab.

You may even stumble upon a whole new category you can dominate that creates tremendous buzz and revolutionizes the way people shop, as Andrew Mason did.

Mason got interested in entrepreneurship early. Barely a teenager, he started a bagel delivery business. It was a pretty simple business. He bought the bagels at a steep discount, loaded them on his red Radio Flyer wagon, and sold them to customers at full price plus a delivery fee.[3]

In graduate school, Mason started developing a new fundraising and social action website based on the concept Malcolm Gladwell branded as the "tipping point." When a certain number of people had signed up, the offer would tip and be activated. Mason called his site The Point. The idea was noticed by a former boss, who gave Mason a million dollars to develop the site.

Most of Mason's efforts on The Point were aimed at social activism and didn't make much money. Before long, Mason's financial backer was pressuring him to monetize the site. The most poplar sections of The Point had to do with group buying, so that was the area he tried to monetize.

A partner of Mason's came up with the name Groupon, made from combining "group" and "coupon," the two key triggers of the flash-sale, group-buying concept.

On October 22, 2008, Mason launched his first Groupon offer, a two-for-one pizza deal at the bar below Groupon's office. Twenty-four people signed up. As he did other offers, Mason realized that it met a need in the market for deals in a bad economy, what he calls "recession chic."

 Creating a new category gives you a breakthrough advantage as the first mover.

Mason's flash-sale, deal-a-day business took off like a rocket. Groupon didn't just fill a consumer need for great local deals, but it met the needs of local businesses, too. So it had two target groups that were driving growth: individuals looking for great deals and shop owners who wanted to participate in Groupon deals because they were an inexpensive way to attract new customers. For the first time, small retailers had a cheap and easy way to acquire new customers at a lower cost of customer acquisition than anything else. According to Mason, "Groupon is a local advertising company for the digital age."[4]

In November 2010, Mason turned down a $6 billion acquisition offer for Groupon from Google. At that sum, it seemed crazy to turn the offer down, especially since copycats were duplicating Groupon's business model. Plus, Groupon was buying up competitors and had to keep expanding into new markets to maintain its dominant position. And Mason's gamble paid off. When Groupon did its IPO on November 4, 2011, it ended the day with a market value of $16.65 billion, and it was the largest public offering for an Internet company since Google's debut in 2004.

ⓉⓂ Find an arena you can dominate—even if it's very small at first.

J. Darius Bikoff found a very different need in the marketplace and a way to dominate the category that paid off big. Feeling rundown one day in 1996, he took vitamin C and drank some mineral water.

As he was drinking, he thought, "Yes, this is nice, vitamins and water. It got me thinking."[5] Bikoff founded Energy Brands in 1996, using his personal savings to do a contract with an aquifer in Connecticut to supply the base water.

Bikoff's beverage concept was to fill the gap between water and soft drinks. In essence, he was creating a new category—enhanced waters—that he could dominate. Bikoff was targeting adults, particularly people who knew they should be drinking more water but weren't. He wanted to create enhanced waters that hydrate and provide essential nutrients and that adults would like to drink. He branded his enhanced water products with the Glaceau name and called the first product, a vapor-distilled water with added electrolytes, Smartwater.

Bikoff was a first mover in enhanced waters, but the early days weren't easy. He had no experience in beverage manufacturing, other than working in an aluminum fabrication factory. He was also getting a divorce and had to file for bankruptcy.

But slowly, Bikoff started building his brand. He wanted to be under the radar of the large beverage companies, who he feared might copy his idea, so at first he distributed through health food stores. He gradually added mom-and-pop neighborhood food stores as he launched Fruitwater in 1998 and Vitaminwater in 2000.

By 2001, he had more than 4,000 retail stores in the New York area, but he was still not seen as a threat by the large beverage manufacturers because of his small-store focus. Then, Bikoff started cultivating independent distributors, planning to go national. In 2002, Glaceau was the top-selling brand of enhanced water because of the runaway success of his best-selling product, Vitaminwater.

Eventually, Bikoff took the classic route of many indie beverage entrepreneurs and first sold a stake in the company to Coca-Cola; in 2007, he sold the entire business to them. Under the purchase agreement, Bikoff and his team run the company independently. In 2008, Bikoff expanded Energy Brands into the United Kingdom, and he's gradually introducing the brand in markets around the world.

 BRAINSTORMER: How can you dominate the market?

3. Figure Out How to Grow and Scale the Business

It's hard to grow big if you can't scale your business. Businesses that scale have leverage. So if you spend more on marketing, R&D, and other operating costs, your revenue goes up at a higher rate, ideally many multiples of what you put in. If you put more money into operating costs and revenue increases at the same rate, then your business does not scale. In short, to scale, your cash flow has to grow more quickly than your expenses.

Technology businesses can be very scalable because you can develop a core set of assets, such as software systems and operations, and then you can monetize them at very low additional cost.

 Your business scales when additional money you put in leads to much higher revenues—a multiple of what you put in.

You also need to strategically determine how to scale your business, including what you can outsource and what you can't. In the early days, Zappos outsourced the shipping and handling for its online shoe business.

It turned out to be a huge mistake. When you think about it, their whole business is based on efficient shipping and handling of a vast variety of merchandise because Zappos has no physical stores. The ability to handle orders and ship merchandise quickly, accurately, and inexpensively is what the company is all about.

When Zappos ceded these processes to outsiders, customer complaints piled up, and there was little that Zappos employees could do to mollify their customers. The Zappos brand didn't take off until they took back control. Now, their motto is "Powered by Service"—and living up to it is their core priority.

Look at the scalability that Google has had with sub-brands like Android and its social networking site, Google+. In the first three weeks after its launch, Google+ had twenty million unique users and more than ten million registered users. And that's in the soft launch, by-invitation-only phase.

Of course, Google+ had a major head start, a large referral base fueled by the hundreds of millions of users of Google, Gmail, and YouTube. With Android, Google gave the software away to smartphone manufacturers so it could quickly scale.

Scalability can fuel growth in retail chains, manufacturers, and other businesses where you develop a winning business model with systems that you replicate or franchise in different markets. To be scalable, you need to build your business model not on people but systems, products, and procedures that can be replicated with reliable results in other markets.

 To scale, build your business on systems, products, and procedures that can be duplicated easily.

Sometimes, you have to create a new platform for your original business idea to scale and fuel growth as a breakthrough brand. U.S. entrepreneur David Overton found his brand magic in his mother's cheesecake recipe.[6]

When he was growing up in Detroit in the 1950s, Overton's mother, Evelyn, served her cheesecake to his dad's boss. The boss loved it so much that he asked her to make twelve cheesecakes to give away over the holidays. That success gave his mom the idea of starting a small cheesecake business in Detroit. Overton, his parents, and his sister worked part-time supplying cheesecake to two local restaurants.

In 1972, Overton's parents moved the cheesecake business to Los Angeles to be near Overton, who was trying to make it in the music business. Realizing he wasn't going to be a rock sensation, Overton decided to focus on expanding the cheesecake business.

Overton knew he had a winning recipe and the "Cadillac" of cheesecakes, but still he was frustrated. The business wasn't growing fast enough. It was hard to fuel growth on that one recipe, tasty though it was.

Then, the solution came to him. What about opening a restaurant to help sell the cheesecake? He named the restaurant The Cheesecake Factory. Now he had a brand name and a physical location to market the brand. He chose Beverly Hills for the first restaurant, to give the cheesecake a classy reputation, but with a twist. The area was known for fine dining, so Overton did the opposite and developed a casual-fare menu for his restaurant.

To prevent copycats, Overton created two barriers to entry: his mom's winning cheesecake recipe was one and the broadest, deepest casual-dining menu around was the other. Today it's a billion-dollar restaurant chain—all inspired by the special ingredients in his mother's cheesecake recipe and a restaurant model he was able to roll out in other markets.

 When you scale with franchising, come up with procedures to preserve the brand.

With its origins as a small burger joint in a suburban Virginia strip mall, Five Guys has become America's fastest-growing restaurant chain, with five new stores opening each week.[7] Even President Obama is a customer, and Zagat's rated Five Guys as having the "best fast-food burger for 2010."

When he started Five Guys in 1985, Jerry Murrell wanted to capture the authenticity of a burger joint in the small town in Michigan where he grew up. He had four sons who didn't want to go to college, so Murrell thought of using the money he had saved for college to start a burger business. He named it Five Guys after his four sons and himself. Five Guys initially focused on a small group of stores in the Washington, D.C., area. Then he had another son but kept the name, and he says it now refers to his five sons.

Five Guys created a new twist on the American classic, the hamburger. The burgers are not mass produced, like they are at McDonald's and Burger

King, but are made to order and served with large helpings of hand-cut fries. Each batch of fries is shaken fifteen times, no more, no less, to ensure they're just right by Five Guys standards. The company used a special bun from a local bakery that's eggier and sweeter than typical burger buns, and they now make the buns themselves. They are sticklers about the way a burger should be made: tomatoes and pickles go on top, onion and bacon go below the hamburger patty.

To underscore its down-home, not-mass-produced roots, Five Guys covers the walls of each restaurant in white and red tiles, leaves the kitchen open for everyone to see, and doesn't change the menu. Most Five Guys restaurants have sacks of potatoes very visible at the back of the store to underscore that the potatoes are hand peeled and fresh fried. The local farm that provided the potatoes is written in chalk on a chalkboard, and customers can munch on baskets of peanuts as they wait for their orders.

In 2002, Murrell's five sons convinced Murrell that they should franchise the business in order to grow, and that's led to explosive growth, with the chain now at more than 2,500 stores. Many franchisees are in sync with the brand, but some stores have been bought back by the Murrells to keep the stores true to the brand promise.

 BRAINSTORMER: What products, procedures, and systems can you develop to scale your business?

4. Enchant Your Customers

At the end of the day, you're only as good as your customers who love and appreciate you, as Five Guys and so many other breakthrough brands know. That's why having a special customer relationship model that's hard to copy can propel your business's growth.

Attentive restaurant service in China is easy to find in expensive, fine-dining establishments, and pretty much nonexistent in inexpensive eateries. That is, until Haidilao came along. Haidilao is a Chinese restaurant chain that specializes in hot pot cuisine, a fondue-like eating experience where you cook thinly sliced meat, seafood, and vegetables in a hot pot at your table.

Haidilao was started by Chinese entrepreneur Zhang Yong, a welder in a small town in Sichuan, the traditional home of hot pot cuisine in Southwest

China. He named the restaurant Haidilao after a term from the Chinese game of mahjong.

No restaurant in China has a better reputation for outstanding service and traditional culture than Haidilao. Because there are often long waits to get a seat, Zhang has a large waiting room in each restaurant where customers are offered free fruit, drinks, ice cream, board games, and television. All the waiters and waitresses have nicknames and only wait on a couple of tables at a time so they can give diners personal service.

 In today's new age of customer care, you need to redefine service to impress customers as part of breakthrough branding.

There are lots of stories about just how great the customer service is at Haidilao. One story that circulated in 2011 in China was about someone who ate dinner there but couldn't finish the fruit dessert. So the customer asked the waitress if he could take the leftover slices of watermelon home. The waitress said the policy at Haidilao didn't allow her to package cut-up fruit to take home. As the customer was leaving the restaurant, the waitress appeared with a whole watermelon and gave it to him to take home. The story surfaced on Weibo, China's Twitter clone, then went viral, as many people forwarded it to their friends.

Zhang has set up a rewards system of bonuses for employees who come up with good ideas on how to improve service. As a result, Haidilao has a turnover rate of about 10 percent compared with 28 percent for the hospitality industry in China.

Now, Zhang has more than sixty Haidilao restaurants in China, and this success story is taught at top Chinese business schools. There's even a top-selling business book, *Haidilao: You Can't Copy It*, about Haidilao's unique customer service model.[8] No wonder Haidilao has created the same intense excitement and following that drew people to McDonald's and KFC when they were first introduced in China.

 BRAINSTORMER: How can you enchant your customers?

5. Put "Growth Agent" in Everyone's Job Title

Business success is a peer-to-peer collaborative process. You can't do it all yourself and you can't be good at everything. There's always someone smarter than you. You'll also find that it's one thing to lead a team and have a strong culture when it's just a handful of employees and quite another when you have to lead a hundred or more people.

Mark Pincus, the founder and CEO of Zynga, the online social game company, found leading relatively easy when his company was small. When it grew to 150 and beyond, Pincus initially had trouble figuring out how to keep everyone productive when he wasn't around.

One day, Pincus put white sticky sheets on the walls and told his employees, "By the end of the week, everyone needs to write what you're CEO of, and it needs to be something meaningful."[9] The lesson Pincus learned was that if you empower people with a big job, they may be a bit scared at first, but they'll find it more fun, and the business gets better faster.

Pincus also uses O.K.R.s to motivate his team and get results. O.K.R. stands for "objective" and "key results" and is a practice used by companies to keep everyone focused on one key objective and three measurable key results.

 O.K.R.s: Objective and Key Results. Have each employee develop one key objective and three key results weekly.

Pincus found that if you achieve two of the three key results, you achieve your objective. If you achieve all three, you've crushed it. At Zynga, everyone knows his O.K.R.s, and this keeps employees focused on the three things that matter, not fifteen things.

Pincus makes it a practice to ask key employees what their three key results are at the beginning of each week and asks them to follow up on Friday with how well they did. In 2009, Zynga grew from 181 employees and 34 million unique visitors at the beginning of the year to 564 employees and 235 million unique visitors by the end of the year. In 2011, Pincus took Zynga public.

Getting the right team focused on the right tasks can dramatically turn around the business dynamics, as the two companies that bought

Skype from eBay discovered. In September 2009, Silver Lake Partners and Andreessen Horowitz bought Skype for $2.75 billion. In May 2011, they sold Skype to Microsoft for $8.5 billion.

How did they increase the value of the company $6 billion in two years?

First, the firms led by Andreessen Horowitz won the confidence of Skype's founders, Niklas Zennstrom and Janus Friis, who owned the rights to the Skype software.[10] The founders sold the new owners the rights for a stake in Skype.

Second, the team brought new management on board, switching out twenty-nine of Skype's top thirty managers. With new talent in place, Skype developed a new vision, new features like smartphone apps, and new partnerships, such as its alliances with Facebook and Verizon, which unlocked tremendous value.

 BRAINSTORMER: How can you make growth and breakthrough brand building a part of everyone's job?

6. Strike the Right Balance between Innovation and Staying True to the Brand

It can be hard to recognize the next hot trend or breakthrough brand because it seems so radically different or the source of the idea is a newcomer. Look how many publishers turned down the Harry Potter books before they found a home and became a runaway success. The same thing happened to Italian rubber sole company Vibram.

Vibram is named after its founder, Vitale Bramani, and is run today by his grandson, Marco Bramani. The company was known mainly for its quality rubber soles used in mountaineering and hiking boots. In 2005, Vibram's U.S. CEO, Tony Post, approached shoe makers in the United States about partnering on producing a radically new five-toe lightweight shoe. The shoe style, with its molded five toes, was so strange that everyone turned Post down. Then he approached retailers. They also gave him a thumbs-down. Nobody was interested.[11]

So Vibram produced the shoe itself, using a breakthrough design by Italian industrial designer Robert Fliri. A mountaineer, Fliri conceived the shoe as a glove for the foot that would mimic the feeling of running barefoot. Vibram named the shoes FiveFingers. Vibram CEO Bramani wasn't sure what the shoes could be used for. Not an athlete himself, Bramani thought they might be good to wear on his boat.

U.S. CEO Post, an avid runner, saw something different than his boss did, and his vision was more akin to Fliri's concept. When Post tested them, he noticed that the shoes allowed his feet to move more naturally and react to the environment. Plus, they relieved his knee pain.

Post positioned FiveFingers as a performance product perfect for fitness training and running and launched the shoes at the Boston Marathon in 2006. Post led the product development team to create new styles for the training and running markets. He created a viral marketing campaign to spread the word in fitness and running circles. Today, Vibram's FiveFinger Facebook page has more than 75,000 fans, and its website has recorded over a million page views in a day. Several well-known professional athletes became fans of the funny-toed shoes and that attracted a lot of attention.

Since its introduction, FiveFingers has seen its sales more than triple each year. In 2011, Vibram expects to sell some $100 million-worth of FiveFingers shoes.

In 2007, *Time* magazine named the shoes one of the year's best health inventions. A big driver of FiveFingers' success was the rise of barefoot running, fueled by Christopher McDougall's best-selling book, *Born to Run*, in 2009. One of the characters in the book is Barefoot Ted (McDonald), whose funny FiveFingers shoes are the focus of a subplot in the book. The next year, a 2010 Harvard study published in *Nature* magazine reported that barefoot runners land on the balls of their feet rather than the heels, and this resulted in less joint stress and fewer injuries.

Instead of leading to a downturn in running shoe sales, the barefoot craze jump-started running shoe sales. It led to the trend toward less shoe and the creation of new running shoe categories such as the minimalist shoe category in 2008 and the lightweight shoe category in 2009, the two areas driving running shoe sales today.

Vibram, once known as a supplier of outsole components for rugged sports, has rebranded itself into manufacturer of cutting-edge finished footwear that has transformed the fitness, running, and outdoor industries. And it's in a race to protect its brand from competitors copying FiveFingers' innovations.

Breakthrough branding involves risk and reward.

It's one thing to launch a successful business and quite another to celebrate the one-hundred-year anniversary of the same business. Business is a long-term game and takes determining the right balance of tradition and innovation. Granted, you will win some years and not do so well others, but you always have to stay focused on what your brand is and what it is not. The business highway is littered with dead businesses and dead brands. Some brands founder because their product is a fad, like Silly Bandz, Rubik's Cubes, and Pet Rocks. Others branch out in new directions and forget the brand promise that made them great in the first place.

Orphaned in his teens, Leon Leonwood Bean devised a boot that he called the Maine Hunting Shoe, which he sold through a simple three-page mailer to holders of Maine hunting licenses. He named his company L.L.Bean and gradually added other items, like a field coat, a chamois shirt, and a canvas boat bag.

L.L.Bean is still going strong today as an independent, family-run business. It has bested other outdoor suppliers, like Eddie Bauer, which built its business around a down jacket and went through many incarnations over the years.[12] It has bested Abercrombie & Fitch, which opened twenty years before L.L.Bean and closed down in 1977, selling its name to The Limited. It has bested Lands' End, which has gone through bankruptcy twice.

Rather than chase the trend of the day, L.L.Bean has remained true to its ancient roots, still selling its Maine Hunting Boot and other iconic outdoor wear. Its years of explosive growth took place under Bean's grandson Leon Gorman, who grew the business from $4 million in 1967 to $1 billion in sales in 2001 when he stepped down. Gorman revitalized the brand by doing market research, increasing mail-order sales, and modernizing the company's operations. Today, L.L.Bean is still selling the one thing that many of its competitors forgot—authenticity.

 Build your business on what you know better than anyone else.

While L.L.Bean stayed true to Maine and to his hunting roots, Will Chase's fortune lay in Herefordshire and potatoes. Dropping out of school at fourteen, Chase went to work on his father's potato farm. Later,

Chase bought the farm, struggled as a potato farmer, and went through bankruptcy.

Discouraged with low prices from the supermarket chains, which began to source cheaper potatoes in Eastern Europe, in 2002, Chase had a small idea, a premium potato chip that was "home grown and hand fried."[13] He bought an oil cooker from a fish and chips store and started production in his kitchen.

Chase named the product Tyrrells Chips after the family farm, Tyrrells Court Farm. He decided to brand them as "chips," in the American fashion, rather than as "crisps," the British term, not to give the product foreign glamour but to telegraph that it was different from mass-produced crisps.

Crisps are made by cutting potatoes very thinly, removing the starch, and cooking the potatoes in a continuous frying batch process. The product is pretty bland and has to be enhanced with chemicals and flavoring. Tyrrells Chips are "cooked on the farm" and go from the field to the kitchen, where they are hand cut and fried in small batches by a cook the same day.

Tyrrells Chips were a huge success in the United Kingdom. In 2003, Chase introduced Parsnip Chips, followed by Mixed Root Vegetable Chips. The packaging features unusual images for salty snacks food packaging, such as vintage photographs, some altered to include oversized illustrations of vegetables; four naked ladies dance on the front of the Naked Chips (no salt). Later, proud of its English roots, Tyrell's decided to embrace local nomenclature and now labels its snacks "crisps," noting that they are "the proper English crisp."[14]

In 2008, Chase sold a major stake in Tyrrells to a private equity firm and launched a distillery to make potato vodka. Chase Vodka is the only English potato vodka in the world. You may laugh, but Chase won the top prize at the 2010 San Francisco World Spirits Competition, beating out Diddy's French-produced Ciroc, as well as Russian and Scandinavian entrants. Chase is expanding with other spirits, all high-margin premium brands distilled in Herefordshire, United Kingdom, which are traditional, authentic, and innovative at the same time.

7. Take Advantage of Good Luck and Bad

The Valley of Death—the start-up period when entrepreneurs struggle to find financing, customers, and resources—creates many obstacles that must be jumped, run around, or overcome. It's your most vulnerable time but also your most opportunistic time, because it is the time when you can create tremendous value for your brand.

Entrepreneur Robin Cook worked at large companies like Procter & Gamble and got his business idea because his wife hated paying the bills. "I had been trained at P&G to find a problem everybody has and that you could solve with technology."[15]

Cook hired a computer science student from Stanford University, who became his cofounder, to study the twenty-plus financial software products on the market. The leading products were slow and didn't work well.

The two named the company Intuit and called their first personal financial software product Quicken. They couldn't get much start-up capital from venture capitalists, so Cook financed the business with about $500,000 of personal savings and retirement money. The business almost went under twice in the early years. They couldn't get stores to carry the product, since they didn't have a marketing budget.

So Cook found an alternate distribution channel. He sold the Quicken software to banks, who would resell it to customers. That gave the company a short financial lifeline to last another year.

Then Cook turned to magazine advertising, using an ad agency. The ad didn't pull in enough business to cover the cost of the media buy. A friend taught Cook how to write a direct-response ad, and he ran it with a toll-free number that drew in orders and profits. Today, Intuit is the leading financial and accounting software company with successful products like Quicken, QuickBooks, and TurboTax.

Breakthrough branding is seeing an opportunity that others overlook.

Sometimes a sprinkling of good luck after bad, along with pluck, can propel your business idea into a breakthrough brand. In 1977, Bill Rasmussen hit rock bottom. He lost his job selling commercial time for the New England Whalers, a World Hockey Association team in Connecticut. To top it off, his son Scott, who was the Whalers' public address announcer, also got the boot.

Without a lot of prospects, the Rasmussens decided to be entrepreneurs. Their small idea was based on their sports obsession. Cable television was just starting at the time. So they began thinking about starting a cable channel focused entirely on Connecticut sports, something they knew and loved.

When they met with a sales rep from RCA's satellite division, the Rasmussens learned they would be able to beam their signal across the whole United States. The rep, Al Parinello, recalled, "They might have been getting sexually excited, I'm not sure. But I can tell that they were very, very excited."[16]

The father-son team realized their small idea for a Connecticut sports channel could be a bit bigger. It could be a cable sports channel covering the whole country.

The Rasmussens called their cable TV network the Entertainment and Sports Programming Network, now referred to solely by its acronym, ESPN. Rather than set up shop in the typical media meccas of New York City or Los Angeles, they set up ESPN in the sleepy town of Bristol, Connecticut, near the Rasmussens' home. In the early days, ESPN was run by the Rasmussens and Stuart Evey, an executive with Getty Oil, the company that bankrolled the network in its early days.

ESPN's trademark show, *SportsCenter*, was launched at the beginning. To fill twenty-four hours a day, ESPN aired college football and basketball games and the sporting events that the networks didn't show, like professional boxing and wrestling. Through the years, they added professional sports like NCAA basketball. (ESPN smartly copyrighted the phrase "March Madness.")

For years, sports commentators and executives hated living in Bristol or even going there, because it was remote and unexciting, but today pro athletes consider it an honor to be invited to Bristol to star in an ESPN "This is *SportsCenter*" ad. Now part of the Disney empire, ESPN has multiple cable channels, a magazine, a radio network, the NFL's *Monday Night Football*, and an avidly followed sports website.

 BRAINSTORMER: What opportunities can adversity lead you to?

Protect Your Brand Assets

The big brands go to great lengths of protect their brand innovations and intellectual property, and so should you.

Moving out West to take advantage of the opportunities of the Internet in its early days, Jeff Bezos settled his company in Seattle. Bezos is an innovative brand entrepreneur who thought of building a big brand every step of his journey. He even looked for a house with a garage so he could say that he had a garage start-up like Hewlitt-Packard, Jobs-Wozniak, and other Silicon Valley tech legends.[17]

At first, he called his internet retailer Cadaba, but when someone thought the name was "Cadaver," Bezos jettisoned it and took the name Amazon. With little money, he didn't advertise much except for a clever and relatively inexpensive ad campaign. He hired mobile billboards to drive by Barnes & Noble stores with a large sign, "Can't find that book you wanted?" It created quite a stir and drove traffic to the Amazon website.

Early on, against the advice of professionals, Bezos allowed customers to post negative reviews. Competitors thought he was crazy. Why would a retailer unsell something he was trying to sell? But Bezos was a counterintuitive entrepreneur and realized, correctly, that he would do more business by creating a must-read forum for making buying decisions.

Bezos is relentless about protecting his innovations. He introduced 1-Click ordering, an innovation that one law journal called "unoriginal software patent." I don't think Bezos cares about that review. Today, you have to pay Amazon a royalty if you want to use a 1-Click ordering option.

Recently, Bezos applied for a new patent: a way to return a gift before it arrives. If you have a relative or friend who gives you unwanted gifts, you can list the person's name, and Amazon will do an intercept and convert all gifts from that person before they are mailed. You can also set up a gift intercept on other criteria, such as "no clothes with man-made fibers." It's a patent that's sure to save Amazon tons of money on mailing charges. The patent cites Mr. Bezos as the inventor.

An Entrepreneur for All Seasons

In order to stay at the helm as your company moves from small idea to breakthrough brand, you need to make the transitions from early-stage start-up to rapid growth to a more mature public phase.

Here are the key drivers for each phase and how you need to grow along with your business brand.

1. The Early-Stage Brand: The Enterprising Entrepreneur

Early-stage brands are in the discovery mode. The early stage is an unstructured period that needs a flexible entrepreneur who can experiment and innovate when everything is fluid and unformed. You need to be a bootstrapper who can operate and turn on a dime.

Key tasks:

▶ Figure out what the brand is and what needs it fulfills in the marketplace
▶ Develop your vision for the business
▶ Overcome obstacles with few resources
▶ Attract early-stage investors, partners, and employees

Classic example: Just about every entrepreneur working anywhere on a business start-up.

2. The Rapid-Growth Brand: The Brand Entrepreneur

The hurly-burly of the rapid-growth phase is an exhilarating ride. You're in an offensive role, launching an attack against the leader and trying to steal market share and break through to being a big brand. You need to develop the brand along with everything else, and you can't micromanage every detail like you could in phase one.

Key tasks:

▶ Develop, manufacture, and distribute the brand's product
▶ Set up systems, structures, and relationships to propel growth
▶ Attract the right talent and establish a vibrant culture
▶ Develop your personal brand to help build the business brand
▶ Attract investors

Classic example: Steve Jobs at Apple, who managed to keep his brands in a rapid-growth phase with lots of cutting-edge products.

3. The Leadership Brand: The Leader Entrepreneur

In the mature-leadership phase of a brand, the brand is still growing, but the rate of growth slows. You're a leader and have an important role in defending your brand's leadership position in the marketplace.

Key tasks:

- ▶ Develop strategies to fend off new competitors
- ▶ Add new bells and whistles to stay ahead of the pack
- ▶ Set up barriers to entry for new competitors
- ▶ Play visible role as industry leader and spokesperson

Classic example: Bill Gates and Steve Ballmer of Microsoft.

4. The Declining Brand: Turnaround Entrepreneur

Usually, brands go through a period of decline, particularly if the founding entrepreneur has left and the original vision of the company has been lost. A special kind of "entrepreneur" is needed at this phase, a turnaround leader who can create something new out of something old.

Key tasks:

- ▶ Revitalize the company
- ▶ Develop a new vision for the future
- ▶ Reorganize and possibly downsize to focus on the company's key jewels
- ▶ Get the right team who can lead the business to new heights

Classic example: Louis Gerstner, who turned around IBM.

The Art of Breakthrough Branding

As much as we might like entrepreneurship or branding to be a science, because it would be simpler that way, it is not. Being a brand entrepreneur, like establishing a brand, is an ever-changing art without easy formulas.

Breakthrough branding may defy carved-in-stone rules, but there are core principles that form the foundation for building any successful enterprise. The wonderful thing about branding and entrepreneurship is that each door you open leads to another hallway full of other doors to open.

It's a journey that will continue until you decide to end it. You can't rest on your laurels and say, "I'm done." Rather, as a brand entrepreneur, you must always be thinking about the next step, the next turn, the next stone in the road, the next phase of your business, and the next phase of your branding. You must always be tweaking your product lineup and finding new ways to grow, new tactics to use to attract new customers, new ways to fend off your competitors, and new ways to do breakthrough branding.

There will always be new problems, new challenges, and new competitors. But there will also be new customers with new needs, presenting new opportunities to tweak your brand, explore a new market, or enchant your customers.

Emergent digital technologies may disrupt your marketing strategy, but once you get your feet wet, you'll find you have a new—and possibly exhilarating—tool in your kit. It's a cliché, but a true one: the only constant is change. And isn't that what makes the entrepreneurial and branding journey interesting?

Say Yes!

The password for entering the entrepreneur crowd is "Yes!"

Realizing the power of yes is easy. What's hard is really harnessing that power—because we're trained from childhood to reject things that seem wild and out of the ordinary. We're wired to see the obstacles, not the cracks.

The breakthrough branding mindset is both strategic and creative and realizes that ideas can come from anywhere. The best ideas often come when two things collide. Look at how many ideas came from a casual observation or an accident or watching the water line rise when sitting in a tub. (Come to think of it, that was the original "Eureka" moment!) Or when you meet someone new or see a demo of a new device or notice an interesting marketing campaign, something is triggered in your mind that leads to a new insight.

Accidental meetings happen all the time. Patterns exist everywhere.

Things that don't work well are in plentiful supply. Traditional approaches often fail. New technologies and new media are being launched every day. There are always creative ways you can tweak and market your brand. There are always new strategies you can explore and tactics you can test in your quest for breakthrough branding.

You'll know you're on your way to growing your small business into a big brand when:

You pick yourself up after setbacks and *find new ways to grow* your brand.

You're building a *breakthrough business brand and a breakthrough personal brand.*

You've created a *special culture of growth agents* and growth is everyone's job.

You *never, ever give up.*

You look at the same things that everyone else looks at and say, *"Yes!"*

From Madison Avenue to Wall Street to the halls of academe, Catherine Kaputa perfected her ability to market products, places, and companies. Catherine first learned brand strategy from marketing gurus Al Ries and Jack Trout at Trout & Ries Advertising. Early in her career she led the award-winning "I ♥ NY" campaign at Wells, Rich, Greene.

For over ten years, Catherine was senior vice president, director of advertising and community affairs at Citi Smith Barney and Shearson Lehman Brothers, in charge of global branding and advertising for corporate, wealth management, and investment banking. And Catherine developed and taught a course on branding and advertising at New York University's Stern School of Business.

Catherine came to appreciate that branding's potential was to help people, not just products. Branding can help individuals to define and own their career identities and create their own performance success. That's why Catherine launched SelfBrand LLC (*www.selfbrand.com*), a New York City–based branding company, and wrote the award-winning book *You Are a Brand! How Smart People Brand Themselves for Business Success*, winner of the Ben Franklin Award for Best Career Book, a bronze IPPY award, and a Top 10 Employee Training Book in China (Chinese language edition). In addition to Chinese, the book has been translated into German, Korean, Japanese, Czech, and other languages. (See www.youareabrandbook.com)

Catherine's last book, on women achieving leadership success, is *The Female Brand: Using the Female Mindset to Succeed in Business* (*www.femalebrand.com*).

Catherine is active as a speaker, workshop leader, and business coach. In her talks and workshop, she specializes in offering dynamic and fun presentations on personal branding, women's leadership, and brand building to a wide range of organizations as part of motivational and group meetings, personal development, sales training, diversity, and women's initiatives.

She also does breakthrough branding programs for entrepreneurs and intrapreneurs who want to transform a small idea into a big brand. She works in various formats: as a keynote speaker, workshop leader, or panel moderator.

Catherine is also a business coach to executives, high-potential employees, and entrepreneurs who are talented and good at what they do but want to work one-to-one in a confidential relationship to maximize their talents and brilliance.

Catherine has been featured on CNN, NBC, and MSNBC, and in *Fortune, The New York Times, The Wall Street Journal, USA Today, The Financial Times*, and *The London Observer*, as well as other media.

Catherine's speaking clients include PepsiCo, Microsoft, Intel, Citi, UBS, KeyBank, Commerz Bank, Unilever, Time Warner, Con Ed, Cardinal Health, Marsh, AT&T, Dow Jones, and others.

SelfBrand is a certified WBENC women's business enterprise.

To learn more, visit Catherine's website, *www.selfbrand.com*, and her blog, *www.artofbranding.com*. You can follow her on Twitter @catherinekaputa and find her on Facebook at Catherine Kaputa. To talk to Catherine about speaking at your event or her coaching services, e-mail *catherinekaputa@gmail.com* or contact *selfbrandpr@gmail.com*. Catherine is always eager to hear from readers who want to comment on the book or share stories.

Acknowledgments

Writing a book is a journey. It's mainly an enjoyable journey, but there are always bits where it seems like the journey is never going to end. Thanks to the encouragement and support of family, friends, and colleagues, the journey does end.

This book couldn't have happened without the family that surrounds me, my husband, Mike, and our son, Ramsey, who got used to me banging away on my laptop early in the morning and late at night. My three sisters, Jean, Joan, and Kevin, are good friends and supporters on this and every other endeavor.

Most of my inspiration in writing this book came from entrepreneurs and intrapreneurs whose stories of launching, branding, and building a business always amaze me. Their individual creation stories for their businesses are as varied as their personalities. Most of them are not people I know personally, but with blogging and social media, I often feel that I do. They are my heroes, all the entrepreneurs and intrapreneurs building businesses around the world.

While the ideas written in this book were written by me, they are not exclusively mine. Al Ries and Jack Trout gave me my first job in branding and advertising, and their thinking, words, and advice are reflected in the book, particularly in my discussion of positioning and brand strategy. Many other books and teachers have inspired me. A recent favorite is Nick Morgan's wonderful book *Give Your Speech, Change the World*, which influenced my discussion of pitching and story in Chapter 9 and now is a constant inspiration as I prepare for every talk.

In helping me develop as a writer and speaker, I want to name Gary Andrew Gulkis, who has the poet's appreciation of words. Gary has not only been been generous with his time, ideas, and wordsmithing, but he pushes me to think bigger and more originally. I also want to name my speaking coach, Tim Davis, who has the comedian's gift for expression. Tim has been persistent in helping me develop my own voice and style and seek fresh examples, stories, and modes of expression. Both Gary and Tim were always willing to take a phone call asking for help on how to make a passage or point in the book more interesting. They both helped me make the book better. I also need to thank Elizabeth Hitchcock, an extraordinary corporate entrepreneur, who's the real deal, brilliantly talented and most generous in every way. Thanks, Gary, Tim, and Elizabeth!

Thanks also to all those friends, colleagues, and entrepreneurs who supported me in writing this book with suggestions, advice, or introductions, including Faith Monson, Jeffrey LaRiche, Sharon Goldenberg, Tom Blanco, Joanne Wilson, Sherrill Smith, Nomi Bachar, Margaret Yelland, Sherry Glazer, Diane Morgan, Marjorie James, Barbara Krafte, Kevin Allen, Harvey Cohen, Laura Berkowitz Gilbert, Pearl Chen, Joe Fabio, and Cathy Lewis.

I also want to thank personal friends who kept me on track when the book writing journey seemed endless, particularly Mary V. Kapka, who edited some of the early chapters. I also appreciate the help of Mengxun Wang and Acong Xi, who were interns at SelfBrand LLC and provided help in researching the Chinese entrepreneurs cited in the book and translating key sources, as well as Laura Ross, who edited several of the chapters and improved them greatly. A special thanks to Jill Klein who prepared marketing materials for this book and SelfBrand talks.

Most especially, I want to thank my publisher, Nicholas Brealey. This is my third book with my publisher, so I am starting to feel like family. Thanks, Nick, for believing in me and this book! And thanks to the rest of the Nicholas Brealey team, especially Vanessa Descalzi, Jennifer Delaney, and Wendy Mainardi for making the editing, production, and marketing process run so smoothly. Thanks also to Susan Lauzau for copyediting the book so skillfully.

Finally, I want to cite the inspiration of my late parents, Carmen and Edward Kaputa, who always told me that I could do anything I set my mind to and to never, ever give up. That's good advice for writing a book as well as being an entrepreneur.

To all of these people, I am deeply grateful.

Introduction

1. Ellen Byron, "Diaper Gripes Grow Louder for P&G," *The Wall Street Journal*, May 14, 2010.

Chapter 1

1. Jim Stenger, *Grow: How Ideals Power Growth and Profit at the World's Greatest Companies* (New York: Crown Business, 2011).
2. http://www.youtube.com/watch?v=iw4BDdoTTcQ for Paul Bloom and his TED talk, "The Origins of Pleasure"; see also his book: Paul Bloom, *How Pleasure Works* (New York: Norton, 2010).
3. Sandra Lee Semi-Homemade, accessed October 23, 2011, www.semihome-made.com
4. Dinah Eng, "The Creative Spark Behind the Viking Oven," *Fortune*, January 17, 2011, 46.
5. Colleen Debase, "Launching Gilt Groupe, A Fashionable Enterprise," *The Wall Street Journal*, December 12, 2010.
6. Tony Hsieh, *Delivering Happiness* (New York: Business Plus, 2010).
7. Jessica Shamboru, "The Honest Tea Guys Look Back," *Fortune*, July 26, 2010, http://money.cnn.com/2010/07/21/smallbusiness/honest_tea_guys_look _back.fortune/index.htm.
8. Elizabeth Olson, "Can Honest Tea Say No to Coke, Its Biggest Investor?" *The New York Times*, July 10, 2010.
9. Daniele Douglas, "Coke Buys Bethesda's Honest Tea," *The Washington Post*, March 1, 2011.
10. Susan Berfield, "Forever 21's Fast (and Loose) Fashion Empire," *Bloomberg Businessweek*, January 24–30, 2011, 91–96.
11. Party Pieces, accessed October 23, 2011, www.partypieces.co.uk.
12. David Kirkpatrick, "Twitter Was Act One," *Vanity Fair*, April 2011, http:// www.vanityfair.com/business/features/2011/04/jack-dorsey-201104.

13. Michal Lev-Ram, "A Twitter Guy Takes on Banks," *Fortune*, February, 7, 2011, 37.

14. Austin Ramzy, "Charles Chao," *Time*, April 21, 2011, http://www.time.com/time/specials/packages/article/0,28804,2066367_2066369_2066392,00.html.

15. Marc Cenedella, accessed October 20, 2011, www.marccenedella.com.

16. Beth Kowitt, "Inside Trader Joe's," *Fortune*, September 6, 2010, 86–96.

17. Ibid.

18. Naomi Schaefer Riley, "What They're Doing After Harvard," *The Wall Street Journal*, July 10–11, 2010.

Chapter 2

1. Lane Wallace, "Multicultural Critical Theory. At B-School?" *The New York Times*, January 10, 2010.

2. Ibid; Melissa Korn and Joe Light, "On the Lesson Plan: Feelings," *The Wall Street Journal*, June 7, 2011.

3. Christina Binkley, "Wanted: a Second Chance," *The Wall Street Journal*, June 9, 2011.

4. "Chris Dawson—The Management Today Interview," The Range, accessed September 20, 2011, http://www.therange.co.uk/fcp/content/chris_dawson_the_boy_done_good/content.

5. Lauren A. E. Schuker, "Struggling Oprah Network to Name New CEO: Oprah," *The Wall Street Journal*, July 13, 2011.

6. Nick Paumgarten, "Food Fighter," *The New Yorker*, January 4, 2010, 36–47.

7. Evan Osnos, "The Han Dynasty," *The New Yorker*, July 4, 2011, http://www.newyorker.com/reporting/2011/07/04/110704fa_fact_osnos.

8. Ibid.

9. Jon Chesto, "Zen and the Art of Zipcar Naming," *The Patriot Ledger*, October 22, 2010.

10. Michael V. Copeland, "Reed Hastings: Leader of the Pack," *Fortune*, November 18, 2010, see: http://tech.fortune.cnn.com/2010/11/18/reed-hastings-leader-of-the-pack/; Michael Blanding, "The Mind of the Entrepreneur," *One Magazine*, Johns Hopkins Carey School of Business, Fall/Winter 2010 http://carey.jhu.edu/one/2010/fall/the-mind-of-the-entrepreneur/.

11. Brian Stelter, "Netflix, in Reversal, Will Keep Its Services Together," *The New York Times*, October 10, 2011.

12. "Being Steve's Boss," *Bloomberg Businessweek*, October 25–31, 2010, 95–99.

Chapter 3

1. Al Ries and Jack Trout, *Positioning: The Battle for Your Mind* (New York: McGraw-Hill, 1981), 3. During my years working for Al Ries and Jack Trout

at their agency, positioning became the buzzword of branding and advertising people, and Al and Jack led the charge on the importance of strategy, not just creativity, in brand success. Working for them has greatly influenced my discussion of brand strategy and positioning.

2. Tony Hsieh, *Delivering Happiness: A Path to Profits, Passion and Purpose* (New York: Business Plus, 2010).
3. Duff McDonald, "The Mastermind of Adrenaline Marketing," *Bloomberg Businessweek*, May 23–29, 2011, 63–70.
4. Ben Paynter, "The Sweet Science," *Fast Company*, April 25, 2011, 112–117. http://www.fastcompany.com/magazine/155/the-sweet-science.html.
5. John Lyons, "Skin-Deep Gains for Amazon Tribe," *The Wall Street Journal*, May 5, 2011.
6. John Colapinto, "Strange Fruit," *The New Yorker*, May 30, 2011, 37–43.
7. Lauren Coleman-Lochner, "Estée Lauder Tries a Hair Makeover," *Bloomberg Businessweek*, April 11–17, 2011, 19.
8. "The Baidu Story," Baidu, accessed June 20, 2011, http://ir.baidu.com/phoenix.zhtml?c=188488&p=irol-homeprofile.
9. Peter Savodnik, "Bigger, Stronger, Richer," *Bloomberg Businessweek*, May 2–8, 2011, 65–67.
10. Matt Ridley, "Three Cheers for the Cheapeners and Cost-Cutters," *The Wall Street Journal*, May 7, 2011.
11. Christina Binkley, "Charity Gives Shoe Brand Extra Shine," *The Wall Street Journal*, April 1, 2010.
12. Dinah Eng, "The Rise of Cirque du Soleil," *Fortune*, November 7, 2011, 39–42.
13. Christopher Kimball, "An American in Paris," *The Wall Street Journal*, December 4–5, 2010.
14. Chrinstina Passariello, "The Illusionist of French Gastronomy," *The Wall Street Journal*, September 17–18, 2011.
15. Sidney Frank, "How I Did It," *Inc.*, September 1, 2005, http://www.inc.com/magazine/20050901/qa.html.
16. "Loro Piana and Vicuna Fur," *The Wall Street Journal*, February 21, 2007.
17. Leslie Robarge, "The Adult Soda," *Bloomberg Businessweek*, June 20–26, 2011, 80.

Chapter 4

1. "Company Name Influences Stock Performance," National Science Foundation, accessed http://www.nsf.gov/discoveries/disc_summ.jsp?cntn_id=107045.
2. Alexandra Jacobs, "Smooth Moves," *The New Yorker*, March 28, 2011, 60.

3. Spanx, accessed September 10, 2011, http://www.spanx.com/helpdesk/index.jsp?display=store&subdisplay=product#16.

4. Clifford Schorer, "Blow: The New York Blow Dry Bar," *Columbia Business School*, 2010, accessed November 4, 2011. http://www4.gsb.columbia.edu/null/download?&exclusive=filemgr.download&file_id=733522.

5. Liu Shiying and Martha Avery, *Alibaba: The Inside Story Behind Jack Ma and the Creation of the World's Biggest Online Marketplace* (New York: Harper-Collins, 2009).

6. Mariel Loveland, "From Jitter to twttr to Twitter, Jack Dorsey Speaks About Twitter's Name," *Scribbal*, July 19, 2011, http://www.scribbal.com/2011/07/from-jitter-to-twttr-to-twitter-jack-dorsey-speaks-about-twitters-name/.

7. Michael Schulman, "Snip," *The New Yorker*, May 9, 2011, 23–24.

8. Victoria Barret, "Dropbox," *Forbes*, November 7, 2011, 83–92.

9. Geoffrey A. Fowler and Yukari Iwatani Kane, "An Article of Faith for Marketers: Place No Faith in Articles," *The Wall Street Journal*, September 12, 2011.

10. Brad Stone, "Comfort Food? There's an App for That," *Bloomberg Businessweek*, June 1, 2011, http://www.businessweek.com/magazine/content/11_24/b4232000961498.htm.

11. Steve Rivkin, "How Did 'Apple Computer' Get Its Name?," *The Naming Newsletter*, http://www.namingnewsletter.com/article.asp?id=156.

12. "New Way to Stream Music Crosses the Pond," *The Wall Street Journal*, July 20, 2011.

13. "Daniel Ek, Founder and CEO of Spotify," Quora, http://www.quora.com/Daniel-Ek/Startup-New-Venture-Origins-Stories/answers; Ben Sisario, "Spotify Music-Streaming Service Comes to U.S.," *The New York Times*, July 13, 2011.

14. Matthew S. McGlone and Jessica Tofighbakhsh, "Birds of a Feather Flock Conjointly," *Psychological Sciences* 11:5 (September 2000): 424–427, https://webspace.utexas.edu/mm4994/www/rhyme%20as%20reason.pdf.

15. Tadashi Yanai, "Dare to Err," *McKinsey Quarterly*, June 2011, https://www.mckinseyquarterly.com/Dare_to_err_2827.

16. "Yu Minhong: From Failure to Success," China Daily, http://www.chinadaily.com.cn/china/2006-11/24/content_742340.htm.

17. Arianne Cohen, "Ode to a Burrito," *Fast Company*, April 1, 2008, http://www.fastcompany.com/magazine/124/ode-to-a-burrito.html.

Chapter 5

1. Don Germain, *Innocent: A Book About Innocent* (London: Penguin, 2009); Jim Stenger, *Grow: How Ideals Power Growth and Profit at the World's Greatest Companies* (New York: Crown Business, 2011).

2. "The Man Behind the FedEx Logo," *The Sneeze*, November 16, 2004, http://www.thesneeze.com/mt-archives/000273.php.

3. "How Genious Works: Michael Bierut," *The Atlantic*, May 2011, http://www.theatlantic.com/magazine/archive/2011/05/michael-bierut/8456/.

4. Lauren Collins, "Sole Mate," *The New Yorker*, March 28, 2011, http://www.newyorker.com/reporting/2011/03/28/110328fa_fact_collins.83.

5. Ibid.

6. Anne Marie Chaker, "The Pampered Countertop," *The Wall Street Journal*, February 8, 2011.

7. Ibid.

8. Bryant Urstadt, "Lust for Lulu," *New York Magazine*, July 26, 2009, http://nymag.com/shopping/features/58082/.

9. Laura Stevens, "The Boss of Big Bold Baby Buggies," *The Wall Street Journal*, August 27–28, 2011.

10. Joshua Robinson, "The Making of a Whiffle Ball," *The Wall Street Journal*, June 20, 2011.

11. Sarah Nassauer, "Art in Aisle 5: Barcodes Enter Expressionist Period," *The Wall Street Journal*, June 22, 2011.

12. Lauren Fedor, "Making Tattoo Indelible," *The Wall Street Journal*, July 16, 2010.

13. Alissa Walker, "Berry, Berry Ambitious," *Fast Company*, December 1, 2007, http://www.fastcompany.com/magazine/121/berry-berry-ambitious.html.

14. Alexandra Alter, "The Self-Taught Mad Genius of Gelato," *The Wall Street Journal*, August 20–21, 2011.

15. Christina Binkley, "How Stores Lead You to Spend," *The Wall Street Journal*, December 2, 2010.

16. John Seabrook, "The Abstractionist," *The New Yorker*, December 21–28, 2011, http://www.newyorker.com/reporting/2009/12/21/091221fa_fact_seabrook.

17. Gwendolyn Bounds, "How Handwriting Boosts the Brain," *The Wall Street Journal*, October 5, 2010.

Chapter 6

1. Johan Berger and Katy Milkman, "Social Transmission, Emotion and the Virality of Online Content," *Marketing Science Institute*, 2010, http://www.msi.org/publications/publication.cfm?pub=1779.

2. Ibid.

3. Douglas Rushkoff, *Program or Be Programmed: Ten Commands for a Digital Age* (New York: Or Books, 2010), 104.

4. Ibid, 13.

5. Lisa Belkin, "Queen of the Mommy Bloggers," *The New York Times*, March 5, 2011.

6. Amanda Fortini, "O Pioneer Woman!," *The New Yorker*, May 9, 2011, 26–31.

7. Geoffrey A. Fowler, "Are You Talking to Me?," *The Wall Street Journal*, May 2, 2011.

8. http://wefollow.com/twitter/entrepreneur, accessed November 5, 2011.

9. David Court, et al., "The Consumer Decision Journey," *McKinsey Review*, June 2009, https://www.mckinseyquarterly.com/The_consumer_decision_journey_2373; David C. Edelman, "Social Media and the New Rules of Branding," *Harvard Business Review*, December 2010, http://hbr.org/2010/12/spotlight-on-social-media-and-the-new-rules-of-branding/ar/1/.

10. Ibid.

11. Douglas Alden Warshaw, "Conan 2.0," *Fortune*, March 15, 2011, http://tech.fortune.cnn.com/2011/02/10/conan-2-0/.

Chapter 7

1. Jefferson Graham, "More Companies Shrinking Sites for iPad, Other Devices," *USA Today*, March 29, 2011, http://www.usatoday.com/tech/news/2011-03-29-mobile-web-sites.htm; http://abcnews.go.com/Technology/companies-shrink-sites-ipad-devices/story?id=13252362.

2. Per Opus Research, cited by Randall Smith and Geoffrey A. Fowler, "Rate This: Yelp IPO Target $2 Billion," *The Wall Street Journal*, November 9, 2011.

3. Katy Finneran, "For Small Businesses, Foursquare is the New Word of Mouth," *Fox Small Business*, June 10, 2011, http://smallbusiness.foxbusiness.com/technology-web/2011/06/10/for-small-businesses-foursquare-is-new-word-mouth/; "Free E-Book Details the Success AJ Bombers Has Had Thanks to Foursquare," About Foursquare, November 23, 2010, http://aboutfoursquare.com/free-ebook-details-the-success-aj-bombers-has-had-thanks-to-foursquare/.

4. "Foursquare Works," SlideShare, http://www.slideshare.net/AJBombers/foursquare-works/.

5. "Keep Up with the Jones, Dude!," *Business Week*, October 26, 2005, http://www.businessweek.com/innovate/content/oct2005/id20051026_869180.htm.

6. "A Startup's New Prescription for Eyewear," *Bloomberg Businessweek*, July 4–10, 2011, 49–51.

Chapter 8

1. Lara Moroko and Mark D. Uncles, "Employer Branding," *The Wall Street Journal*, March 23, 2009.

2. Sue Shellenbarger, "Better Ideas Through Failure," *The Wall Street Journal*, September 27, 2011.

3. Gregory Berns, *Iconoclast* (Cambridge: Harvard Business Press, 2008).

4. Johan Lehrer, "Social Networks Can't Replace Socializing," *The Wall Street Journal*, August 6–7, 2011. The research study was done by Isaac Kohane at Harvard Medical School. The quality of the papers was measured by the number of citations each paper received in scientific journals.

5. "Cranium Creator Richard Tait Shares Tips for Success," *Zillow Blog*, April 13, 2011, accessed November 4, 2011, http://www.zillow.com/blog/2011-04-13/cranium-creator-richard-tait-shares-tips-for-sucess/.

6. Stephanie Clifford, "Burnishing a Brand by Selecting an 'Idol,'" *The New York Times*, December 24, 2009.

7. Liz Welch, "The Way I Work: Paul English of Kayak," *Inc.*, February 1, 2010, http://www.inc.com/magazine/20100201/the-way-i-work-paul-english-of-kayak.html; Kayak, accessed November 5, 2011. www.kayak.com.

8. Douglas Edwards, *I'm Feeling Lucky* (Boston: Houghton Mifflin Harcourt, 2011).

9. Ibid.

10. Ibid.

11. Teri Evans, "Entrepreneurs Seek to Elicit Workers' Ideas," *The Wall Street Journal*, December 22, 2009.

12. Krish Raghav, "We Paint Our Own Walls," *The Wall Street Journal*, June 10, 2011.

Chapter 9

1. Craig Lambert, "The Psyche on Automatic," *Harvard Magazine*, December 2010, 48–52.

2. Ibid; Dana R. Carney, et al., "Power Posing," *Psychological Science*, September 21, 2010, http://pss.sagepub.com/content/21/10/1363.short.

3. Russell H. Granger, *The 7 Triggers to Yes* (New York: McGraw-Hill, 2007).

4. http://www.youtube.com/watch?v=yWyLaXCV2_s.

5. June Kronholz, "Talk Is Cheap in Politics, But a Deep Voice Helps," *The Wall Street Journal*, December 3–4, 2007.

6. Alex French, "Tony Robbins Is Disappointed," *New York*, November 1, 2010, 14.

7. Ori Brafman and Rom Brafman, *Click: The Forces Behind How We Fully Engage with People, Work, and in Everything We Do* (New York: Crown, 2011).

8. Ibid.

9. Benedict Carey, "You Remind Me of Me," February 12, 2008, *The New York Times*.

10. Nick Morgan, *Give Your Speech, Change the World* (Cambridge: Harvard Business Press, 2005). This book has a wonderful discussion not only on how to give a speech but on the five story formats that influenced my discussion in this chapter.

11. Ibid. See Morgan's discussion of the stranger-in-a-strange-land story, which influenced my discussion.

12. Jerry Weintraub, *When I Stop Talking, You'll Know I'm Dead: Useful Stories from a Persuasive Man* (New York: Twelve, 2011).

13. Nick Morgan, *Give Your Speech, Change the World* (Cambridge: Harvard Business Press, 2005). See his discussion of the love story format that influenced my writing.

14. Beth Kowitt, "One Hundred Million Android Fans Can't Be Wrong," *Fortune*, July 4, 2011, http://tech.fortune.cnn.com/2011/06/16/100-million-android-fans-cant-be-wrong/.

15. "Words of Wisdom: Joseph J. Plumeri," *The New York Times*, June 12, 2011.

16. Jill Lepore, "Objection," *The New Yorker*, May 23, 2011, 38.

17. Ori Brofman and Rom Brofman, *Click* (New York: Crown Business, 2011), 81 ff.

18. Nick Morgan, *Give Your Speech, Change the World* (Cambridge: Harvard Business Press, 2005).

Chapter 10

1. "We Remember Bad Times Better Than Good," *Science News*, August 28, 2007, http://www.sciencedaily.com/releases/2007/08/070828110711.htm.

Chapter 11

1. Gary Vaynerchuk, *Crush It!* (New York: Harper Studio, 2009).

2. John Warrillow, "Will Gary Vaynerchuk Crush His Business?," *Inc.*, May 9, 2010, http://www.inc.com/articles/2010/10/gary-vaynerchuk-on-personal-branding.html.

3. Lauren Etter, "Groupon Therapy," *Vanity Fair*, August 2011, http://www.vanityfair.com/business/features/2011/08/groupon-201108.

4. Ibid, 71.

5. Andrew Davidson, "Coke's Water Man J. Darius Bikoff Gushes Forth," *The Sunday Times*, May 25, 2008.

6. Dinah Eng, "Cheesecake Factory's Winning Formula," *Fortune*, May 9, 2011, http://money.cnn.com/2011/05/02/smallbusiness/cheescake_factory_david_overton.fortune/index.htm.

7. Karen Weiss, "Five Guys' Biggest Struggle Is to Stay the Same," *Bloomberg Business Week*, August 16, 2011, http://www.msnbc.msn.com/id/44138062/ns/business-us_business/t/five-guys-biggest-struggle-stay-same/.

8. Tieying Huang, *Haidilao Ni Xue Bu Hui* (Beijing: Citic, 2011). http://www.chinaacc.com/new/287_294_/2009_10_10_wa2400292401010190029280.shtml, http://money.163.com/11/0508/23/73IN9HPI00253B0H.html.

9. "Are you a C.E.O. of Something?," *The New York Times*, January 31, 2010.

10. Kevin Maney, "Skype: The Inside Story of the Boffo $8.5 Billion Deal," *Fortune*, July 25, 2011, http://tech.fortune.cnn.com/2011/07/12/skype-the-inside-story-of-the-boffo-8-5-billion-deal/.

11. Ira Boudway, "FiveFingers," *Bloomberg Businessweek*, August 11, 2011, http://www.businessweek.com/magazine/fivefingers-08112011.html; Tony Post, "The Idea Conference," *Ad Age*, http://amiga.adage.com/ideacon10/10-TonyPost.php; "Barefoot Shoes Try to Outrace the Black Market, *CNN Money*, http://money.cnn.com/2010/08/13/smallbusiness/vibram_fivefingers/index.htm.

12. Wayne Curtis, "The Man Who Lived on a Shoe," *The Wall Street Journal*, August 4, 2011; James L. Witherell, *LL Bean* (Gardiner, Maine: Tilbury House, 2011).

13. Jane Martinson, "Will Chase: Farmer Making a Packet Out of Knobby Crisps," *The Guardian*, July 28, 2006; "Will Chase: Crisps and Vodka: the Proof Is in the Potato, *The Independent*, March 2, 2008; Michael Kavanaugh and Harriet Stilles, "Tyrrells Founder Discovers Vodka and Crisps," *The Financial Times*, July 25, 2010.

14. http://www.tyrrellscrisps.co.uk/blog/2011/05/17/the-tyrrells-big-screen/ accessed November 5, 2011.

15. Sarah E. Needleman, "For Intuit Co-Founder, the Numbers Add Up," *The Wall Street Journal*, August 18, 2011.

16. David Kamp, "It Came from Bristol," *Bloomberg Businessweek*, June 20–26, 2011, 86.

17. Richard L. Brandt, "Birth of a Salesman," *The Wall Street Journal*, Octobr 15, 2011, http://online.wsj.com/article/SB10001424052970203914304576627102996831200.html?mod=WSJ_hp_LEFTTopStories.

Index

Commercials, 155
Community, 166
Company culture
  copycat syndrome in, 169–170
  customer service-based, 165–166
  employee brand, 160
  employer brand, 159–160
  failure in, 162
  groupthink in, 169
  innovative, 161–163
  key markers of, 168–169
  shared mission atmosphere of, 161
Company-driven branding, 128
Competence, 172–173
Competition
  brand name different than, 82
  description of, 15–16
Competitive advantage, 47
Compound name, 76
Consequences, 46
Consumer insight, 140
Consumers
  feedback from, 149
  power of, xviii
Cook, Robin, 237
Copycat syndrome, 169–170
Corona, 62
Corporate entrepreneurs, xiii, xvi
Coulombe, Joe, 21–22
Cranium Control, 163–164
Creation story, 87–88, 187, 208
Creative brief, 136–140
Creativity, 43, 51, 113–114, 161–163
Credibility, 38
Crush It!, 224
Customer(s)
  analyzing of, xxi
  branding participation by, 148
  enchanting of, 230–231
  engaging of, xxi
  internal. See Employee(s)
  loyalty of, 129–130, 149

negative reviews from, 132
pass-alongs by, 116–117, 143–144
perceptions by, 37–38
reactions from, 39–40
rewarding of, 149
Customer persona, 139–140
Customer service
  company culture focus on, 165–166
  description of, 6–7
  example of, 230–231
  feedback about, 39–40
Cyber reputation, 211–212
Cyberbranding, 119–123, 133, 154–156, 223

D

Damage control, 132
Danielson, Antje, 38
Darrow, Clarence, 195
Data mining, 31
David versus Goliath story, 186–187
Dawson, Chris, 34, 192
Dax Gabler, 34
Declining brand, 241
Defining moment, of purpose story, 89
Delivering happiness, 48
Delivering Happiness, 208
Dell, Michael, 50
Demand, 118
Design(s)
  description of, 7
  experience, 101–102, 109
  modernizing of, 112
  of packaging, 104–105
  of products, 106–107
  prototypes, 109–110
  trademark, 111
  updating of, 112
Dialogue, 181
Different, 5–6, 46, 72
Digg, 79–80
Digital conversation, 130–131

Mateschitz, Dietrich, 51–52
Maverick positioning, 54–55
Maybank, Alexis, 12
McCollough, Jack, 79
McDonald's, 37, 78, 113, 164, 229
McDougall, Christopher, 234
McFerson, Zanna, 55–56
Media
  engagement in, 142–143
  new, 119–120, 133
  pitching stories to, 152–153
  "read-only," 119–120
  "read-write," 119–120
  seeking of, 207–208
  social, 119, 125, 151, 153–154
  traditional types of, 117–118
  transformation of, 117–118
Mediagenic, 207–208
Mehta, Sonny, 107–108
Melt, The, 81–82
Memorable, 46
Mendelsund, Peter, 107
Meta-narrative, 179
Metaphor, 195–196
Michaels, Bret, 61
Microblogging, 19–20
Microsoft, 54, 76–77, 79, 241
Middleton, Carole, 16–17
Midler, Bette, 59
Mimicry, 175–176
Mindshare, 141–142
Mirror neurons, 176
Mistakes, 40–41
Mitchell, Mike, 130–131
Mizrahi, Isaac, 61
Mobile app, 147
Mobile marketing, 146
Monson, Faith, 99
Morris, Kit, 67
Morris, Shireen, 67
Moskovitz, Dustin, vii
Mother Teresa, 161
Mrs. Meyer's Clean Day, 103–104, 224

Mullany, David, 106
Mullany, Stephen, 106
Mumm, 85
Murrell, Jerry, 229–230
Music, 109, 113
Mycoskie, Blake, 63

N
Nalebuff, Barry, 14–15
Name. *See* Brand name
Nassif, Monica, 103–104
Negative reputation, 211
Negative reviews, 132
Nestlé, 107
Net effective reach, 155
Net-a-Porter, 52
Netflix, 40–41, 129
Networking
  advisory board, 205
  description of, 201
  economy of, 202–203
  strategic, 203–204
Neuromarketing, 58–59
New media, 119–120, 133
New Oriental Language and Technology
    Group, 88
Niche, 50, 224
Nike, 84
Nintendo, 73
Nonprofits, 22–23
Nordstrom's, 7

O
Obama, Barack, 229
Objective and key results, 232
O'Brien, Conan, 130–132
Omidyar, Pierre, 76
One Drop Foundation, 64
1-Click ordering, 239
O'Neill, Tip, 197
Online reviews, 132
Openness, 173
Orman, Suze, 89–90